The Civil War and the Limits of Destruction

# THE CIVIL WAR

### AND THE

# LIMITS OF DESTRUCTION

Mark E. Neely, Jr.

HARVARD UNIVERSITY PRESS

Cambridge, Massachusetts

London, England

2007

*Library of Congress Cataloging-in-Publication Data*

Neely, Mark E.
The Civil War and the limits of destruction /
Mark E. Neely, Jr.
p.   cm.
Includes a bibliographical references and index.
ISBN-13: 978-0-674-02658-2 (hardcover: alk. paper)
ISBN-10: 0-674-02658-6 (hardcover: alk. paper)
1. United States—History—Civil War, 1861–1865—Destruction and pillage.
2. United States—History—Civil War, 1861–1865—Casualties.
3. Violence—United States—History—19th century.
4. War casualties—United States—History—19th century.
5. Death—United States—History—19th century.
6. United States—History—Civil War, 1861–1865—Social aspects.
7. Racism—United States—History—19th century.
8. United States—Race relations—History—19th century.
I. Title.
E468.9.N438 2007
973.7—dc22       2007017981

⤜⤙

# Contents

The Civil War and the Limits of Destruction

# INTRODUCTION

## Destructiveness in the Civil War

In the late summer of 1863 Americans stood at a crossroads in their civil war. Any reader of the contemporary press could see it. All eyes then focused on Charleston, South Carolina. U.S. forces besieging the city were on the verge of capturing it. Northerners could hardly wait for this cradle of secession to fall.

There was good reason for Northern optimism. Masonry fortifications had crumbled helplessly under assault from modern rifled artillery, and U.S. General Quincy Gillmore now had heavy batteries close enough to damage the target. For the vengeful, the situation was all but delicious: the Confederate commander of the threatened Charleston defenses was none other than P. G. T. Beauregard, the general who had gained credit for the humiliating Rebel victory at Bull Run two years earlier. And Gillmore had a flaming surprise in store for the impudent general with the French accent. His arsenal included new experimental artillery shells intended not to penetrate masonry but instead to rain "Greek Fire"—a highly flammable substance that could not be doused with water—down on the extremists who started the war.[1] These were the creation of the Yankee inventor Levi Short and had the blessing of the president of the United States himself. Abraham Lincoln had helped Short get his incendiary shells an audition before the army's ordnance experts more than a year earlier.[2] Lincoln was—indirectly—on the verge of reducing Charleston to ashes.

The bombardment of Charleston failed to cause the city to surrender. Even had the attack succeeded, the victory would not have been militarily decisive in the Civil War. The crossroads in the war was not that kind of turning point. The new direction the war might take after this siege was toward destructiveness and wanton, fiery, and indiscriminate loss of life, civilian and military. When Greek Fire fell on Charleston, then, did the Civil War take its fateful turn toward the mind-boggling destructiveness of the twentieth century?

We know better now than to look exclusively at the eastern theater of the war for an understanding of the overall conflict, but the news from the Civil War's western front pointed in an equally destructive direction in the late summer of 1863. In the midst of reading about the incendiary shelling of Charleston Americans also learned about the Lawrence Massacre. On August 21, 1863, Confederate guerrilla leader William Quantrill led a raid on the Kansas border town and murdered some 150 men and boys, all civilians.

With East and West linked in hideous and fiery destruction of cities and slaughter of unarmed civilians, the picture of the future of war in North America seemed grim indeed. The moral barriers as well as the technological ones to the advent of truly destructive and indiscriminate warfare had been breached decisively. Would there be no turning back?

⊶⚍⊚ ⚍⊶

Readers of modern books on the Civil War naturally expect the worst. When we move to the final sixteen months of the Civil War, 1864–1865, we should encounter slaughtered innocents and incinerated countryside that have given the war its modern reputation for "brutality." Invocations of that term and others like it to characterize the American Civil War are now routine. In the textbook I assign in my Civil War survey course, for example, the index, under "Civil War," has only some fifteen headings, one of which is "reasons for length and brutality of."[3]

In this book I will investigate the question whether the American Civil War can accurately be characterized as brutal—"grossly ruthless" or "unfeeling" in its conduct, "cruel" and "cold-blooded."[4] I will attempt to measure how far the country plunged after reaching the precipice of destructiveness in August and September 1863. To answer such questions I will move back and forth in time and method.

In the first chapter I will seek the roots of Civil War behavior in the American past, by examining the Mexican-American War of 1846–1848, often regarded as a "rehearsal" for the greater conflict to come fifteen years later. We will listen to the voices of the American soldiers in Mexico, from Winfield Scott and Zachary Taylor down to the lowliest enlisted man. In the second chapter I will return to the Civil War, in particular to Missouri and Kansas (the scene of Quantrill's raid in 1863). We will see whether the last great Confederate effort in Missouri, Price's Raid in 1864, provoked further deterioration in the restraints imposed by the laws and customs of war. In that chapter I rely mostly on the reports of general officers published in the government's official records of the war. In the third chapter I return to Mexico, but to the time sixteen years after the Mexican-American War when citizens of that unhappy republic were fighting to drive out of their country the Austrian Emperor Maximilian, placed on the throne by an invading French army. Mexican reactionaries had invited Maximilian into the country, and the resulting conflict was a civil war also. Since it occurred simultaneously with the great conflict in the United States, it constitutes the civil war closest in time and place to the American Civil War. The Mexican conflict of

1862–1867 thus offers the best basis for fruitful comparison of the nature of civil wars in republics in the middle of the nineteenth century. In that chapter I will examine what people in the United States thought of the "brutality" of the fighting in the republic to the south of them to see whether in any way it reminded them of the excesses of their own civil war.

In Chapter 4 I will move back to the United States and to the eastern theater in the Civil War, to General Philip Sheridan's Shenandoah Valley campaign of 1864. In that chapter I will test the extent of destructiveness of that campaign, acknowledged to be among the most destructive of the war. We will take a close look at what exactly was destroyed in the valley, who destroyed it, and in what spirit those destroyers acted. In the fifth chapter I will return to the borderlands near Missouri, to examine the legacy of the Sand Creek Massacre to see what parallels we can find between the Confederacy in flames and the Plains Indian wars. Here, as in the study of the Mexican-American War, we can examine again the effects of racial perceptions on the destructiveness and violence wrought by U.S. soldiers. Finally, in Chapter 6 I will examine the viewpoints of Congress and the administration that oversaw the conflict as they debated the war issue that would arouse the rawest emotions for years to come, the mistreatment of prisoners of war.

In the brief conclusion I will draw on the insights gained from the previous chapters to assess the accuracy of the image of destructiveness of the American Civil War given readers in modern histories.

Each chapter is aimed at answering the simple question: How destructive was the American Civil War?—how destructive when compared to the previous war nearest in time?—how destructive when compared to another civil war on the same continent?—how destructive when compared to Indian wars? How do eastern and western theaters, heartland and border, of the Civil War compare in destructiveness? Readers will not find a tabulation of destruction, though close consideration is given to what was targeted and actually destroyed in the fires set in the Shenandoah Valley in 1864, and the conclusion will include a reconsideration of the casualty figures from the Civil War. Precise calculations and recalculations of destruction and death will, I hope, become the work of econometricians and demographers in future books on the Civil War.[5] In this book I attempt to understand how destructive the protagonists in the Civil War wanted to be or dared to be, under the assumptions of that genteel and sentimental age.

A key assumption of the age was that "race" mattered. From Mexico in 1846 to Virginia in 1864 Americans saw the world's peoples as divided into races, and they associated levels of civilization and barbarism with them. Among civilized peoples, they assumed, warfare had been increasingly restrained in ferocity, but with barbarians it was different. People in the United States were keenly aware that Maximilian was attempting to hold sway over a people of another race. These were the most fundamental intellectual abstractions on which the people in the period shaped their day-to-day behavior in peace and war. In the end, then, this book, like many others concerned with the American Civil War, is a book about racial beliefs as a major determinant of behavior in the era.

*⟞══ 1 ══⟝*

# THE MEXICAN-AMERICAN WAR

## Republicanism and the Ethos of War

THE EARLY LITERATURE on the Mexican-American War—histories emphasizing diplomacy, generals, and strategy—casting it as a "rehearsal" for the greater conflict of the later Civil War, is fast being replaced by a newer literature that focuses on the common soldier and on his cultural perceptions of the enemy. Historians of the Civil War have not yet digested this new history of the Mexican-American War or considered the many implications that lie in the contrasts suggested by it. Historians now have available to them, in addition to the familiar printed diaries and letters of men who became major figures in the Civil War (such as George B. McClellan), newly published sources from more obscure soldiers who campaigned in Mexico. It may well be that we can reach a better understanding of the Civil War by viewing it from a long-range chronological perspective than we can by following the lead of recent scholarship on the Civil War, examining single battles day by day, adding detail, and putting a relentlessly microscopic focus on the events. Instead of the microscope, in this chapter I will employ the wide-angle lens of comparison in an attempt to capture the essence of the American Civil War.[1]

⟞══ ══⟝

1. *Mexico*, 1855. Acquisitive interest in Latin American lands remained high even after the end of the Mexican-American War in 1848. The inset detail map of the Isthmus of Tehuantepec, a route favored in proposals for Latin American passages to California, reveals what people in the United States found most interesting on maps of Mexico.

The advent of popular national wars after the French Revolution meant that warfare could no longer be a matter merely of diplomacy and dynastic or ministerial objectives. Whatever the national leaders may have desired to accomplish in their conflicts with other countries, they had now to oversee a popularization of their goals within their own. With the republicanization of war in the New World, such popularization of war aims grew still more important. The result for wars of the nineteenth century can aptly be termed the advent of "ethos" in war.

That wars in the United States had a "distinguishing character" or an "overriding belief," to invoke the dictionary definition of "ethos," is made clear by the Mexican-American War. When I read Paul Foos's *Short, Offhand, Killing Affair,* I first realized that point. "Manifest Destiny," whatever fig leaf of republicanism adorned it, was at bottom acquisitive, aggressive, and aggrandizing, as Foos has been at pains to prove.[2] Somehow, this ultimate rationalization for the Mexican-American War reached the common volunteer and affected his actions.

The behavior of U.S. volunteers in the Mexican-American War has been gaining an increasingly notorious reputation. At the time, it astonished even the highest-ranking U.S. generals who commanded the soldiers in that war, men with presidential ambitions who had every reason to flatter the volunteers. Zachary Taylor, who would succeed in riding the reputation he gained from the war to the presidency in 1848, and Winfield Scott, who made a similar but unsuccessful attempt in 1852, hated each other and saw eye to eye on very little involving the war, but both are on record as having testified to the rapacious behavior of U.S. volunteers in Mexico.

Winfield Scott's testimony comes from his own hand. He informed Secretary of War William L. Marcy on January 16, 1847:

2. *Genl. Scott's Entrance into Mexico,* 1851. A hint of the guerrilla war that soon followed the fall of the city to U.S. forces can be seen in the shadows at the lower left, where a ragged Mexican reaches for a rock to throw at the American soldiers. Within an hour of the scene of victory depicted here, ugly guerrilla violence erupted in the city.

Our militia & volunteers, if a tenth of what is said be true, have committed atrocities—horrors—in Mexico, sufficient to make Heaven weep, & every American, of Christian morals *blush* for his country. Murder, robbery, & rape on mothers & daughters, in the presence of the tied up males of the families, have been common all along the Rio Grande. I was agonized with what I heard—not from Mexicans, and regulars alone, but from respectable individual volunteers—from the masters & hands of our steamers. Truly it would seem unchristian & cruel to let loose upon any people—even savages—such unbridled persons—freebooters, &c., &c.[3]

Taylor's contemptuous attitude toward volunteers was well enough known to endanger his later presidential campaign. The documentary record for him is not as plain as it is for Scott, but the language Taylor used to express his views is remembered as plainer, as befits his rough and ready image. Early in 1847 Taylor lost his temper with a group of Ohio volunteers, and one version of his outburst is: "You are all a G___d d___d set of thieves and cowards; you never came here to fight, but to rob and plunder, and will run at the first sight of the enemy."

Obviously, the source for the Taylor quotation is second hand, and in its most colorful version, given above, it stems from the presidential election of 1848. Yet the man who was the source for the remarks was, like Taylor, a Whig who served as commander of an Ohio regiment during the Mexican-American War. Samuel R. Curtis apparently heard Taylor call Ohio troops "thieves and cowards."[4] It would be difficult to imagine modern generals in charge of U.S. forces in the Middle East, for example, characterizing the behavior of American volunteers in a foreign land as Scott and Taylor did.

It might be tempting to dismiss the generals' observations as the product of the prejudices of old professional soldiers had Scott's attitude not left a permanent and indisputable institutional legacy: trials by military commission. Scott was in earnest when he said he was agonized by the spectacle of rapine and plunder, and he set about solving the problem. To his practical mind, the root of the problem lay in the fact that there was "no legal punishment" for the "atrocities." "By the strange omission of Congress," he noted, "American troops take with them beyond the limits of their own country, no law but the Constitution of the United States, and the rules and articles of war. These do not provide any court for the trial and punishment of murder, rape, theft, &c., &c.,—no matter by whom, or on whom committed." Scott's Field Order 20, of February 1847, brought to

American history and jurisprudence for the first time the military commission. These military courts could try soldiers for "offenses, any one of which, if committed within the United States or their organized Territories, would, of course, be tried and severely punished by the ordinary or civil courts of the land." He enumerated such crimes as "assassination, murder, poisoning, rape, or the attempt to commit either; malicious stabbing or maiming; malicious assault and battery, robbery, theft; the wanton desecration of churches, cemeteries or other religious edifices and fixtures; the interruption of religious ceremonies, and the destruction, except by order of a superior officer, of public or private property."[5]

What the generals saw when they complained about plunder and robbery was the effect of the ethos of the Mexican-American War on its eager American volunteers. We are permitted a rare glimpse of the articulation of the war's acquisitive allure in a description of the election of officers in an Illinois regiment in 1846. The witness was Samuel E. Chamberlain, a poor farm laborer who rushed to the colors and participated in the election himself. The election of colonel took place in a ten-pin alley, and the winner of the election for colonel achieved victory by providing whiskey for the soldiers who elected him. Chamberlain wanted to be first lieutenant in the regiment, but, he recalled later, "I found I had no chance to win—my money was all gone—but I made a spread eagle speech, with plenty of the 'Halls of Montezuma' and 'Golden Jesus's' of Mexico, but alas, the 'Suckers' [people from Illinois] preferred whiskey present to Jesus's in the future."[6] Thus had some of the volunteers internalized the acquisitiveness as a justification for the war, and young Chamberlain knew to hold out the lure of supposed crucifixes made of gold to be found in the Catholic churches of Mexico. General Scott's provisions for military commissions specifically singled out desecration of places of worship.

The common soldier's hope of financial gain from war, one of the fundamental motivations explored—in the case of medieval soldiers—by the great military historian John Keegan in his seminal *Face of Battle,* could still lurk in the modern wars of the nineteenth century.

⊷⟺ ⟺⊶

More important than the ethos of the Mexican-American War was the perception of the enemy as another race, and one with a parasitic religion. These views proved adequate to obliterate in the minds of most American soldiers the kinship of republicanism shared by Mexico and the United States in the middle of the nineteenth century.

The record from the Mexican-American War is remarkably uniform in that regard. In the rest of this chapter, I will draw on the ideas and observations of eleven articulate soldiers, men of differing politics, military rank, and geographical origins, to help us understand the U.S. experience in Mexico. To begin with, Samuel Ryan Curtis, colonel of the Third Ohio Volunteers in the Mexican-American War and later a general in Missouri and Kansas in the Civil War, complained in his diary entry for August 13, 1846, of the "lenient conduct" of General Zachary Taylor toward the Mexican civilians in the northern part of the country. It seemed to Curtis that "war to them . . . can have no terrors conducted as it now is. *Subjugation* or *devastation* is my view of the matter. The people are semi savage and they must be made to acknowledge our sovereignty or this war will never end."[7] As the next chapter will reveal, Curtis's attitudes toward the enemy in the Civil War fifteen years later were quite different.

The modern editor of Curtis's Mexican War diary singled the Ohio colonel out because he "lacked the extreme cultural bias so often found in the contemporary diaries and letters of American soldiers stationed in this area." The editor also praised the American administration of occupied Mexico, saying that "Curtis and others in authority managed to avoid total anarchy by using common sense, diplomacy, and expressions of good will toward the people of Matamoros and their existing civil government. This was the model of governance applied almost universally by the military as they strove to manage occupied northern Mexico."[8]

Yet to a reader fresh from the study of the Civil War, Curtis's diary seems remarkable for its unsympathetic references to the enemy's culture. "This is Sabbath," the colonel wrote on August 9, 1846. "The bell rang for matins in Matamoros this morning, but how can we expect religion in such a den of thieves robbers and assassins! I believe the place ought to be cleansed with *fire*."[9] Curtis moderated his opinions somewhat when faced with the practical responsibility of acting as military governor of various Mexican villages. He came to cooperate with local Mexican officials and lawyers to keep a lid on violence and disorder. But he never retracted his summary views of the Mexican people as semi-barbarous.

Like Curtis, George B. McClellan was trained at West Point and destined to become a Civil War general. His brief but incisive diary from the Mexican-American War focused on two subjects: lessons of technical military expertise and the depredations of the volunteers. "You never hear of a Mexican being murdered by a regular," McClellan told his mother while he was on campaign, "or a regular by a Mexican. The volunteers carry on in a most shameful and disgraceful manner; they think nothing of robbing and killing the Mexicans."[10] The regulars' emphasis on the undisciplined depredations of the volunteers had the practical effect of causing the regulars' descriptions of their own experiences in Mexico to seem rather mild, but in fact most of these Americans shared a similar racial outlook. They thought the country was underdeveloped economically because the people were lazy and unenterprising. They thought the religious institutions kept the people in superstitious ignorance.

They thought a tiny and reactionary religious and aristocratic-military elite dominated and skimmed the wealth of the country. The resulting backward economy of scarcity and the inadequacy of the religion to inculcate morality led the society to be plagued by bandits and brigands. McClellan, for example, upon his first encounter with Mexicans near the Rio Grande, made the customary observation on their lack of enterprise: "The Mexicans appear to cultivate nothing whatever but a little Indian corn (maize). They are certainly the laziest people in existence—living in a rich fertile country (the banks of the river at least) they are content to roll in the mud, eat their horrible beef and tortillas and dance all night at their fandangos." He lapsed easily into the use of the pejorative "greasers" to describe Mexicans.[11]

George Gordon Meade, another West Pointer, agreed with McClellan in his view of the depredations of the American volunteers: "They rob and steal the cattle and corn of the poor farmers, and in fact act more like a body of hostile Indians than of civilized whites."[12] In another letter Meade complained, "Already are our guardhouses filled daily with drunken officers and men, who go to the town, get drunk and commit outrages on the citizens."[13]

Since the volunteers' answer to the regulars' charges was not always denial but instead the counter-accusation that the regulars behaved in the same way, the historian has a sobering body of contemporary eyewitness testimony to the behavior of American soldiers in Mexico in 1846–1848. The accusations against the volunteers permeated the regular army from the very highest ranks of command to the lowly field officers. Zachary Taylor termed the behavior of the volunteers "licentious."[14] Winfield Scott, when he first met Samuel R. Curtis in Mexico, gave him "a long talk on the subject of the abominations committed by our troops." Curtis, though trained at West Point, was commanding volunteers. Incensed by Scott's charges,

Curtis's answer was to point out the behavior of some regular dragoons who "robbed many of the local jacals [huts]" and "tried to violate the women." He recorded later that in another instance of depredation in northern Mexico by U.S. troops, not specified as regulars, "more than a hundred . . . huts have been burned to ashes."[15]

Even those soldiers who disapproved of depredations by American forces, and there were many, shared cultural assumptions not far removed from those that animated the more aggressive soldiers. Sergeant Thomas Barclay, of the Second Pennsylvania Infantry, marched under the strictly restraining orders of General Winfield Scott, and the Pennsylvanian thought the destructive behavior of American soldiers who defied the letter and spirit of Scott's orders was counterproductive. Barclay commented on the controversial actions of Captain Samuel H. Walker. Walker had been a member of an ill-fated invasion into Mexico in 1842–1843, called the Mier expedition, and, as Sergeant Barclay noted, had "an inveterate hatred against the Mexicans." On the campaign march from Jalapa to Puebla, Walker's horsemen set fire to all the ranches within striking distance of the road on which the American army marched, in retaliation for recent guerrilla attacks. "It looks as if we were departing from our general rule when property is thus destroyed and the smoke arising from all directions in this beautiful valley does not produce in my mind very pleasant feelings." Barclay did "not think it . . . very good policy to permit the gallant captain to thus exasperate the whole people, for every man of common sense knows that we should conciliate as well as fight and prevent by every possible means the arousing of the Mexican nation. Against the government and war party we must be successful, but if the whole people are once aroused either by an attack upon their religion or property, a resistance will be made similar to the Spanish campaigns of 1813 & '14."[16]

Cold, calculating reason, however, could produce as unhappy conclusions in thinking about Mexico as the rage of racist passion. Sergeant Barclay, once he reached Mexico City, predicted that Mexico's "downfall" was "inevitable." Torn "by civil internal convulsions, pressed by a foreign war, the center of her territory invaded and in possession of the foe," Mexico could "only preserve her nationality by sacrificing territory to her affectionate sister of the north" (whether that reference to the republican United States was meant to be ironic is difficult for a modern reader to tell). Mexico could borrow time for a brief continued national existence by surrendering territory to the north, but "the time is approaching," the victorious sergeant predicted, "and the young of the present generation may see the day when the 'Stars and Stripes' which now float in triumph over the City will be the banner under whose folds the inhabitants of all Mexico will find shelter and protection." There followed in his journal a full-fledged racialist explanation of the future:

> The Anglo Saxon race, that land loving people are on the move. In an incredible short time they have overrun an immense territory in the north. Long since have wishful eyes been cast towards the fertile plains of Mexico. And the same people who have driven before them the various Indian tribes and have in Texas come in contact with the Spanish race will soon land like a wave over the province of Mexico. No embankments, no treaties can prevent the inundation. A contest between the races will follow and the Anglo Saxons have never been conquered. If they once obtain a footing, entire possession will be the result.

Familiar cultural assumptions underlay these predictions. The church and the army in Mexico divided the country's "power and wealth." The "inquisition" came immediately to Barclay's mind in describing the sumptuous tyranny by which these two obnoxious powers ruled Mexico. There was no flourishing "commerce, manufactures or agriculture"; only banditry and robbery were left to the people. Sergeant Barclay then reached a conclusion unusual for one reasoning from the common prejudices of the United States against the Mexican republic. "At the present time . . . much [as] we would deplore such a retrograde movement, there is no doubt but that a monarchial government would be best suited for this country. A sovereign at the head of the army and the throne supported by the clergy would without difficulty suppress all the internal dissensions and in course of time by correcting abuses in the laws, encouraging the arts and protecting the property of all, Mexico would occupy that station which her fertility, her position and her great resources entitle her." He thought the more likely result would be absorption by the United States.[17] Echoes of Barclay's startlingly nonrepublican attitudes toward Mexico, as we shall see in Chapter 3, would be heard again in the United States years later when the emperor of France attempted to place on a throne in Mexico the Austrian prince Maximilian.

Sergeant Barclay was a lawyer in civilian life, and the militia unit of which he had been a member, the Westmoreland Guards, which formed a part of the Second Pennsylvania Infantry, was composed of the elite of his county. Private Thomas Tennery was a simple farmer from Illinois enlisted in that state's fourth infantry regiment, but he held views similar to Barclay's. On November 12, 1846, while campaigning in northern Mexico, Tennery described his strange surroundings:

Everything appears dull, the houses, the inhabitants little above savages and without energy or business of any importance going on. This appears to be caused by the want of commerce, with the indolence of the inhabitants and perhaps the want of a settled government that will secure property. But to bring about this change the country must be inhabited by a different race of people. The Spanish and Indian do not make a race of people with patriotism and candor enough to support a republic, much less to form, sustain and establish one out of the present deranged fabric called the Republic of Mexico.

Tennery laid blame for Mexico's plight not only on race but also on "their religion": the government would always be distracted while "a prey to priestcraft."[18]

In the army of the West, which set out from Missouri to invade New Mexico, the allure of gain was perhaps more pronounced. Richard Smith Elliott, a sometime newspaperman from St. Louis and now a lieutenant in Laclede's Rangers, part of the western force, regularly sent back lively letters for the *St. Louis Reveille.* Elliott later recalled the feeling of anticipation on the eve of first contact with the enemy's territory: "Were we to fight, and if so—how much? Was the land anywhere populous, and if so—how much? Was it rich in gold and silver, and if so—how much? Were the people more civilized than savage, and if so—how much?" Gold, silver, and semi-savagery, common themes in the U.S. encounter with Mexico, popped immediately into the clever journalist-soldier's head. Elliott's unit and others from St. Louis remained in New Mexico to occupy Santa Fe and Taos, but Colonel Alexander Doniphan led the rest of the army of the West to capture the Mexican state of Chihuahua. While occupying Chihuahua, American forces there established an English-language newspaper. They named it the *Anglo Saxon.*[19]

It obviously seemed important in the midst of the Mexican enemy to assert distinction of race. Racial differences were matters of nearly ubiquitous observation by U.S. soldiers in Mexico. McClellan, when he entered Mexico City, professed relief at seeing the light-skinned upper-class women there. "They formed a pleasing contrast to the black and brown complexions of the Indians and negroes who had for so long been the only human beings to greet our sight," he noted.[20]

Although awareness of race increased in the years following the Mexican-American War, the only Civil War newspaper in the North to embrace a racialist masthead was John Van Evrie's *Caucasian*, published in New York City and virulently *opposed* to the war. Race did not work in the Civil War North to evoke images of an alien enemy or to provoke hatred of the Confederate foe.

⊷═⊙ ⊙═⊶

Comparison of the Mexican-American War with the Civil War not only calls our attention to the acquisitive and aggressive ethos and racial interpretation of the earlier conflict, but also reveals sharp differences in the level of discipline of the soldiery involved in the two conflicts. The regulars in Mexico exemplified greater restraint in dealing with the local populace and Mexican dwellings and property than did the volunteers. The difference between volunteers and regulars lay in military discipline. The army controlled the regulars by a violent discipline that sickened and appalled the volunteers, who saw in it something entirely alien to American political culture. In fact, it seems clear that stern discipline could override the ethos of the war and keep in check the brutal impulses fired by cultural beliefs. Certainly the regulars, as we have already observed, held similarly racist and anti-Catholic and nonrepublican views of Mexico.

If we think of discipline as a deterrent to desertion, then it is surprising that the U.S. Army had to invest any effort into discipline in Mexico. Desertion proved to be a modest threat once the Americans got to Mexico, for the opportunities were slim. The society into which the discontented soldier might escape spoke another language and, with the exception of the minority Catholic soldiers, some of whom did desert and form the famous San Patricio battalion, worshiped at alien altars. The landscape was harsh and offered only a life-threatening scarcity of water and food in most places. American soldiers were a very long way from home, and the transportation network was inadequate and unfamiliar.

That may be one reason that volunteer regiments put so little emphasis on discipline. The more important underlying reason, apparent in the observations of the era, was the extremely free political culture of the United States. Camp discipline makes this point clear. Consider a famous scene from the war in Mexico: After Zachary Taylor's victory at Buena Vista, the Americans entered a demoralizing period of garrison life in a camp near Saltillo. As the historian Paul Foos describes it, "[Colonel Robert T.] Paine countered with tightened discipline over his battalion, and with a menacing, though largely symbolic, step: the erection of a wooden horse in front of the North Carolina regimental headquarters."[21] The wooden horse, familiar to all Civil War historians interested in the life of the common soldier, was an instrument of excruciating punishment, a bar suspended in the air that the condemned soldier had to sit astride for long periods of time.

Volunteers in the Mexican-American War would not tolerate its use. They rioted rather than submit to the threat of the horse, and indeed Paine's wooden horse was never used. To the Civil War historian that scene is astonishing, for the use of the horse, bucking and gagging, and other agonizing and limb-straining punishments were standard in the later conflict.

Flogging was different. The triumph of popular indiscipline in the volunteer army of Mexico came with a nearly universal hatred of whipping. That punishment was freighted with tremendous symbolic meaning for republicans in a society that tolerated slavery. The members of the Second Pennsylvania Infantry on May 19, 1847, assembled for one of the most dramatic incidents of garrison life in Puebla:

This afternoon the troops in the City were formed and marched to the plaza. Four soldiers had been court-martialed and found guilty of robbery. They were to be punished today and whipping was part of the punishment. The culprits were three regulars and Drummer Revelon of Co. B of the 2nd Pa. Vols. Three muskets were stacked and the prisoners stripped to the pants and tightly tied to the stack . . . [A]mid much writhing the prisoner received 39 well and slowly laid on. He was then taken from the stack and the same ceremony was gone through with the rest. They were then taken back to the guard house. The object of assembling the troops was that they might profit by the example. There was among all however a general feeling of disgust. The men no doubt were scoundrels who deserved punishment, but everyone regretted that such a punishment could be inflicted under the laws of our country. Barbarous and cruel is such a punishment. Instead of reforming, culprits by the exposure are hardened. Spectators forget the crime in sympathy for the sufferers and our country is lowered in the eyes of all her children when she forgets the principles of humanity and modern government and permits a punishment which is only known in cruel savage nations or in most barbarous times.

The witness, Sergeant Barclay, was a lawyer. Private Richard Coulter, also of the Second Pennsylvania, said more succinctly, "The performance was, I thought, cruel and had a bad effect upon the Mexicans, many of whom saw it. It is the first instance of a volunteer being whipped during the war and has raised considerable excitement and caused the uttering of many hard expressions against the officers of the Court Martial."[22]

Discipline was on its way even in Mexico in 1847: the scenes of the horse and the flogging were firsts for volunteers. So were Winfield Scott's trials by military commission. Surely more discipline would have come in Mexico had the war not ended so soon. But the protests by the volunteers revealed the obvious incompatibility of flogging with republicanism. The Pennsylvania soldiers were correct in their assessment of popular feeling, and flogging did not last past the middle of 1861. Discipline, however, was there to stay.

→→◎ ◎←←

Just as the American soldier in the Mexican-American War enjoyed a lack of disciplinary restraint that allowed incursions on the local civilian populace, so too did the soldier in that conflict have an incentive for destructiveness that was largely absent in the Civil War years later: revenge. What nineteenth-century Americans remembered about Mexico was the Battle of Goliad, of March 19–20, 1836, part of the Texas revolt against Mexico. Texans captured in this battle were executed on the orders of General Santa Anna. The poet Walt Whitman devoted six stanzas to the martyrs of Goliad in *Leaves of Grass*, published in 1855. Whitman told "of the murder in cold blood of four hundred and twelve young men." After their ammunition ran out and their colonel was wounded, they had "treated for an honorable capitulation, received writing and seal, gave up their arms, and marched back prisoners of war." On Sunday, March 27, 1836, they were "brought out in squads and massacred." The Mexicans burned the bodies afterward. Whitman did not mention the word "Goliad" or "Mexico" for that matter, but presumably most of his readers knew what he was talking about.[23]

Whitman, a Democrat and expansionist, did not tell the whole story. In fact, the Mexican general, José Urrea, who captured the Texas revolutionaries, was apparently embarrassed by Santa Anna's policy and wished to treat the captives as prisoners of war, but Santa Anna would have none of it, and ordered the men executed.[24] People in the United States did not blame Santa Anna in contradistinction to General Urrea. They blamed Mexico instead.

Among soldiers in the Mexican-American War, ten years after the Texas revolution, another matter of irritating cultural memory was the Mier expedition. In 1842 a small group of Texans invaded northern Mexico and were captured by superior Mexican forces at the town of Mier. Somehow they escaped for a time, but they were recaptured. At that point the Mexican soldiers had the prisoners draw from a container of beans, one in ten of which was black. They shot the men who drew the black beans and imprisoned the rest.

The incident moved Samuel H. Walker, one of the leaders of the Mier filibuster who was imprisoned and later released, to rejoin the army for service in the Mexican War of 1846. Other U.S. volunteers seem to have felt the same urge for revenge he did. Sergeant Barclay, of the Second Pennsylvania Infantry, for example, in the summer of 1846 visited the building in Perote, Mexico, where Walker and the other surviving Texans had been imprisoned. Barclay knew the meaning of the place in American memory full well: "The Castle possesses a melancholy interest to our army. It was here that the prisoners after having been marched in triumph over the greater part of Mexico were confined. Here is showed the hole from which Capt. Walker and a part of his companions escaped. And when we consider the sufferings to which these men were exposed, abused in the grossest manner, a number of their party murdered while prisoners in cold blood, the feeling of retaliation which influences the survivors is in a great degree palliated and cannot be violently condemned." The story, as Barclay knew of it, included an anecdote of distorted national retribution: "An American prisoner while here confined was obliged to repair or rig a flag staff. While at the job it is said he deposited a coin under the staff and hoped he might see the day when he could remove it and see the American flag waving over the fortress. He has had his wishes gratified."[25] The Mier expedition's forces came from independent Texas and would not have been dreaming of the U.S. flag in 1842 necessarily, but the imagined connections between them and citizens of the United States were strong, especially in juxtaposition to their Mexican adversaries, regarded as another race.

Robert W. Johannsen's longtime standard work, *To the Halls of the Montezumas: The Mexican War in the American Imagination*, which makes a case for the popularity of the Mexican-American War in the United States, does not mention the Mier prisoners and the infamous black bean lottery.[26] But soldiers at the time knew the story well. Captain Franklin Smith, a quartermaster serving with the Mississippi Rifles, met "one of the Mier prisoners," a man named Raga serving as an interpreter in 1846, while Smith was stationed at Camargo. Smith learned from Raga another of the legendary stories associated with the ill-fated expedition:

> It will be remembered that while being conveyed to Mexico they [Walker's men] rose on their guard and beat them off but getting lost afterwards were recaptured and decimated—One of his friends [was] a Texian with a large family having drawn a black bean—Raga went to the Mexican officer and enquired whether he might not be shot in his stead which was agreed to his friend was plunged into the greatest distress. Raga came to him and told him to cheer up that he would be shot in his place—that he should yet see his wife and children—and as for himself he had none and did not care about dying at all. The man embraced him and said not for the world would he allow such a thing—and marching out with the rest died with the utmost firmness—This instance of Roman fortitude and magnanimity which I get from a reliable source I have thought worthy of being remembered.[27]

The regular soldier Daniel Harvey Hill, of the Fourth United States Artillery, when he found out his camp lay near the town of Mier, wanted to visit because it had "some historical associations."[28]

Cadmus M. Wilcox, a West Point graduate who served in Mexico, recalled the Goliad and Mier atrocities as rallying points for eager Texas volunteers in the Mexican-American War of 1846:

> Scattered throughout the country, especially in the Southern and Western states, were many who had taken an active part in the Texas struggle for independence and returning home were objects of attention, notably at barbecues and mass meetings, so dear to the American heart, where their denunciation of Mexican oppression and cruelty, and their descriptions of the heroic sufferings of the Texan martyrs never failed to touch a responsive chord. There was scarcely a fireside in the land unfamiliar with the barbarous massacre of Fannin's men at Goliad, of the Spartan-like defense of the Alamo . . . There was scarcely a hearthstone where the details of the ill-starred Mier expedition had not been listened to with horror . . . Of Ampudia [the Mexican general who captured the Mier invaders] it was related that in the Yucatan . . . his adversary, General Santmenal, fell in his hands, and without . . . a trial he had his head cut off and boiled in oil and his body mutilated beyond recognition.[29]

The motive of revenge for the Mier prisoners and the image of Mexican cruelty that animated many American soldiers were not regionalized and applicable only to Texans, Southerners, or Westerners. Pennsylvanians, as we have seen, knew about the episode as well.

The role of those who had themselves been Mier prisoners proved considerable. Raga served as an interpreter and as a legend spreader. Samuel H. Walker played an even more marked role. He was a scout in the northern campaign under Zachary Taylor and a contra-guerrilla in Winfield Scott's campaign against Mexico City.[30] Mexicans killed Walker, who was associated with episodes of atrocity, outside Mexico City, and, in turn, his death provoked an incident of wanton retribution against the enemy. Moreover, the identities of those who killed the Mier prisoners were apparently known specifically among American soldiers in 1846–1848 and probably were circulated by Walker and other Mier escapees.[31]

The emotions that swept over the common soldiers did not necessarily affect leaders, the politicians and the generals. General Pedro de Ampudia, for example, reviled in American popular memory as perpetrator of the Mier atrocities in 1842–43 and as a mutilator of bodies, commanded the Mexican armies against Zachary Taylor at the Battle of Monterrey, fought September 20–23, 1846. General Taylor, far from treating General Ampudia as a war criminal, met him in person to negotiate an armistice interpreted by many Americans, most important among them President James K. Polk, as lenient toward the Mexican army.[32]

⊷⊷◎ ◎⊷⊷

What is noticeable in all this is the contrast with the American Civil War. Let us return now to each point for comparison. For by taking this long perspective on the Civil War in the context of previous American wars, it will be easier to see it in a new light.

If we recall Scott's and Taylor's denunciations of the behavior of the volunteers in Mexico, it is striking that one cannot recall similar characterizations of Civil War soldiers by their own generals. Likewise Samuel Chamberlain's depiction of the election of officers in an Illinois regiment formed a vivid part of a larger tale of gambling, drinking, knife fights, and atrocities, not all of which can be entirely believed. Still *My Confession,* as Chamberlain's book is titled, remains a standard source for the Mexican-American War. When his memoirs were published in Great Britain, they were given the title *The Recollections of a Rogue.* There may exist an analogous rogue's-eye-view memoir of the American Civil War, but I am unaware of it, and certainly no such memoir has attained the prominence as a documentary standard in the study of the Civil War that Chamberlain's confessions hold for the study of the Mexican-American War.[33]

Perhaps such a long view may serve to free Civil War history from the present tight focus in the literature concerned with the common soldier on the question, as the historian James M. McPherson expressed it, "Why did so many of them fight like bulldogs?"[34] A now vast literature has addressed that question, and historians can safely move on to other questions.

If we think of Civil War soldiers as compared to their forerunners in the Mexican-American War, we immediately notice that the Civil War soldiers were nearly all volunteers, and therefore the regular army, crucial in the Mexican-American War, played a negligible part in the later war. And who would say that the American soldiers in Mexico did not also fight like bulldogs?—not the Mexicans, certainly. Yet, even without the regulars present to police them, the Civil War soldiers behaved differently toward the enemy.

In the first place, the ethos of war was different. The ideals of Union and liberty were different from "manifest destiny." The ideals of defending Southern hearth and home were different too. The appeal of financial gain to be wrested from the enemy was less common in the later war. The appeal was more patriotic and idealistic in the Civil War, and the ideological and political struggles leading up to the war in the 1850s made it unlikely that Union soldiers would be enlisting in the hope of looting golden religious objects. For one thing, the South was characterized by an evangelical Protestantism as relentlessly opposed to papal splendor as any Northern sect; there was not much to be gained from the South's plain Baptist churches. More important, the steady denunciation of the South by the Republican party in the 1850s had constructed an image of the slave states as societies plagued by economic backwardness and poverty.[35] Mexico seemed economically underdeveloped too, but the fabled wealth of its churches in Protestant caricature and the get-rich-quick allure of its supposedly undeveloped silver mines loomed more vivid than the possibilities of plunder on the plantations of the great Slave-ocracy of the Southern Confederacy later.[36] Moreover, cities had stood in history, since the fall of Rome to the barbarians, as the targets of sacking, and the rural Confederacy aroused few visions of beauty and booty in decadent urban settings. As for the motives of the Con-federate soldiers, they could always be roused to defend home and hearth from the Yankee invader.

Even more important than the ethos of the wars was the factor of perceptions of race. Racial constructs help explain the unrestrained passions or the unfeeling contempt exemplified by the American vol-unteer in Mexico, and racial constructs likewise explain the restraint of white Civil War soldiers fighting other white soldiers. At least one historian of the Mexican-American War has also made the compari-son, but the reigning myths about the Civil War kept him from reaching the compelling conclusion. James M. McCaffrey concluded his able and balanced study of the common soldier in the Mexican-American War by rating the destructiveness of those soldiers as "probably no worse than average . . . in comparison with other nine-teenth-century armies." Then he made this comparison to the Civil War: "In Mexico there was no need to wage all-out war, as General Sherman did in Georgia in 1864. Conventional methods were very successful. And it was probably this success that went a long way to-ward preventing the type of destruction of civilian property that en-sued during the Civil War. The American troops had not become embittered by a long, costly war. They had, after all, won every bat-tle they fought. The absence of this bitterness probably saved a lot of Mexican property from the torch."[37] Unfortunately, such a con-clusion serves to undermine the whole point of studying the well-described "Army of Manifest Destiny" of the title of McCaffrey's fine book. The American troops in the Mexican-American War were embittered not by length of service but by ethnocentrism, racial constructs that were necessarily absent in most of the campaigns of the Civil War later.

There is a notable contrast between the behavior of the American volunteer in Mexico in 1846–1848 and the U.S. volunteers in the Confederacy in 1861–1865, but the differences all ran in the opposite direction. Robbery, rape, religious hatred, and the lure of pelf can hardly be found in the Civil War. The reason the subject of William T. Sherman's campaign in Georgia came to mind was that it provided a notable exception to the rule of the Civil War in regard to the private property of the enemy—and that rule was broken on Sherman's campaign only on the strict orders of the commanding general and not against orders in an individualistic quest for golden crucifixes.

Nor can we ignore the role of military discipline. The Mexican-American War proved, among other things, that military discipline could restrain soldiers' behavior no matter what the aggrandizing and prejudiced ethos of the war might be.

Discipline has proven a difficult subject for American historians to write about. Not surprisingly, the subject is usually dealt with from a libertarian perspective.[38] The very description of military discipline seems in American historical writing to be a call for reform. It is seldom closely considered as a successful means of altering behavior.

It is true, as James M. McPherson says of Civil War soldiers, that "American white males were the most individualistic, democratic people on the face of the earth in 1861," and that "they did not take kindly to authority, discipline, obedience."[39] Yet the same was true in 1846 as well as in the rest of the nineteenth century. Still, there were clearly differences in the systems of discipline imposed on American soldiers at different times and in different wars.

One major difference between the Civil War and Mexican-American War armies' behavior, never heretofore pointed out, lies in the quiet and gradual victory of discipline. Of course, at first the swamping of the regulars by volunteers in the Civil War meant that indiscipline marked the military. High rates of desertion plagued both Union and Confederate armies throughout the war, but these are not comparable with Mexican-American War experience because of the nature of the societies and landscapes into which soldiers had to desert in the two conflicts.[40] The Civil War soldier skulked away into a familiar landscape and temperate climate. He spoke the same language and worshipped for the most part at the same altars as the residents. He wore the same style of clothing in civilian life. The transportation system worked on familiar principles. Private John D. Billings, of the Tenth Massachusetts Battery in the Civil War, witnessed executions of deserters but believed nevertheless that the punishment did nothing to halt the escape of men from the ranks. The "opportunities to get away safely were most abundant," he observed.[41]

The Civil War lasted four long years, and the armies of that war had time to learn from experience and to change their practices. Discipline was the hidden lesson of the Bull Run defeat for the Federal armies at the end of June 1861. The Northern press was replete with calls for its institution. "What is the value of free . . . institutions if they do not make us more valiant men?" asked the *New York Evening Post*. "The cause of the late panic at Bull Run . . . was not want of personal courage . . . [but] want of discipline." U.S. volunteers needed "an immense deal of thorough schooling."[42]

Figuring out the lessons of the Bull Run defeat became a journalistic cottage industry for a time, but the conclusions commonly reached can be easily summarized. In addition to the need for discipline, newspapermen, surprisingly, came to believe that the military should ignore the popular press when it urged precipitate action and that the country should rely on officers professionally trained in military "science." Such men, of course, would be akin to the West Point officers in Mexico in their views on discipline, and without an intrusive press looking for abuses of the individual rights of common soldiers, one can imagine the sort of discipline such men would introduce. And introduce it they did, apparently.

But first the Congress had to deal with the problem of flogging. Discipline may have been a widely recognized need of the post–Bull Run Union army, but the country needed an army in the field to discipline. Congress had to assure a steady supply of volunteers. That could be done in part by improving the unattractive aspects of military life. Thus in the special session of Congress that met after July 4, 1861, to deal for the first time with the Civil War, one of the unheralded measures taken was to abolish flogging in the army.

This was most likely a recognition that the war would be fought on a large scale and thus by volunteers and not by regulars. President Abraham Lincoln signed into law the bill outlawing flogging in the army on August 5, 1861. A miscellaneous catchall from the Committee on Military Affairs, the bill dealt mainly with fortifications. The statute in the end carried no explanatory preamble and there was no roll call vote on the measure. Historians must guess at the motivations of the members of Congress in this case. It seems likely that the legislation shared the purpose of other military measures passed in that special session, to make service more attractive to potential volunteers. Likewise, it appears that the measure was made possible by the absence from the halls of Congress of the representatives of the South's planter class—now departed to the Confederacy—who were likely to stand up for the symbolic prowess of the lash. The two U.S.

senators who seemed most interested in the bill were antislavery stalwarts, Henry Wilson of Massachusetts and John P. Hale of New Hampshire.

To end flogging in the army was to say to the potential volunteer that he was not being asked to descend into the slavery of the professional soldier in the ranks. Otherwise, the measure ran counter to what lay in store for the eager volunteer. In the end, the Civil War armies proved to be closely disciplined. The institution of regular discipline was one of the keys to the "organizational" genius of George B. McClellan. Though routinely noted, that quality of genius is seldom analyzed. One thing seems clear from the record: McClellan was consistently stern on matters of discipline. The examples to be found in the work of the first great student of life in the Union army, Bell I. Wiley, should suffice to make the point. When Joshua C. Ward was court-martialed for sleeping on guard duty, the officers found him not guilty and cited a long (and unimpressive) string of extenuating circumstances for his behavior: Ward was tired from marching, the post he guarded was not very important, and his unit had low discipline on the whole. "Little wonder," remarked Wiley with his customary common sense, "that this finding called forth a blistering rebuke from McClellan!" Wiley also cites an example from the time shortly after McClellan assumed command of the Army of the Potomac, when the general complained sharply of the imposition of only light punishments for serious offenses. "It has seldom happened that military delinquencies so grave have been visited with punishments having so much the appearance of intending to sanction future violations of good order and discipline . . . Military crimes to which the articles of war annex the heaviest penalties are treated as if they were the most venial misdemeanors."[43]

Obviously McClellan had been appointed to remedy the faults of the Bull Run army and understood his role in that regard perfectly.

it was carried on by both officers and privates. In one command, at least, where this vice was interdicted, culprits in the ranks were punished by having one-half of the head shaved — a most humiliating and effective punishment.

ON A WOODEN HORSE.

Then "back talk," as it was commonly called, which, interpreted, means answering a superior officer insolently, was a prolific cause of punishments. It did not matter in some organizations who the officer was, from colonel or captain to the last corporal, to hear was to obey, and under such discipline the men became the merest puppets. In theory, such a regiment was the perfect military machine, where every man was in complete subordination to one master mind. But the value of such a machine, after all, depended largely upon the kind of a man the ruling spirit was, and whether he associated his inflexibility of steel with the justice of Aristides. If he did that, then was it indeed a model organization; but such bodies were rare, for the conditions were wanting to make them abundant. The master mind was too often tyrannical and abusive, either by nature, or from having been suddenly clothed with a little brief authority over men. And often when nature, if left to herself, would have made him a good commander, an excessive use of "commissary" interfered to prevent, and the subordinates of such a leader, many of them appointed by his influence, would naturally partake of his characteristics; so that such regiments, instead of standing solidly on all occasions, were

3. Illustration of the wooden horse punishment by Charles W. Reed in John D. Billings, *Hardtack and Coffee: The Unwritten Story of Army Life,* 1887. Punishments such as this that could have caused mutiny among U.S. volunteers in the Mexican-American War had become routine in the more disciplined armies of the American Civil War.

We know from his Mexican War diary that he was well suited to that part of the task. He worked wonders, apparently. The result was a surprising routinization of discipline among American volunteers, whether it was primarily the work of McClellan or, as is more likely, the work of many sensible officers after the Bull Run defeat. John D. Billings's *Hardtack and Coffee: The Unwritten Story of Army Life,* as standard a source for the Civil War as Samuel Chamberlain's *Confession* is for the Mexican-American War, stands as a monument to the changed discipline of the American volunteer. Billings served as a private in a Massachusetts battery in the Army of the Potomac, and his charming memoir includes a substantial chapter, complete with illustrations by Charles W. Reed, titled "Offences and Punishments." A reader fresh from the study of Mexican-American War diaries and letters will be quite surprised at the long list of standard punishments for camp offenses and the matter-of-fact mention, in the course of making that list, of what in the Mexican-American War had provoked mutiny: lashing to "a tall wooden horse which stood perhaps eight or nine feet high."[44] In a similar way, the wooden horse provoked no special attention from the great historian of the life of the common soldier, Bell I. Wiley. He mentioned it only in passing as one of the lighter penalties for common and minor offenses in the Union army.

Historians agree substantially that discipline improved—that is, harshened—as the Civil War progressed, but the comparison across wars makes a more important point: it helps to put the whole Civil War experience in perspective. Civil War volunteers were much more disciplined and therefore more restrained than their predecessors in the Mexican-American War.

⋰⊨⊜ ⊜⊨⋰

Nor was revenge a significant factor in explaining the behavior of most Civil War troops. The Union army did not enter battle with the cry "Remember Sumter." No one died in the Confederate shelling of the Union fort that began the war. It is true that considerable feeling rankled in the Northern breast against South Carolina as the political cradle of secession, but that proved to point to specific targets, first the siege by "Greek Fire" of Charleston in 1863 (a subject further examined in Chapter 5) and later by the general destructiveness perpetrated on the march of William T. Sherman's army through South Carolina in 1865. There were special and local wrongs to be righted, but nothing held sway over memory in the Civil War armies as did Goliad and the black bean lottery of the Mier prisoners.

⊶≡◎ ◎≡⊷

I have been seeking the key to the character of Civil War violence and destructiveness literally for decades. Ever since I wrote "Was the Civil War a Total War?" and called into question the assertion that Northern soldiers deliberately targeted Southern civilians for destruction, I have been looking for the factors that explain the restraint of the Civil War soldiers. What I had written was long on taking apart the old assumption but short on explaining what kept the soldiers from the bloody and brutal outlook erroneously attributed to them by historians.

The influence of evangelical Protestantism was an obvious possibility, but as the historian Harry Stout accurately observes, the clergy were "cheerleaders all."[45] Internalized religious restraints specific to the war did not always hold the soldiers back, though general rules of morality about stealing and killing might have played some role. True, the enthusiastic nationalism of the Protestant denominations could, as in the times of the religious wars, fuel atrocity, but the Civil War soldiers were not fighting Roman Catholics, as in Mexico. It was neither a religious war nor a religiously restrained one. Self-righteousness rather than humanistic restraint was the obvious effect of Civil War religion.

The assumptions of the age in regard to the laws and customs of war, as people at the time often referred to the restraints inherited from the Enlightenment, were frequently mentioned by Civil War soldiers. And it is certainly true that the literature on the Civil War has paid too little attention to those. Although vague, the terms "laws and customs of war" came readily to the lips of most Civil War officers and embodied some relevant ideal of legal and moral restraints imposed by civilization. Their overlooked importance becomes clear when we realize that these laws and customs achieved their first official codification in the very midst of the Civil War in General Orders No. 100.[46] The law professor Francis Lieber drafted the code, and the Lincoln administration imposed it on the Union armies and made it known to the Confederates in 1863. That surprising initiative was an attempt to reverse a breakdown of traditional restraints that seemed to be threatening to turn the war in a savage direction in 1863. But Lieber's code was itself a rough-and-ready affair, allowing much leeway for abuse and simply not often enough mentioned by officers and soldiers in the field to be considered a practical restraint holding back the passions aroused in a great national and civil war. Like religion too, the laws and customs of war were invoked against the enemy, most often, and seldom used to search the behavior of one's own side.[47]

Only when I turned away from the Civil War and began looking back into American history to gain perspective on the problem, did I come to realize that the answer lies substantially in perceptions of racial differences and racial *similarities*. Historians of the Civil War have long recognized that when soldiers perceived the enemy as being of another race, as in the case of Confederate soldiers fighting African American troops, atrocity was an all but certain outcome.[48] But no historian has stressed the obvious corollary: When Civil War soldiers perceived the enemy as being of the same race, that perception acted as a restraint. In other words, the most powerful cultural force restraining white American volunteers on both sides in the Civil War was the perception that the enemy was of the same race. The historian Mark Grimsley has come the closest to placing proper emphasis on this factor, arguing that historians should regard racism as a "psychological phenomenon" as well as an excuse for economic exploitation and a cultural invention.[49] As a psychological factor, racism triggered one type of ideas and impulses in people who perceived the enemy as another race and aroused different feelings in people who regarded the enemy as members of their own race. Most of the Civil War was fought by white volunteers against white volunteers, and under the ugly assumptions of the age, that made a considerable difference. It made so much difference, in fact, that it led from its ugly premises to a generally beautiful conclusion. No-quarter policies were regarded as unforgivably extreme. Women and children, the aged and infirm, were strictly exempted from direct and deliberate targeting for destruction. Civilized belligerents eschewed certain kinds of destructive actions—when dealing with others regarded as civilized belligerents.

Moreover, the perception of sameness was such that it need not— did not—evoke assertion. In other words, the perception was so universally present, like air one breathes, that no one bothered to comment on it. It is therefore the sort of thing historians are likely to overlook, so much a part of the mindset of the age that it hardly ever had to be asserted. The racial outlook was, surprisingly, already firmly embedded at the time of the Mexican War. That conflict preceded the sharp sectional controversy over slavery among the political parties in the 1850s and the consequent hardening of white supremacist affirmations in the Democratic party. But when people were confronted with a strange society, the racist assumptions were easily and promptly brought to the surface in rationalizing racial speculations on the fate of Mexico.

It is surprising to find the assumptions so easily articulated by both Whigs and Democrats and by the politically unengaged on campaigns in Mexico. Examined closely, however, the diaries and memoirs and letters reveal the bedrock of comfortable assumptions about race. For example, in the quest for entertainment in the garrisons and camps, the American soldiers turned to amateur theatricals. What proved both diverting and comforting was the familiar humor and song of minstrel shows. Richard Smith Elliott, in occupied Santa Fe, noted the creation of a thespian group among the men from St. Louis in camp. They performed a tragedy. "After the tragedy," Elliott said, "came the Virginia Minstrels, led by [John T.] Neal, one of the [Laclede] Rangers, their songs being interspersed by negro lectures conundrums, &c., all in a style of broad extravaganza."[50] Luther Giddings, describing "enchanting" nights around the fire in camp, remembered the singing of the German Americans in his Ohio regiment. "There were those too," he added, "in the ranks who delighted in the Ethiopean style of minstrelsy, long popular in the United States, and who awoke the echoes of the grove with the untutored but not unpleasing, music of the banjo and the bones."[51]

Civil War soldiers from the North enjoyed minstrel entertainments at least as much as their Mexican-American War predecessors. But in their case reminders of supposed racial differences in the world served, in most instances, to unite them with the enemy rather than to separate them. A revealing incident occurred when Tattnall Paulding, an officer in the Sixth United States Cavalry, was captured by Confederates in 1863 and taken under guard to Richmond, Virginia, to be kept in Libby Prison. The route the Union prisoners followed went south through the Shenandoah Valley to Staunton and then through the gap in the mountains near Staunton eastward to Richmond. In the northern part of the Shenandoah Valley, already the scene of many Civil War battles, the local residents had seen many Yankees, but when the prisoners reached as far south as Staunton, the residents were more curious to see the foe. At the train station in Staunton, as the prisoners awaited transportation, the citizenry turned out to gawk at the Union soldiers. "Quite a crowd gathered," wrote Paulding, "to see the live Yankees and were much amused at the 'Lemcum Gunboats' and 'Three Black Crows' with which we favored them, the Adjut. of the 4[th] Michigan being principal musician."[52]

Thus it occurred immediately to the officers of the Union army, faced with the curious crowd, to forge a bond with them through an appeal to racial prejudices held in common. Such an appeal helped ensure the prisoners' safety among the possibly hostile local populace in Virginia. The strategy worked well for the Union soldiers and amused them in the bargain. Once they reached Libby Prison, the soldiers continued their minstrel entertainments, as Paulding recalled: "A Negro minstrel band has come into existence. It is a little annoying to me to see with what proficiency some of our officers take to the role of the nigger. The performance was amusing at first but is played out. Our cousin Kindall is 'Brother Bones.'"[53] Though the crude minstrel shows may have grown tiresome to Paulding, they had their utility. On Christmas Eve, 1863, for example, the Union prisoners of war in the Libby Prison in Richmond, all of them officers in the U.S. Army, presented a program of the Libby Prison Minstrels to the Richmond citizens.[54] In the Mexican-American War minstrel entertainments were comforting reminders of home that said nothing in particular about the enemy in Mexico but that testified to the belief that the world was arranged in races. In Virginia in 1863 minstrelsy was rooted in a belief that the white enemies shared in common—like the Christmas spirit itself but not benign.

A historian could study a great deal of the vast documentary record of the Civil War and never find mentioned overtly the most important factor in shaping behavior toward the enemy. The mindset of the era is sometimes perceptible only from a perspective outside the era itself. Examined from the perspective of a war in which the mindset was suddenly thrust into unfamiliar circumstances, as in Mexico, the assumptions become clear. Common beliefs in racial identity restrained the Civil War soldier from the exploitive and rapacious excesses of the U.S. volunteers in the Mexican-American War.

The quiet perception of sameness and racial equality among whites in the Civil War was nearly everywhere reinforced by the constant presence of African Americans in Southern society. The white soldiers thus encountered regular reminders of their whiteness and of the whiteness of the adversary. The perception fundamentally dictated the tone of the conflict.

## 2

## PRICE'S RAID

### Limited War in Missouri

No BOOK has had more influence on the modern writing of Civil War history than Michael Fellman's *Inside War: The Guerrilla Conflict in Missouri during the American Civil War,* published in 1989. In a little over a decade after its publication, Civil War history was so transformed that what had once been regarded as a "sideshow" to the great national conflict, guerrilla warfare, had stolen the show.[1] The vivid and innovative studies that followed the trail Fellman blazed have gone a long way toward giving the Civil War an appearance of remorselessness and grisly violence that respected no persons or property. This body of literature, if not comprehensive, is certainly substantial enough to allow us to stand back from it and to put it in perspective. And one of the best ways to accomplish that is to return to Missouri, where Fellman began this little revolution in writing Civil War history.

I will look first at one of those incidents that by 1863 seemed to be leading the country down the path to merciless and unrestrained warfare, the Palmyra Massacre. That incident will set the scene for the focus of the remainder of the chapter, the return to Missouri of Confederate General Sterling Price on a raid in 1864. The raid caused the Union commanders in Missouri to turn from their preoccupation with guerrilla butchery to face the Confederate foe once again, in gray uniformed array. What ensued provided a test: What was the effect of experience in guerrilla warfare on fighting a conventional enemy?

⋆⟿ ⟾⋆

What happened in Missouri during the American Civil War drew notice all over the world. In 1863 the London humor magazine *Punch* printed John Tenniel's cartoon entitled "Extremes Meet," comparing the Lincoln administration's effort to conquer the Confederacy to Russian attempts to suppress Poland. The irony of friendly diplomatic relations between czarist Russia and the most advanced democracy on earth underlay the image of Lincoln and Alexander shaking hands. Behind the cartoon figure of Lincoln, "Greek Fire" rains devastation on Charleston, South Carolina. The Russian army slaughters civilians in the scene that provides the czar's backdrop. A satirical poem accompanying the cartoon catalogued a litany of atrocities commonly attributed to the Union cause at the time. Obviously the comic editors at *Punch* thought the United States had already taken the fatal turn toward destructiveness posed as a possibility in the Introduction to this book.[2]

In the cartoon Lincoln boasts to the czar of the work of "General McNeil." John McNeil is a symbol of Yankee atrocity mostly forgotten, but in the middle of the Civil War he ranked with "Greek Fire" as a symbol of atrocity in war.[3] In this book I aim to recover the sense of limits to warfare that governed the era of the Civil War, and McNeil and Greek Fire obviously more than tested those limits at the time. (Greek Fire will be discussed again in Chapter 5.) John McNeil's infamous career provides a good way to introduce the problem of unconventional warfare.

On September 18, 1862, in Palmyra, Missouri, McNeil had ten hos-

4. *Extremes Meet, Punch,* October 24, 1863. President Lincoln and Czar Alexander II shake hands warmly amidst the ashes of a city reduced by bombardment with "Greek Fire" and scenes of civilians slaughtered by imperial soldiers.

tages executed. He had been holding these ten men, selected from guerrillas taken prisoner, pending the return of a Unionist prisoner named Andrew Allsman, who had been captured by Confederate guerrillas led by Joseph C. Porter. Allsman, who was around sixty years old, had long resided in the area and performed valuable services as a guide, leading Union forces to guerrilla hideouts, and as an informer, identifying disloyal people in the area. McNeil did not regard Allsman as the kind of man the Union could afford to let the Confederates kidnap without showing great concern. So he had a letter printed in the *Palmyra Courier* demanding Allsman's return in ten days' time on pain of the execution of ten hostages. He gave a copy to Porter's wife, who lived in the area and was rumored to be in regular contact with her husband.

Nothing happened and Allsman was presumed dead. At the designated deadline McNeil had the prisoners shot. Naturally, the *Palmyra Courier* covered the grim event. Newspapers passed readily between the lines during the Civil War, and the Confederate *Memphis Appeal* picked up the story from the Missouri paper. On November 2, 1862, an aide to General Sterling Price, a Missourian in Confederate service, sent President Jefferson Davis the Memphis clipping. The aide recommended that Davis demand a satisfactory explanation from the Union authorities or the surrender of McNeil to Confederate justice. Failing that, the Confederates should execute Union prisoners of war in retaliation. On November 17 Davis enclosed the clipping with an order to General Theophilus Holmes, then the commander of the Confederacy's Trans-Mississippi Department, to send out, under a flag of truce, a demand for explanation. If Holmes received none, and McNeil was not handed over to him, he was to execute the first ten Union officers to fall into his hands as prisoners of war. Davis later received more protests about McNeil in a letter written by outraged citizens of northeastern Missouri, who alleged a long train of abuses by McNeil. They held him responsible for a hundred prisoners' deaths.[4]

News of the atrocity at Palmyra quickly reached as far away as London, England, and was put to damaging use against the United States. Newspapers hostile to the Union cause, such as the *Times* of London, naturally made the most of it, but so did the usually friendly *Star*. At that point, the London correspondent for the Republican *New York Times* took alarm and warned of the "Effect of Terrorism" on British views of the war in America:

> There is one matter worthy of the attention of the Government at Washington. It is the effect produced in Europe by such acts as the Military execution of the prisoners of war at Palmyra, Mo., not for acts of their own, but for the supposed acts of others. Every such act of simple terrorism alienates thousands of friends and embitters millions of enemies. The South is made more hostile, and the restoration of the Union more hopeless. If a National General in Missouri shoots ten prisoners for one man suspected to be killed, why should not a Confederate General shoot a hundred prisoners—carrying out the same proportion—for these were known to be killed; and so on until all prisoners on both sides are butchered in cold blood as soon as taken!

In the same issue of December 1, the editors in New York denounced the act of General McNeil.

Yet McNeil was never surrendered to the Confederates, and General Holmes apparently never followed up with the dire threats in Jefferson Davis's order. Enthusiasm for retaliation among high-ranking military and political leaders almost always ebbed with the passage of time. They did not tend to nurse grudges and injuries of that sort, let alone transfer a sense of outrage to other officials. Revenge, as we have seen in the case of the American volunteers and the Mier and Goliad martyrs, moved the rank and file but not the general officers.

Before anything happened in the McNeil case, Holmes was replaced as Confederate Trans-Mississippi Department commander by General Edmund Kirby Smith. Kirby Smith followed up on the problem, but months had passed. Holmes had written Union general Samuel R. Curtis about McNeil, for the Mexican-American War veteran Curtis was then in command of the Department of the Missouri. Curtis replied vaguely. When Kirby Smith forwarded the correspondence to Richmond, he revealed his true feelings. "In consequence of the time that has elapsed since the alleged murder," he said, "the effect of retaliation now could not be so salutary as if made at an earlier day."[5] In the end the Confederate president could only put the whole unfortunate affair to use as propaganda. In his annual message to Congress of December 7, 1863, Jefferson Davis commented, as usual, on the "savage ferocity" of the enemy, in this instance putting McNeil in the infamous company of General Benjamin F. Butler, the "Beast" of New Orleans, and General John B. Turchin, whose men pillaged the town of Athens, Alabama, after capturing it early in 1862.[6] So ended the Confederate part in the McNeil affair.

On the Union side, the army did look into the Palmyra executions. Early in December 1862, after the spectacular international criticism, General Curtis asked McNeil for an explanation. McNeil sent the clipping from the *Palmyra Courier* as exoneration and added his own defiant narrative to his defense. The executions, he insisted, were "done to fix & emphasize & make sacred the life of a Union man. I refer to the still of the country for the effect. I refer to God for the Justice of the act." He did not refer to law.

Perhaps because the correspondence in the *New York Times* had already divulged as much, McNeil volunteered information on more atrocities than the one at Palmyra. "The morning after the battle of Kirkmill," he said, "I shot fifteen violators of parole—the next day an officer was tried & shot for being a spy & a Garilla subsequently at Macon City Genl Merrill shot ten men for the same cause." The Southern-sympathizing citizens of northeastern Missouri who wrote Jefferson Davis may not have exaggerated greatly in their catalogue of a hundred executions by General McNeil.

McNeil insisted that none of the guerrilla leaders in northeast Missouri really held commissions from the Confederate government. That claim required rather close calculation. Some of those who once held commissions, he argued, resigned them before returning to Missouri (guerrillas went to the Confederacy in the winter months when there were no leaves on the trees in Missouri to hide their movements). The rest lost their commissions when commands were consolidated, or enjoyed commissions contingent upon raising troops in Missouri not yet raised. "As to giving me up," he added in one last defiant note, "I suppose I will have something to say about being given up. My own government can try & punish me for my acts, none other can untill we relapse into barbarity. The proposition is decidedly Indian."[7]

While the army and the Lincoln administration decided what to do, others went to work to exonerate McNeil. They did more than that, in fact; they sought to make him a national hero. A prominent Unionist in Missouri wrote his senator to urge McNeil's promotion.[8] Hundreds of Missourians from small towns signed printed petitions that were sent to the president of the United States urging him not to surrender McNeil to Jefferson Davis. One group of citizens in New York sent from their "remote distance" a letter of encouragement and a sword in honor of his acts.[9]

McNeil must have realized that the tide of public opinion was running in his favor. On Christmas Eve he wrote General Curtis a remarkable letter, asking his superior in an outraged tone whether he would be "shut off from promotion" on account of the Palmyra incident.[10]

McNeil's practical argument, one widely invoked by his defenders, was that his stern action brought peace to northeast Missouri. It is difficult to tell, but we are able to catch occasional glimpses of the effect of the Palmyra affair in his later military campaigns in Missouri. Naturally, his name became a byword among Confederates operating in the West. Colonel G. W. Thompson of the Sixth Missouri (Confederate) Cavalry referred to McNeil in a report in May 1863 as "the criminal outlaw and tory leader," and expressed his special determination to win a victory over him.[11] Northern officers added their own testimony to the existence of special motivation for Confederate forces when they fought against McNeil. Colonel R. R. Livingston, of the First Nebraska Volunteer Infantry, operating in Missouri in April, noted in his report of the campaign that the enemy "battle cry was 'Hurrah, now for McNeil!'"[12] Here was a Civil War incident that stirred local motives of revenge.

McNeil himself had to admit to some ill effects of his actions. He described his operations near the Arkansas border in March with this observation: "I administered the oath to over 100 citizens, and could have done so to many times that number had they not been scared off by extravagant reports of our killing unarmed and innocent persons. The covers being over our guidons, for it rained most of the time, they were taken for black flags, and the story that we were marching under that peculiarly Southern emblem widely circulated. Rape and murder were charged on us, causing the men to flee to the swamps. The women alone stood their ground."[13] By his own admission, his fame had preceded him. McNeil did receive his promotion, but his military career was confined to Missouri and he never moved on to a more important theater of operations.[14]

President Lincoln saw all the correspondence concerning the incident at Palmyra and did nothing.[15]

The Palmyra Massacre brought together explosive elements of atrocity. It caused citizens for months literally to imagine they saw the black flag of merciless death raised over Union military columns. It immediately conjured up images of a chain of retaliation and counter-retaliation that might result in the execution of all prisoners of war on both sides. Talk of "barbarity" and "Indians" was in the air. Could it be said that Palmyra marked a little-known turning point in the American Civil War? Was the policy of the Lincoln administration becoming more callous in 1863, since General McNeil not only escaped punishment but was promoted? Have we witnessed the hardening of attitudes of generals faced with guerrilla warfare?

It is impossible to judge the Civil War by any single incident. It is always difficult to identify "policy," let alone discover the events that provoked its formulation. Lincoln did not condemn, but he did not necessarily draw some drastic new strategic conclusion, either. The public did not know exactly what his previous policy was, or whether he was changing to a new one. In reality, nothing much changed, for better or worse. General McNeil continued to be quite a fighter and gave tough public orders, threatening to deal "summarily" with certain offenses and offenders.[16] Yet he negotiated under a flag of truce sent by Confederate General William Steele in Arkansas on December 9, 1863, and explained earnestly the "proper subjects of intercourse by a flag of truce between hostile armies," insisting on adhering to "the laws of civilized warfare" and "the interests of our common humanity."[17]

Just as we cannot with any confidence judge the Civil War by any single incident, so we cannot judge the Civil War from any single campaign or even from a single department of operations. Certainly we cannot judge it by what happened in Missouri, for many different things happened there, and the lessons drawn by the participants from the events of the war varied.

⚬⟫ ⟪⚬

Price's Raid, which began in September 1864, was the opposite of the Palmyra Massacre. It presented the return of traditional combat situations to Missouri after more than two years of unconventional and brutal warfare. Thus Confederate General Sterling Price's invasion of Missouri two years after the Palmyra Massacre affords the historian a rare opportunity to examine Union policy at work against two kinds of enemies at the same time and place. Suddenly the Union generals and politicians who had been waging war against guerrillas now faced a traditional Confederate enemy, Price's invading army. At the same time the Union forces faced an energized enemy in the rear: Price's Raid roused the virulent guerrilla forces and bushwhackers of Missouri to cooperative action.

The Union generals and politicians treated the two threats as separate problems and dealt with them in different ways. There was no transfer of skills, techniques, or attitudes from one front to the other. By modern standards, the Union forces exhibited a sort of military schizophrenia. By the standards of the nineteenth century, they fought the "civilized" enemy by customary means and the "barbarous" enemy by suitably unpleasant means. This phenomenon is all the more remarkable given the nature of Price's Raid.

Price's Raid into Missouri was a desperate military campaign if ever there was one, eloquent testimony to the dire straits of the Confederacy in 1864. President Jefferson Davis had been pleading with General Kirby Smith to send troops from the West across the Mississippi River to help the forces in Georgia directly or at least to initiate some action farther west to divert Federal attention from the relentless campaigns in Georgia and Virginia.

Price's Raid was the ultimate pitiful result. Under strength, the expedition began with as few as 9,000 men (but more likely 12,000). Astonishingly over 20 percent of them—perhaps as many as 40 percent—were unarmed![18] The dreamy idea was to capture weapons in Missouri to equip the men, along with even more unarmed recruits expected to rally to the Confederate banner once Price's army appeared in the state.

Anyone who would invade enemy territory unarmed was surely desperate. The unarmed combatants were the very dregs, wretched men that might shame the old European armies in the darkest days of impressment.[19] By the admission of the Confederate high command itself, not only the 2,000 to 4,000 unarmed men but some

2,000 of the rest of the invading army were "deserters and conscripts, officered by men of their own kind."[20] Modern historians conclude that they were motivated by the lure of booty or the desire for revenge or that they were forced into the ranks.[21]

The discipline of this army fell below even the rough standards of the far-western Confederate armies, and nearly everyone concerned on the Confederate side admitted it. The army was desperate not only for arms and ammunition but also for food and forage. Consequently, it was common practice on the march to authorize "scouting," foraging the countryside for food and fuel—which, as many admitted later, was little more than looting. In some instances, of course, it resulted in "marauding," committing violent crimes against the civilians in the countryside.[22] General Price issued the customary cosmetic orders forbidding such practices and on at least one occasion condoned the execution on the spot of a Confederate marauder by an officer, but there was little systematic disciplinary muscle available to enforce the orders.[23]

Price had traveling with him a politician named Thomas C. Reynolds, the so-called Confederate governor of Missouri, who hoped to be installed in office in Jefferson City on the raid. Reynolds was sorely disappointed when Price decided not to lay siege to the Missouri capital, and thereby Price created a bitter and articulate critic. Upon the return of the Confederates to Texas, Reynolds drafted a scathing letter alleging Price's incompetence to command such a venture. He described the army's march through Missouri with unforgettable images:

> The disorder in his army was terrific . . . It would take a volume to describe the acts of outrage; neither station, age nor sex was any protection; Southern men and women were as little spared as Unionists; the elegant mansion of General Robert E. Lee's accomplished niece and

the cabin of the negro were alike ransacked; John Dane, the first civilian ever made a State prisoner by Mr. Lincoln's Government, had his watch and money robbed from his person, in the open street of Potosi, in broad day, as unceremoniously as the German merchant at Fredrickstown was forced, a pistol at his ear, to surrender his concealed greenbacks. As the citizens of Arkansas and Northern Texas have seen in the goods unblushingly offered them for sale, the clothes of the poor man's infant were as attractive spoil as the merchant's silk and calico or the curtain taken from the rich man's parlor; ribbons and trumpery gee-gaws were stolen from milliners, and jeweled rings forced from the fingers of delicate maidens whose brothers were fighting in Georgia in Cockrell's Confederate Missouri brigade.[24]

Governor Reynolds went on to describe Price's infamous wagon train, a fine symbol of the whole operation: "Numerous wagons which the soldiers believed to contain untold wealth of plunder by staff officers and dead-heads, had dangerously augmented his train, so that it numbered over five hundred vehicles, and, shockingly controlled and conducted, often stretched out eight or ten miles in length. Marched in the center of the army, flanked, preceded or followed by a rabble of dead-heads, stragglers and stolen negroes on stolen horses, leading broken down chargers, it gave to the army the appearance of a Calmuck [Mongol] horde."[25]

No assaulting force in American history was more worthy of being regarded by defenders as a barbarian invasion than Price's raiders. Such an army, if it can be called that, invited Union forces defending their homes and hearths in Missouri to fight without restraint. Missourians had already been tried beyond the breaking point by three years of hideous atrocities perpetrated by guerrillas acting in the name of the Confederacy. They surely had little patience to spare for forces such as Price commanded. The invaders burst into the state, equipped only for living off the land, and fully intending to seek help

5. *Battle of Bull Run,* 1889. Fears of the Southern cavalier magnified the presence and prowess of the Confederate cavalry in the Northern imagination. The unit depicted in this chromolithograph, the First Virginia Cavalry, did not actually sweep through the New York Fire Zouaves (recruited from the fire departments of the Northern city) in the first great battle of the Civil War, fought in 1861.

from the most notorious of the guerrilla groups already operating in Missouri, those led by William Quantrill and "Bloody Bill" Anderson.[26] Moreover, most of the force was mounted and thus required more in the way of supplies than columns of infantry would.[27]

The initial reaction to the raid was predictable, under the assumptions of the era. Unionists in Missouri at first mistook some of the invading enemy for savages. Rumor had it that the Confederates included Indians among their forces, and Missourians fled in panic. Rumors, of course, do not make good history, but they reveal the fears and stereotypes held by those who believe them. Missourians did not, as Federal forces in the eastern theater of war sometimes did, express their fears by seeing imaginary "cavaliers" charging on fine Virginia horses.[28] In the West they feared savagery.

Union generals were careful to sort out the facts about the enemy from the rumors. General Thomas Ewing wrote for information from a major stationed near the invading armies at Pilot Knob, Missouri, asking about a particular Confederate unit said to be among the invaders: "I suppose it is the command which includes the Indians, the reports of the presence of whom have been stampeding the people."[29]

In fact the intelligence had come in part from people fleeing in the face of Price's army and was found to be erroneous.[30] As it turned out, Price commanded no Indian units, but the Union side recruited Indians to meet the Confederate invasion—in Kansas under martial law—and not the other way around.[31]

⊶≡◎ ◎≡⊷

Savagery and barbarism have long since ceased to be anthropological classifications, and their invocation can no longer be taken seriously. But Lincoln's generation thought they knew what barbarism and civilization were. The initial emergence of "savagery" as a factor in the Civil War early in 1862, even in the remote western theater of the conflict, appears to have taken most people quite by surprise. No one expected savagery to intrude on this epoch-making struggle for national existence. It is true that allegations of atrocities committed by Confederate soldiers emerged immediately after the first Battle of Bull Run and were investigated by the Joint Committee on the Conduct of the War in the U.S. Congress. They faded rather quickly from memory, carrying as they did the scent of routine vilification of the opposition. But actually confronting military forces of Indians on a Civil War battlefield—people notorious to most Americans for not

6. *Battle of Pea Ridge, Ark,* 1889. Fears of savage warfare in the American West magnified the importance of the small contingent of Indian troops deployed by the Confederates at this battle fought in 1862.

being ruled by the laws and customs of war—was difficult to interpret. This had already happened once in the Missouri theater of operations.

The use of Indian soldiers in the Confederate forces at the Battle of Pea Ridge, just across the border from Missouri in Arkansas on March 7–8, 1862, proved so shocking that it became a symbol of Confederate ruthlessness. It was memorialized in 1889 in the famous series of chromolithographs issued by the Chicago firm of Kurz & Allison by one image depicting a charge of mounted Indians at the Battle of Pea Ridge.

Historians of the battle insist that the image is "wildly inaccurate," and say that no Indians participated in the Confederate cavalry charge at the battle. But the symbolic meaning of the event—the shock of the possibility of barbarism intruding on a war between "civilized belligerents," as Abraham Lincoln and most of his generation regarded the two sides in the Civil War—deserves more attention. In fact, members of one or both of the two Confederate Cherokee regiments at the battle did scalp and mutilate some of the dead from an Iowa regiment, and testimony is mixed on the presence of Indians in the cavalry charge early in the battle.[32]

The evidence of the scalping incident (an officer had the bodies in question dug up for examination after the battle to make certain) led to accusation and protest.[33] The day after the battle, in the customary correspondence between opposing sides to arrange for disposal of the bodies lying on the field, Union General Samuel R. Curtis told Confederate General Earl Van Dorn that "on the battle-field, contrary to civilized warfare, many of the Federal dead . . . were tomahawked, scalped, and their bodies shamefully mangled." Curtis expressed "a hope that this important struggle may not degenerate to a savage warfare."[34] Van Dorn's reply was out of character for exchanges involving allegations of atrocity. Instead of issuing a blustering denial, the Confederate general insisted that "the Indians who formed part of his forces" had "for many years been regarded as civilized people." Still, he promised Curtis that he would "most cordially unite with you in repressing the horrors of this unnatural war."[35] General Albert Pike, the Confederate commander of the forces brought from Indian territory to the Pea Ridge campaign, was an unusual man with exceptional ideas about Indians, and he later admitted to Curtis outright his chagrin at the behavior of his own troops.[36]

Less than two weeks after the Battle of Pea Ridge, General Van Dorn moved to the east and left General Pike to defend the whole territory from the enemy. "You may reward your Indian troops," Van Dorn said, "by giving them such stores as you may think proper when they make captures from the enemy, but you will please endeavor to restrain them from committing any barbarities upon the wounded, prisoners, or dead who may fall into their hands."[37] Van Dorn obviously did not really believe these Indians had become "civilized people," and he was uncomfortable in his alliance with them.

General Curtis, who would later himself form an uneasy alliance with Indians friendly to the Northern cause in order to defend against Confederate invading forces, abetted exploitation of the Pea Ridge incident for the Union cause. When the Joint Committee on the Conduct of the War got wind of the atrocities, it sought information from Curtis, and he finally replied in April, to Senator Benjamin F. Wade, that "the warfare was conducted by said savages with all the barbarity their merciless and cowardly natures are capable of."[38] Curtis's correspondence with Van Dorn had been even more revealing. Responding to a counter-allegation made by Van Dorn that German American soldiers in the Union army had killed Confederate prisoners at Pea Ridge, Curtis denied it and then went on to say:

> Exceptions may undoubtedly occur, as we have murderers in all communities, but the employment of Indians involves a probability of savage ferocity which is not to be regarded as the exception but the rule. Bloody conflicts seem to inspire their ancient barbarities, nor can we expect civilized warfare from savage foes. If any presumption has been raised in their favor on the score of civilization it has certainly been demolished by the use of the tomahawk, war club and scalping knife at Pea Ridge . . .
>
> Believing the general commanding the opposing army is equally anxious to suppress atrocities which are too often coined by our species the general commanding the army hopes Indians will hereafter be excluded from your forces.[39]

Perhaps the remark he made in his first letter to Van Dorn on the subject was the most revealing of all: he had said that they surely did not want this "important struggle" to degenerate into savage warfare.

In the view common to the era, fighting against savages or by means of savage tactics threatened the very significance of the great Civil War between the civilized belligerents of the North and South. Let us leave the Indians out of this, Curtis seemed to be saying, or else we will damage our chances at making history. No one in the American Civil War much wanted a merciless or pitiless struggle, though all were perfectly willing to wage a long, determined struggle by the traditional means associated with civilized belligerents.

⊷⟞⟜⟝⟞⟜

Although Indians did not return two years later with Price's forces to the Missouri theater of operations, some of the people's worst fears did come true. The guerrillas Quantrill and Anderson, now operating under Price's orders, murdered prisoners (against all orders). Scalps dangled from saddles and bridles. Confederate marauding was commonplace and plundering unstoppable.[40]

Civilians certainly were in danger of victimization, but not as much as the circumstances might suggest. Yet in a key action at Pilot Knob, General Price eschewed the strategy that would have cost him the smallest number of casualties because Missouri citizens informed him that the Union garrison inside Fort Davidson, guarding the approach to Pilot Knob, had taken prominent Southern sympathizers, old men and young boys from the college of Arcadia, inside the fort. If General Price had placed field artillery on the high ground overlooking the ill-sited fort, he could have quickly shelled it into submission, but he would have shelled the friendly Missouri citizens as well. After the costly assault that took the fort, Price's chief engineer found dead civilians inside.[41]

At Fort Davidson and elsewhere, the Confederates, despite their unruly resemblance to a Calmuck horde, fought with disciplined restraint that cost them precious lives and precious time. Most enemies captured by Price's forces were treated as prisoners of war and paroled by the Confederates, who, already underfed, had no way to retain them on their fast-moving raid. So conspicuously proper was Confederate behavior in this case that Union General Clinton B. Fisk, a fierce veteran of Missouri's guerrilla conflict, at one point wrote a message to a Confederate from Price's forces who had guarded captured Union soldiers, mostly Missourians, complimenting him on the treatment of his men.[42] Price had reason enough for revenge. His aide, after all, had brought the Palmyra Massacre to Jefferson Davis's attention. Nothing had been done. Like many other wounds in Price's beloved Missouri, that one was still open. But Price showed no impulse for revenge.

Fisk's response shows that the Union side fought with restraint as well. Neither side fought without restraint. Neither unleashed the full fury of unbridled wrath.[43] Events remained under control.

When Fisk dealt with the guerrillas in Missouri before Price's Raid, he almost always spoke of them as "fiends in human shape." They were to him "barbarians."[44] But the possibility of calling Price's Raid a "barbarian invasion" apparently never occurred to him. Price's men were, technically, different. General Price was a commissioned general officer in the Confederate army under orders from the department commander and, ultimately, President Davis himself. Dealing with guerrillas was not a hardening experience that was likely to lead Union commanders to treat proper Confederate armies—or Confederate civilians—the same way they treated irregulars. Guerrilla war was sui generis.

The forces hastily assembled on the Union side to defend Missouri were, if not the mirror image of the Confederate invaders, at least not up to the customary standard of discipline. The Kansas forces brought into the state had a reputation for abusing prisoners of war from Confederate Missouri units and could not be trusted to guard them at the rear.[45] The invading Confederates could report that villages had been looted by Union forces retiring in front of them before the hungry and underarmed Confederates came in to scavenge among the leavings.[46] Union officers admitted the poor discipline and looting by some of their own troops.

But as soon as a "legitimate" army came into view, however far below standard in discipline, the old and familiar rules and customs of "civilized warfare" were reapplied without thought. True, the Union army may have been up to that time fighting guerrillas by means reminiscent in some ways of the ruthless campaigns against Plains Indians, largely without the rules of "civilized warfare." But with Price's Raid, scrupulous procedures for taking and paroling prisoners were followed. War resumed its customary Victorian and controlled guise.

The guerrilla war in Missouri proved an exception, not a learning ground. No one took as a tactical or strategic model what the Union commanders in Missouri felt compelled to do from day to day to deal with guerrillas—and that went for the Union commanders themselves when meeting Confederate armies in Missouri again in the autumn of 1864.

⇥⇤

"Fiends in human shape" was a term commonly used in Union generals' and Republican politicians' dispatches and letters dealing with guerrillas in Missouri. By and large, it was a term reserved for them alone. When they denounced other Confederates, they used other terms.

General William S. Rosecrans, who was commanding the Missouri District at the time of Price's Raid, held the same sort of contempt for the guerrilla enemy that other commanders of longer tenure and experience in the region had. In his colorful final report on the campaign against Price, not issued until December 7, 1864, he denounced the internal enemy animatedly:

> Previous to and pending these events the guerrilla warfare in North Missouri had been raging with redoubled fury . . . traitors of every hue and stripe, had warmed into life at the approach of the great invasion. Women's fingers were busy making clothes for rebel soldiers out of goods plundered by the guerrillas; women's tongues were busy telling union neighbors "their time was now coming." General Fisk, with all his force, had been scouring the brush for weeks in the river counties in pursuit of hostile bands, composed largely of recruits from among that class of inhabitants who claim protection, yet decline to perform the full duty of citizens on the ground that they "never tuck no sides." A few facts will convey some idea of this warfare carried on by Confederate agents here, while the agents abroad of their bloody and hypocritical despotism—[James M.] Mason, [John] Slidell, and [A. Dudley] Mann in Europe—have the effrontery to tell the nations of Christendom our Government "carries on the war with increasing ferocity regardless of the laws of civilized warfare." These gangs of rebels, whose families had been living in peace among their loyal neighbors, committed the most cold-blooded and diabolical murders, such as riding up to a farmhouse, asking for water, and while receiving it, shooting down the giver, an aged, inoffensive farmer, because he was a radical "Union man." . . .
>
> About the 1st of September ["Bloody Bill"] Anderson's gang attacked a railroad train on the North Missouri road, took from it twenty-two unarmed soldiers, many on sick leave, and after robbing placed them in a row and shot them in cold blood. Some of these bodies they scalped, and put others across the track and ran the engine over them. On the 27th this gang, with numbers swollen to 300 or 400, attacked Major Johnston with about 120 men of the Thirty-ninth Missouri Volunteer Infantry, raw recruits, and, after stampeding their horses, shot every man, most of them in cold blood. Anderson a few

days later was recognized by General Price at Boonville as Confederate captain, and with a verbal admonition to behave himself, ordered by Colonel Maclean, chief of Price's staff, to proceed to North Missouri and destroy the railroads, which orders were found on the miscreant when killed by Lieutenant-Colonel Cox about the 27th of October ultimo.[47]

When I first read that, I assumed Rosecrans was preparing the ground to excuse his army for retaliating with unrelenting fury and with perhaps some excusable lapses here and there. What followed in Rosecrans's report, however, was no such tale but a routine description of a standard campaign in the American Civil War. Little more was said of atrocities. The general had made his point, and then he moved on to the conventional civilized warfare with which he normally dealt in his after-battle reports.

Rosecrans had displayed the customary contempt for "fiends in human shape" without using the term. He made contemptuous fun of the ungrammatical excuses of the hypocrites who pleaded neutrality and then helped the rebels as soon as they were strong again (as though all the people fighting against the guerrillas were masters of the King's English). Scalping put in its customary appearance as a reminder of warfare with "barbarians." He was able to forge a crucial link with the Confederate commissioned general Sterling Price because of the orders found on "Bloody Bill" Anderson when he was killed. Yet even then, Rosecrans had to admit that Price had given at least a verbal warning to Anderson about his methods. In the remainder of the report Rosecrans wrote nothing to besmirch the reputation of the Confederates who invaded Missouri.

In the end, Rosecrans somewhat spoiled the effect of this small part of his report meant to answer the Confederate propagandists in Europe. He included as an addendum the general order he issued after the death of Anderson. In addition to commending the humble Missouri militiamen who had brought down the notorious marauder, the order described the special rewards coming to the Missourians:

> In consideration of their gratuitous services, and as a reward for their gallantry, it is therefore ordered that the property taken by these citizens from the robbers be distributed . . . as follows:
>
> The horse ridden by Bill Anderson and the watches and arms taken will be given to the several officers of the command, to be retained as honorable trophies. The money captured will be given in just proportions to the wounded of the command and to the families of such as were killed in the affair.[48]

Taking such property was not allowed by the laws of war.[49] Legal niceties abounded in the case: the militiamen served as emergency volunteers without pay, and Anderson and his men were hardly regarded by the Union side as ordinary soldiers rather than guerrillas. Still, it might have served Rosecrans's international purpose rather better to edit out of his report the reference to this irregular reward system, not unlike the thieving one embraced by the guerrillas themselves.

General Rosecrans was not the only Northerner with an awareness, however incomplete or flawed, of the propaganda value of descriptions of the exploits of "Bloody Bill" Anderson. As soon as the guerrilla was killed, Major James Rainsford, assistant adjutant-general in the Seventh Military District of Missouri, wrote his superior to describe the orders found on Anderson's body. The point was to show that they clearly linked him directly to General Price.[50] Anderson's propaganda value was great in another way: to prove he had been killed was important for Missouri Unionist morale. Rainsford had photographs of Anderson's dead body taken and forwarded to his superior as well.[51]

Before the news of Anderson's death made its way up the chain of command to General Rosecrans, he had sent the following remarkable letter to Sterling Price himself via a Confederate lieutenant who had been brought into Union lines under a flag of truce by some captured Union soldiers:

Lieutenant Graves, C.S. Army, with forty enlisted men, bearers of flag of truce, arrived here on the 20th instant from escorting Colonel Harding and prisoners captured by you at Glasgow to Boonville. The escort to this flag was clothed in our uniform. I have always adopted as a rule, necessary for my own protection, that soldiers of your army captured in our uniform, should be treated as spies. The necessity of this rule must be obvious to you. I cannot object to your wearing captured clothing, provided its color is changed so it cannot deceive me. I have not interfered with Lieutenant Graves, for he was protected by the flag he carried. I am not unmindful, general, of your humanity and courtesy toward federal prisoners in times past, but I consider it my duty to express my regret that you permitted this practice, which exposes your men to the rigorous punishment demanded by military prudence as a protection against surprise. Permit me also, general, to express my surprise and regret that you have allowed to associate with your troops bands of Missouri guerrillas, without principle or feeling of nationality, whose record is stained with crimes at which humanity shudders. It is unnecessary to enumerate what these crimes are. The newspapers have not exaggerated. You and I, general, have tried to conduct this war in accordance with the highest dictates of humanity and the laws of war among civilized nations. I hope the future will make no change in this respect.[52]

The explanation for the mildness of Rosecrans's report on Price's Raid and of the mildness of the Union military response to the raid in general lies in the hope expressed in this letter.

Presented with the evidence of Price's complicity with "Bloody Bill" Anderson, Rosecrans gave his Confederate opponent's reputation an "out." He gave Price the benefit of hearsay evidence that he had at least verbally admonished Anderson to behave by the laws of war. Then, instead of publishing as an addendum to the report's sensational news that Anderson had been killed the full text of the orders found on his body linking Anderson with Price, Rosecrans published his own rather unfortunate orders rewarding Anderson's killers with captured personal property.

However we interpret Rosecrans's final report, one thing is clear from the episode of Price's Raid: Union generals fought Confederate generals one way and guerrillas another. They distinguished clearly between them as individuals and they distinguished clearly between the tactics and strategies to be employed against the different enemies, even when they appeared in the same theater of operations at the same time. Rosecrans thought of Sterling Price and "Bloody Bill" Anderson in entirely different compartments of his military mind. And so did nearly everyone else on the Union side.

⟶⟹ ⟸⟵

The way the generals chose to fight the conventional Confederate armies such as the one led by General Price was the way most generals chose to fight on most fields in the American Civil War. There is a growing tendency among historians to think otherwise. We have been told, for example, that events in Missouri "set the pace for the transformation from a limited to a total war, radiating outward and southward from Missouri." "Most of the Union commanders," it has been observed, "who subsequently became famous as practitioners of total war spent part of their early Civil War careers in Missouri— including Grant, Sherman, and Sheridan. This was more than coincidence."[53] Contra-guerrilla methods of fighting did not "set the pace" even in Missouri, let alone in the rest of the embattled country. When renewed invasion of the state in 1864 caused it to become an important theater once again and armies returned to Missouri and generals were sent to fight the invaders, the Union forces resumed the strategies and tactics associated with conventional warfare in the middle of the nineteenth century. Nor was it only generals who were transferred from the East to fight Price who behaved with such restraint. The generals who had been fighting in Missouri all along and remained to fight Price likewise resumed the accustomed restraints of mid-century warfare among "civilized" belligerents.

When General Rosecrans addressed citizens of northwest Missouri in the middle of summer of 1864, he chided them: "citizens, situated as you have been, who will tolerate a species of—I will not call it warfare, but outrage, which finds no parallel in the annals of our Indian wars, must expect the vengeance due to such moral dereliction among a free and professedly Christian people."[54] The work of fighting guerrillas in Missouri was extremely distasteful to generals such as Rosecrans and constituted a sort of exile. He was sent to Missouri after having lost the Battle of Chickamauga in 1863.

In fact, fighting guerrillas in the Civil War was the penalty for failure. Generals were transferred to Missouri if they failed at the war's important tasks. By 1864 the Union high command in Missouri was an assemblage of losers.

General-in-chief Ulysses S. Grant had no respect for the department commander, General William S. Rosecrans, whom he had replaced after Chickamauga. Samuel R. Curtis, whom Lincoln had removed from the Missouri Department in 1863 (though, it must be said, mostly for political reasons rather than ones of battlefield competence), headed the less important Department of Kansas (and played a role in turning Price back from that state when his escape route led that way). The Union cavalry force that pursued Price was led by Alfred Pleasonton, whom Grant obviously considered Philip H. Sheridan's inferior. Pleasonton was sent to Missouri when Sheridan became head of the cavalry in the East.[55]

Success and the reward of departure from Missouri for more important theaters of the war did not come to those who learned the lessons of hard guerrilla warfare in Missouri. Let us briefly examine the careers of the Union generals in Missouri in 1864–65. Most, like Rosecrans himself, learned quickly to deal harshly with guerrillas, but most remained in the Missouri theater to continue the application of their special skills. After Rosecrans allowed Price's army to escape, Grant relieved him of command and replaced him with Grenville M. Dodge (Rosecrans's report on the raid was written on December 8, the eve of his departure from St. Louis after Dodge replaced him).

Dodge might well be considered a professional soldier, a graduate not of West Point but of the military academy run by Alden Partridge in Norwich, Vermont. He proved to be an able engineer and moved to Iowa to develop railroads; he began his Civil War service there. Dodge was hardly a military failure, but he was twice wounded, the second time in the Atlanta campaign. Missouri was also a place to send a man who might not be able to operate at full capacity for command in a critical area. Dodge went to Missouri.[56]

Of the highest-ranking generals in Missouri late in the war, Dodge appears to have had the most unrelenting attitudes, and there is some evidence that they left a mark on his attitudes ever afterward. His favorite policy to save the state was exile of the families of guerrillas.[57] Many years later he would defend the infamous water torture applied by U.S. troops to Filipino prisoners and other tough policies directed against the Philippine Insurrection at the turn of the century, saying that they "simply followed the plan of war that was pursued by Grant, Sherman, and other commanders in the Civil War."[58]

The district commanders who served in Missouri under Rosecrans or Dodge shared a tough outlook in their fight against guerrillas in the state. The others were Thomas Ewing, Jr., John McNeil, Egbert B.

Brown, Clinton B. Fisk, John B. Sanborn, and John F. Phillips.[59] Ewing was the author of General Orders No. 11, of August 25, 1863. These dictated the abandonment of four counties in Missouri, near the Kansas border, as retaliation for William Quantrill's raid on Lawrence, Kansas, and as a way of removing the civilian population from whom such guerrilla groups drew their sustenance. Of the various Missouri schemes for "removing the inhabitants of certain counties *en masse;* and of removing certain individuals from time to time," President Lincoln said only that he was "not now interfering," hardly a ringing endorsement.[60] Ewing was well connected politically, but he finished his military career in Missouri.

Clinton Fisk was of the "fiends-in-human-shape" school of thought on guerrillas. A St. Louis businessman, not a professional soldier, he was an abolitionist and a teetotaler, and his moral approach to war in Missouri included closing grog shops in his area of command and burning bawdy houses along with guerrilla safehouses. To Fisk, Missouri had become a land of "villainy and corruption," plagued with "fiends," and he feared that "military law . . . will have to be supreme in Missouri for a long time to come."[61]

Egbert Brown, when he organized his Rolla district for self-defense after the failure of Price's Raid, organized unpaid citizen guards of "unconditional loyalty" who were "to assist in a war of extermination, by lawful means, of all guerrillas, bushwhackers, robbers, thieves, and rebels, or other disturbers of the peace and quiet to the country." They were to have broad powers to seize private property, and there were provisions as well to send the disloyal out of the district.[62]

John B. Sanborn tried not to mix politics and war, but he did have to answer a letter sent by a woman named Mrs. Sarah M. Scott, protesting her expulsion from his district in the middle of winter. "Whatever is necessary to be done," he replied, after pointing out how skewed toward the disloyal were her views of charity, "to enable the Government to exercise its authority and protect its subjects in all places of its dominion will be done without regard to the suffering of any particular class, or even that of a whole generation."[63]

John F. Phillips, who never rose above colonel's rank, also advocated transporting out of his district "immediate families of men who are in the rebel army and those who have gone South." Otherwise the Confederate soldiers would surely attempt to return to Missouri to see them. "This may seem harsh," Phillips explained, "and in some cases might work injustice, but war is full of severity. These people invoked war; let them reap its harvest."[64]

By and large, these practices and attitudes remained in Missouri with the embittered and frustrated Union commanders who held them. These soldiers did not go on to other theaters and greater exploits, bringing their vicious skills with them. Readers have probably not heard of most of them before seeing this chapter. They labored in obscurity on the borders.

⊷═◉ ◉═⊷

It is important not to review Union policies in Missouri, the worst case of guerrilla warfare in the whole conflict, in isolation from other events of the Civil War. If we keep our eye on other events occurring simultaneously we see the two faces of combat in Missouri—and in the whole Civil War. When legitimate Confederate forces raided the state, under orders from Jefferson Davis and Kirby Smith and under the field command of Sterling Price, the Union forces immediately resumed their accustomed respect for the laws and customs of war. They resumed their curious but benign mindset of military chivalry, scrupulously taking care of prisoners of war and addressing each other as fellow aristocrats acting to keep the violent contest within bounds, leaving women, the aged, the underage, and the ill largely undisturbed. If they heard rumors of atrocities committed by Price's rebels, they nevertheless restrained themselves from retaliation in kind. General Curtis affirmed to Pleasonton the obligation to obey the laws of war: "I am . . . well informed by intelligent men of our militia, who have been in their camp as prisoners for three or four days, that our prisoners in Price's hands are treated very badly. Several have been shot down in the presence of the provost guard. Most of them are driven along on foot, after being robbed of their clothing, including their shoes. All this, however, must not provoke us to acts of barbarity toward our prisoners, but will be a matter of settlement when we secure the commander, which I trust will not be long postponed."[65]

It does not quite capture the essence of these simultaneous strategies and attitudes to characterize them as well-considered utilitarian options, applied in rational response to enemy actions, as the historian Mark Grimsley would have us understand them.[66] We do not see General Rosecrans, for example, calculating the superiority of traditional methods in meeting Price's Raid and condoning from a different process of military calculation less restrained strategies and tactics in actions against the likes of "Bloody Bill" Anderson. Instead, we glimpse a worldview formed well before the American Civil War and destined long to survive it. The world was made up of civilized people and barbarians, and soldiers fought them by different methods. If otherwise civilized people chose for some reason to fall from grace and embrace the methods and outlook of savages, as the Missouri guerrillas appeared to Unionists to have done, then they too were dealt with in savage ways.

But such savage tactics were an exception. Missouri was itself an exception. No one looked there for clues to conducting successful warfare against the Confederate States of America. The very conventional warfare that ensued when Price invaded Missouri in 1864—including sieges, refusals to bombard towns or fortresses with civilians in them, paroled prisoners of war—gives the lie to any notion that Missouri was a training ground for the drastic warfare of the future. General Pleasonton was reluctant to send the Confederate generals John S. Marmaduke and William L. Cabell, captured near the end of Price's Raid, along with other captured officers, to Kansas and General Curtis's department under escort of the untrustworthy Kansas troops.[67] Pleasonton even put some of the high-ranking Confederate prisoners up in a hotel while waiting the opportunity to resolve the dispute by referring it to General Rosecrans.[68]

Drastic warfare was employed against guerrillas, all right. But as soon as the enemy was clothed in legitimacy, the Missouri generals fought them just as any general from the Army of the Potomac might have. For the most part, Missouri and other limited areas of guerrilla warfare elsewhere in the American Civil War remained sideshows, fought by generals of limited military promise with methods no one wanted to see imitated.

## ⋅→≡ 3 ≡←⋅

# EMPEROR MAXIMILIAN'S
# BLACK DECREE
## War in the Tropics

IN 2003 the editor of *Civil War History* made a plea for considering "the international dimension of the war" and suggested, among other avenues of approach, examining "the similarities and differences of civil wars in the nineteenth century."[1] Such a comparative approach offers a new avenue to address the question of destructiveness broached in this book. The beginning of this book has already pointed us in the direction to be taken, south of the border. There the civil war most proximate in time and place raged side by side with the American Civil War. And "rage" is the proper verb to employ, for war in the tropics had already proved, back in 1846–1848, to be a breeding ground of guerrilla violence and contra-guerrilla atrocities. What people in the United States thought of that warfare in the period of French intervention in Mexico during the American Civil War has never been examined.[2] Did they see in Mexico a mirror of their own destructive Civil War?

⋅→≡ ≡←⋅

Amzi Wood, the U.S. commercial agent in Matamoros, Mexico, was a firsthand observer. The warfare he saw from day to day in Mexico did not in any way remind him of conflict the United States. Here is a typical scene. Wood went out for a walk early on Thursday morning, May 4, 1865, and, as he described it,

> had only proceeded a little ways when I see a procession approaching me from a quarterly direction, they were advancing in a hollow square & in the center was a well dressed Mexican soldier, a prisoner from the outside party, a young man about six feet high straight, walked erect bearing the cross in his left hand, a priest by his side, reading & he re- peating after the priest, they moved in a slow & solemn manner, I walked along with them for about one hundred rods when the fellow was caused to kneel, have his eyes bandaged & the soldiers at a given signal drew their pieces in position & shot the poor fellow dead—The soldiers were about ten feet off.[3]

The French army and the loyalist Mexican General Tomás Mejía had only recently turned back a Liberal siege of Matamoros, and the town witnessed such scenes regularly. "All the prisoners taken they shoot early in the morning," Wood observed, "& the next morning after their capture."

About five months later, in Mexico City, Emperor Maximilian codi- fied the practice Wood had so often witnessed. The first article of what came to be known as the "Black Decree" of October 3, 1865, stated: "All persons forming a party or band, or an armed gathering existing without legal authority, whether or not they proclaim a po- litical pretext, whatever may be the number of those who form the band, the organization of the latter, the character and the denomina- tion it takes—shall be judged militarily by court-martial; if they are found guilty, even if it be only of the act of belonging to an armed band, shall be condemned to capital punishment, and the sentence shall be executed within twenty-four hours." Because a war was rag- ing in Mexico at the time, such a decree meant that men who consid- ered themselves soldiers in organized military units fighting for their country might be executed, if captured, simply for being soldiers in an army. Article two specified that when members of such "a party or band . . . shall be made prisoners in battle," they would be "judged by the commander of the force into whose power they may fall." The article reiterated the threat of capital punishment and the brief period of time to elapse after sentencing, but called for the minimal requirement that there be a "procès-verbal"—an official record of the case written down. The officer also had to "procure spiritual aid for the condemned" and "forward the *procès-verbal* of the enquiry to the Minister of War."[4]

Article five greatly enlarged the net of guilt. It stipulated that those who voluntarily provided money "or any other kind of succour for the *guerrilleros*," those who had "given them any warning, news, or advice," and those who had knowingly procured them arms, horses, or provisions were to be considered as belonging to the category described in the first article. So fierce in intent was the emperor's decree that it even limited his own imperial power. The prisoners were to be executed without being allowed to petition for pardon from the emperor.[5]

The Black Decree was not a desperation measure. Maximilian issued it at the very height of his power in Mexico. In a proclamation issued the day before publishing the Black Decree, he described as a failure the revolutionary cause of his opponent Benito Juárez and boasted of the extent of the imperial military and political success by the autumn of 1865:

Mexicans!

The cause which Don Benito Juárez upheld with such constancy and valor has succumbed both to the national will and to those very laws invoked by the rebel chieftain in support of his titles. To-day even the banner under which that cause degenerated has been abandoned by its leader who has left the fatherland.

The National Government has long shown indulgence and clemency to those recreants who ignored true facts as well as their chance to join the majority of the Nation in a return to duty. Even so the Government has achieved its purpose; honest men have rallied to our flag and accepted the just and liberal principles of our policy. Disorder is maintained by only a few brigands misled by unpatriotic passions and supported by a demoralized rabble, as well as that unbridled soldiery constituting the sad dregs in all civil life.

From now on the struggle will continue merely between the honest men of the Nation and those hordes of criminals and bandits. Indulgence must cease, lest it encourage the desperadoes who burn villages, rob and murder peace-loving citizens, persecute the aged, and violate defenseless women.

The Government, strong in its power, will henceforth show itself inflexible in punishment, for such are the demands made by the precepts of civilization, the rights of humanity, and every moral canon.[6]

Even as he prepared to violate the laws and customs of war, Maximilian paid fealty to them by proclamation, noting the disapproval of "civilization" for burning towns, killing civilians, victimizing the aged, and raping women.

Estimates vary greatly of the number of Mexicans killed as a result of the decree and of the lawless practices that had preceded it that were openly embraced by the decree. They range from 11,000 to 40,000.[7]

There is, of course, nothing analogous to the Black Decree in the annals of the national government during the American Civil War, either in words or in deeds. It is difficult to imagine Abraham Lincoln signing his name to such a document, and that makes claims of his merciless approach to fighting the Civil War ring hollow. Realizing the difference between the Black Decree and the sort of document Lincoln issued to the enemy when *he* was optimistic of success, the Proclamation of Amnesty and Reconstruction of December 8,

1863, for example, with its famous 10 percent plan for reconstruction, is important for understanding the true nature of the American Civil War.

The differences between these two famous documents seem to be instructive, but they do not, in fact, tell us what any person in the United States thought of the Black Decree and the drastic sort of warfare it prescribed. Did people in the United States believe that Maximilian was merely bringing to self-conscious and avowed policy statements the fierce and destructive methods of the American Civil War? The importance of that question makes it worthwhile to examine American attitudes toward the French incursion in Mexico.

To do so is not as simple as it sounds. One problem is to locate sources of articulate opinion on the question. Newspapers in the United States followed the war in Mexico, but they were consistently distracted by their own Civil War and the momentous problems of Reconstruction afterward. Extended commentary on Mexico is hard to find in the press. To supplement views expressed in newspapers in the United States, I will rely here particularly on letters written about the Mexican situation to Secretary of State William H. Seward. These contained the observations and policy recommendations of people who evinced more than ordinary knowledge of or interest in Mexico.

Even with these materials as evidence, an obstacle remains: In Chapter 1 I discussed the great problem of interpreting what people in the United States said about Mexican politics and society. Basic attitudes toward Mexico, grounded in racist opinions and anti-Catholicism, had not changed one bit. But the political situation had changed dramatically. The idle speculation, which entered at least one Pennsylvania soldier's head during the Mexican-American War of 1846–1848, that monarchy might solve Mexico's problems in the short run, had become a genuine possibility. But that imposition ran afoul of the Monroe Doctrine and of the republican sentiments that undergirded it. Surely now Mexico loomed in the Northern imagination as a sister republic in a way the country had not in the heyday of Manifest Destiny. And what would be the impact of those resurgent republican sympathies on the perception of warfare and atrocity observable now in Mexico?

Finally, it is as difficult to discover what exactly happened in the countryside when the French invaded Mexico as it is to discover exactly what happened in the forests of Missouri in the myriad confrontations between guerrillas and Union authorities. How, in fact, do the two wars compare in levels of atrocity?

⋆━◉ ◉━⋆

When diplomatic historians last surveyed U.S. relations with Maximilian, the assumptions of consensus history reigned, and with them the notion that ideological differences ended at the country's shores. Dexter Perkins, for example, writing a triumphal history of the Monroe Doctrine, thought it was "clear that the American people viewed with intense feeling the presence of the French in Mexico" and that there were but "a few exceptions to the general rule" of support for ousting the emperor.[8] Looked at today, under different assumptions, public opinion in the United States on the French venture looks much more divided and the reasons raised by apologists for Maximilian more significant.

Anyone who reads the observations of people in the United States on the French intervention in Mexico in the 1860s is sure to be surprised by the weakness of the role played by "republicanism" in shaping their ideas. From the foundations of the United States in the Stamp Act crisis and the succeeding Revolution down to the middle of the nineteenth century, American politics was strongly animated by common beliefs in republicanism and by common fears of foreign and domestic conspiracies against individual liberty in the United States. The pattern of beliefs and attitudes may have been losing some potency by the time of the Civil War, and the effect of republican beliefs and attitudes on foreign policy and views of the greater world has never been clearly worked out by historians. Still, the belief that liberty was the goal of organizing political society and that liberty was a fragile commodity perpetually threatened by power, even by monstrous plots and conspiracies, had a long history in the United States.[9] It was not dead yet, and it must have retained some ability to make people in the United States think well of Mexico as a republic and to fear for Mexico's safety when threatened with the imposition of a foreign emperor put into power by mercenaries, the standing army of an Old World power, and reactionary aristocrats and clericals.

Yet opinion on the French incursion in Mexico was sharply divided. The Republic of Mexico had many apologists and sympathizers above the Rio Grande, but not as many as it should have had if republicanism were a potent belief. In truth, what is most striking about the opinions expressed is that Maximilian had many apologists in the United States. That was true from the distracting beginnings of the Mexican intervention at the beginning of the American Civil War to its bitter conclusion in 1867, when people in the United States could focus on the Mexican adventure.

In the beginning, in 1861, foreign intervention in Mexico was a multinational project with no overt political aims: France and other European creditor nations began landing troops on Mexico's shores at the end of that year in order to collect debts owed by the country, long troubled by civil wars. France, however, quickly unveiled plans to establish monarchical government. Opportunity, of course, stemmed from the distraction of the United States with its own civil war, which made the Monroe Doctrine and the threat of forceful expulsion of European invaders a dead letter for all practical purposes. The French emperor, Napoleon III, claimed to be creating a rallying point for the "Latin races" against the ever-present threat of An-glo-Saxon hegemony over the continent. Whatever the real reasons, French troops had landed in substantial numbers by 1862, fighting Mexican republican forces loyal to President Benito Jaurez and cap-turing Mexico City in 1863. France then arranged to have an Aus-trian Hapsburg, Archduke Maximilian, assume an imperial throne in Mexico in 1864. He came in part at the invitation of embattled Mexi-can conservatives, and therefore the ensuing struggle for national in-dependence is also viewed as part of a continuing civil war in Mex-ico.[10] Maximilian came only with the assurance that a "plebiscite," like the one that created the French empire under Napoleon, had en-dorsed the Austrian's accession. The extent of French control of the country was hardly enough to make any such popular vote more than farcical.

Maximilian's reign lasted three years. The French presence had never avowedly been perpetual, and when the American Civil War ended, steps to withdraw French troops quickly materialized. They were formally announced to the United States in 1866, and Maxi-milian was left to the protection of the small reactionary contingent that had rallied against the republicans from the start and a hand-ful of "volunteers" from Austria and Belgium (his wife, Carlota, was a Belgian princess). At Querétaro, less than 150 miles northwest of Mexico City, republican forces captured Maximilian after a brief siege. A court-martial soon sentenced Maximilian, General Miguel Miramón, and General Tomás Mejía to death, and the Mexican re-publicans executed them together, by firing squad, on June 19, 1867.

The U.S. government had long since officially recognized the re-public and never wavered or recognized Maximilian. It always in-sisted on the withdrawal of French troops. It did not have recourse to military action, however, as the Monroe Doctrine might suggest it would. After the war, the United States could finally mass troops on the Rio Grande in 1865 and threaten the imperial government. The French departed, and in the end, Secretary of State Seward attempted to prevent the republicans' execution of Maximilian, considering it a disservice to republicanism itself. Revenge ended with the executions at Querétaro, by and large, and the aftermath of the war against Maximilian's forces, almost as much as the American Civil War itself, was remarkable for its lack of bloody retribution.[11]

The official position of the United States on the French intervention in Mexico was simplicity itself, but the attitudes of individual Americans who followed the action in Mexico were not so simple. Amzi Wood provides a good example. His job as commercial agent in Matamoros was patronage made available by the famous citizen of his hometown Auburn, New York, William H. Seward, secretary of state under both Abraham Lincoln and Andrew Johnson. Wood was an ardent patriot, whose hatred of the Confederacy knew hardly any limit. His natural human sympathy for the Mexican prisoners of war executed before his very eyes offered no clue to his political conception of the brutal conflict unfolding before his eyes in Mexico.

Wood said he had many personal friends among the native population, but his general opinion of the country's inhabitants was low: "In a word, the whole race, except a portion of the wealthy are in a state of ignorance & their minds are without education, without culture & one can only look upon them in pity & with disgust, their love of money is great & their desire for its accumulation is large provided it does not cost them extra labor to obtain it. There are a great many negroes who have fled from Texas here & I think a cross with the Mexicans would improve the stock."[12] He rather admired Imperial General Mejía's stern administration of Matamoros, and he shared in a loose way the Imperial view of the resistance in the Mexican countryside. "The whole land is a blaze of Revolution, & the revolutionists are bands of Robbers & Murderers."[13] He said little about the political aspects of the Liberals' cause.

Wood's foreign policy views, if they could be dignified by that name, were grounded more in religious and racial assumptions than in political faith in republicanism. He referred to the Mexican people as a "race" and his references to their ignorance was standard Protestant rhetoric for referring to Catholic peoples. When the Liberals returned to besiege Matamoros again, Wood expressed privately his wish to "have both sides whip[ped]." The "whole nation," he added "is a set of miserable God forsaken wretches & ought to be allowed to fight the thing out without any interference from any quarter, except to help both sides fight until not one cuss was left to disgrace the Earth with their damd homely shadows, & then introduce a race of Babboons to inhabit this."[14] When Wood was in other moods, such contempt naturally lent itself to imperial ambitions. Disgusted by the Mexican war's atrocities, Wood once observed:

> All persons in the interest of the imperial govt caught by the liberals are hung up by the feet & left to die & rot, tis a common sight (as I am informed) to see them hanging along the road side. How long this state of things will continue, depends upon the fact, whether the United States government will take this infernal motley crew of beings under their protecting care, any government who does that thing & establishes, what I doubt can be maintained peace, order & security will be conferring a great blessing on the nation, & country. The people are no more capable of self government than the animals nor are they capable of any uniform government.[15]

In short, Wood's views were those of an intense patriot, but their republican content was vestigial and essentially negative. He extolled the American flag and the American eagle this way to his wife: "The emblems that point the soul from Earth to heaven, blest of God & under his wise guidance Elevates the soul in the celestial worlds on high, emblems which rebels [i.e., Confederates above the Rio Grande] & their deluded & misguided al[l]ies, the Copperheads, despise, crowned heads fear & from the Luster of its Magic power, Monarchs fear & tremble . . . I love to boast of my country, its government, its institutions, its wealth, its resources, its power, its greatness, its ability to whip the world & all the rest of mankind."[16] Republicanism revealed itself mainly in a hatred of monarchies, but it did not lead Wood and others like him to love other republics. Mostly, he reveled in growing American national power.

‑‑◉ ◉‑‑

In truth, Wood's views were not far removed from those of more thoughtful politicians of more benevolent aspect. When Abraham Lincoln rallied citizens to defend the Union by describing it as the "last best hope of earth" for republicanism, he was hardly accurate. There were many other republics in the New World, and Lincoln knew it. Here he departed from the sympathies of his political hero Henry Clay. In a eulogy on Clay in 1852, Lincoln said: "Mr. Clay's efforts in behalf of the South Americans, and afterwards, in behalf of the Greeks, in the times of their respective struggles for civil liberty are among the finest on record, upon the noblest of all themes; and bear ample corroboration of what I have said was his ruling passion—a love of liberty and right, unselfishly, and for their own sakes."[17] By the time of the Civil War such views on the outside world had receded in the United States.

The fact of the matter is that Mexico never figured in the American imagination primarily as a republic, let alone a model one. Instead, Mexico more often represented abundant natural resources, undeveloped. In other words, Mexico figured in the American imagination less as a republic than as a silver mine.

The natural resources were conspicuously of the glitteringly alluring sort: mineral wealth, especially gold and silver. And their "undeveloped" state was as important in the image as the resources themselves, for in that part of the image lay a moral tale often repeated.

The Mexican people had proved too lazy to develop the resources, according to this point of view. Such an outlook was so widely and thoughtlessly embraced that even Abraham Lincoln, a Whig who had opposed the U.S. war against Mexico in 1847 and 1848, nevertheless held that view too. In a lecture on the subject of discovery and invention, which Lincoln delivered in Illinois several times in 1859, he celebrated the "*habit* of observation and reflection" as a prelude to discovery and then cited this example: "But for the difference in *habit* of observation, why did yankees, almost instantly, discover gold in California, which had been trodden upon, and over-looked by indians and Mexican greasers, for centuries?"[18]

<hr>

Early in 1865 the Mexican republic briefly played a major role in the halls of power in Washington. Francis Preston Blair, Sr., concocted a scheme involving policy toward Mexico to bring about the end of the American Civil War. The proposal led eventually to the Hampton Roads Peace Conference between President Lincoln, Secretary of State Seward, and emissaries sent by President Jefferson Davis. Blair's scheming led only indirectly to the conference, and neither Lincoln nor Davis showed serious interest in the Mexican part of it, but Blair did get a hearing from the most important men on the continent for the idea of bringing about peace between the North and the South by somehow uniting them in a crusade to evict Maximilian and the French from Mexico.

Lincoln allowed Blair to contact Davis in person, and after returning from Richmond, Blair briefed the president on his conversation with Davis. Blair had suggested to Davis that he lead a Confederate army, amnestied under Lincoln's famous proclamation of December 8, 1863, to the Rio Grande. Blair boasted that he knew Matías Romero, the Mexican minister to the United States, and that his son Montgomery Blair was "intimate" with the "able" and "patriotic"

Mexican. Montgomery Blair was convinced that Romero "could induce Juárez to devote all the power he can command on President Davis—a dictatorship if necessary—to restore the rights of Mexico & her people and provide for the stability of its government."[19]

The slippage of political ideas was typical, even among sophisticated political thinkers such as Blair. A scheme to save a neighboring republic transformed itself into a plot to make Jefferson Davis another Maximilian in Mexico, propped up by a renegade Confederate army—all in the span of one memorandum. Like Amzi Wood's republicanism, Blair's came down to an inveterate hatred of foreign monarchies, not a love of other republics. "This scion of the House of Hapsburg," Blair railed in typical fashion, "must have inherited from a line of Ancestors extending to the Dark ages, the very innate instincts of that despotism which has manacled the little Republics of Italy and the little principalities of Germany."

Nor could Blair resist the lure of expansionism. "If in delivering Mexico," he explained to Lincoln, Jefferson Davis "should model its States in form & principle to adopt them to our union and add a new Southern constellation to its benignant sky while rounding off our possessions on the continent at the Isthmus, and opening the way to blending the waters of the Atlantic and Pacific, thus embracing our Republic in the arms of the Ocean, he would complete the work of Jefferson."[20] The historians Alfred Jackson Hanna and Kathryn Abbey Hanna have observed with cool accuracy: "Here Blair's line of persuasion degenerated from the heights of patriotic fervor over the Monroe Doctrine to the depths of a filibustering adventure."[21]

Though Blair now acted with the Republicans, he had, of course, played a major role in founding the Democratic party a generation earlier, and expansionism lay near the heart of that party's beliefs. For an informed and articulate view of Mexico at the time of the French incursion from an old Whig rather than an old Democrat, we can examine the opinions of Henry Shelton Sanford.[22] During the Civil War, Sanford served as minister to Belgium. Unlike the insular old Marylander Blair, Sanford had long enjoyed an extremely cosmopolitan life, including years of travel in Latin America. In Europe during the American Civil War and Reconstruction, he moved regularly between Brussels and Paris and dined with royalty and the diplomatic aristocracy.

In the end, what all Sanford's experience came down to in the case of Mexico was a sophisticated contempt based on grandiose racial assumptions about the world. He could recall a conversation he had held with the great German geographer Alexander von Humboldt in Berlin, when news of General Zachary Taylor's victories in Mexico reached Europe. Humboldt assumed that Taylor's victories would lead to acquisitions further south and even to the conquest of Brazil, but these would only "ensure your ruin as a united Republic," he warned the credulous Sanford. "A Republic," Humboldt said with a tone of scientific authority, "as you now understand one, is not possible south of the fifteenth parallel—the laborious, virtuous energetic races of the temperate zone become effete & enervated under the influence of the tropical sun & the absence of necessity for labor—for labor develops the virtues & makes man capable of self government."[23]

With such intellectual baggage in tow, travel was not really broadening. "I have often in traveling since in Central & South America," recalled Sanford, "among the splendid ruins left by the Spaniards where for weeks I would fail to meet a single pure blooded white, & looking upon the effete, listless copper colored remains of those vigorous Conquistadores, called to mind the prediction of Von Humboldt."[24]

Like many Americans, Sanford was at bottom an expansionist, but ethnic prejudices channeled his expansionist hopes in certain directions and left him hostile to some forms of imperialism.[25] When Seward acquired Alaska, that stroke of diplomacy truly inspired Sanford, who urged the American secretary of state:

> Complete your work, give us the whole of that Pacific Coast line from California up & the command of the Pacific is ours, & you will have soon a rival New England with its hardy mariners & fishermen & laborious population to develop that magnificent field—I dread acquisitions further South—the climate unfits the race for our institutions—but I have just the contrary opinion with regard to the country north of us . . . There is a population in those British provinces which we need, to help make head against the celtic & germanic races which are overrunning us; hardy, saving, laborious protestant—It is New England over again—the very stuff we need in every particular but its fanaticism—to correct & give tone to the whole mass—The Isthmus I take it we must one day take or control . . . with constant steam communication & flow of northern people through it, we may keep up Yankee energy there—but I hope we shall be chary of adding other territory south of us—You see the fate of the Spanish race in tropical countries. Our people would become equally enervated & run into the Negro & Indian blood in a few generations.[26]

Republicanism repeatedly took a back seat to religion and ethnicity in evaluations of Mexico made by people from the United States, whether their political origins were Whig or Democratic.

People of different political outlooks managed to make apologies for Maximilian. William Need, for example, lived in Las Vegas, New Mexico Territory, and had traveled widely in the state of Chihuahua. He expressed the belief in early October 1865 that "*Maximilian's* rule will be acceptable to the great mass of the population." Writing at the nadir of the republican cause in Mexico, Need began thinking of an alternative role for Juárez, whom he called the "Ex-President" of "the late Republic of Mexico." Perhaps the former president could be made the "head of the Great Railroad scheme" to link Memphis, Tennessee, through El Paso, Texas, with Chihuahua. He could thus "effect a compromise with the Emperor *Maximilian,* which will be advantageous to himself, the United States and Mexico." Need predicted eventual U.S. hegemony over the region: "I believe in process of time (within the next century most assuredly) the Government of the United States will extend to the Isthmus of Panama, and the English language be spoken as the accepted language of the people that far down on the Continent." Seward should support that mission, Need thought, but both the United States and Mexico had had "enough of war" and the desired result should come about through "Peaceful Negotiation, Treaties, and not wars."[27]

Willful ignorance sometimes played a role in creating inaccurate, one-sided, and unflattering images of the republic to the south. Robert Anderson Wilson, who had written a book about Mexico in the 1850s, professed to be an expert on its population.[28] He solemnly warned the secretary of state against forming policies based on the population estimates of the Mexican Liberal politician Miguel Lerdo, who had put the country's population at 7,000,000. It came nowhere near that number, Wilson insisted: it stood instead at 2,500,000.

Wilson began his calculation with the population statistics for New Spain in 1796, 4,500,000, and added to that 500,000 as an estimate of population from areas not then counted but a part of modern Mexico. Putting the 1800 population at 5,000,000, Wilson then subtracted from it 2,500,000 as the "loss by nearly 60, years of civil war." That left the "present population" at 2,500,000, he insisted. As a work of demography, this was laughable, but as a dramatic example of the skeptically dismissive attitude of many in the United States toward Mexico, it was symptomatic and revealing. In the view of many, Mexico was a country decimated by internal wars.[29]

Modern estimates put the population of Mexico in 1850 at

7. *Mexican Dresses* [*sic*], Mexico, 1863–1864. This depiction of Mexican revolutionaries from the decade preceding the French invasion and the imposition of Maximilian testified to the centrality of civil war in Mexico's political image. The lithograph equated republicanism and the national costume of Mexico with factional militias, bristling with bayonets, lances, and sabers.

7,600,000, but Wilson's absurd calculation serves to show the exaggerated place civil war played in imagining Mexico's history and politics.[30] Factional strife was the storied cause of the downfall of republics lacking a virtuous citizenry, and thus traditional republican beliefs themselves undermined sympathy for the sister republic. Also at issue was the type of warfare waged in Mexico. The country was notorious for guerrilla warfare.

People in the United States despised guerrilla warfare. During the Mexican-American War of 1846–1848, Secretary of War William L.

8. *A Stage Coach Attacked,* Mexico, 1863–1864. Maximilian's Black Decree equated the military opposition to his regime with the sort of banditry pictured here.

Marcy had stated flatly, "The guerrilla system is hardly recognized as a legitimate mode of warfare, and should be met with the utmost allowable severity."[31] But even the uniformed armies of Santa Anna fought with what was regarded as Hispanic cruelty.[32] The sort of warfare typically waged in Mexico by Mexicans seemed to lack honor or heroism. What many Americans remembered about warfare in Mexico was the Battle of Goliad and the Mier expedition. And guerrilla warfare was widely equated with banditry and brigandage.

Though not central to the image of Mexico—race and religion came first—warfare did figure in opinion of Mexico. It symbolized its republican failures and its foundation on peoples of no virtue or honor. The attitude persisted into the era of the American Civil War. In November 1865 George J. Potts, surgeon of the 23rd regiment of the United States Colored Troops, serving under General Godfrey Weitzel near Matamoros, was aggrieved by his treatment at the hands of his commanding officer and wrote complaining letters to Washington alleging Weitzel's corruption in running guns illegally to the republicans. Potts denounced Weitzel but dwelled less on the illegality of the operation than on its lack of political wisdom. Potts began with a pro forma gesture toward republican values:

> There cannot be a man in the Union whose heart does not sympathize with the cause of Republicanism in Mexico as well as in any other part of the World. But the Question arises, who are these for whom we would risk the peace of our country—These very men who are represented as [Republican] Generals [Mariano] Escobedo[,] [Juan N.] Cortinas [sic], & others have no sympathy with our cherished institutions. Their system of warfare is that of robbers and they subsist in predatory bands. The peculiar character of the Mexican unfits them for stable Government and representation by such men as Cortinas [sic] Escobedo and others Offers little hope or promise to that unfortunate country. Whatever love may be in our hearts for this glorious cause of liberty and Free Government for the maintenance of the first attribute of Mans Nobility—still there remains a greater principle namely A Love of Law and order.[33]

It is true that even Mexican patriots acknowledged the country's common resort to guerrilla warfare and sometimes celebrated it as a distinguishing feature of their national history. A Mexican told a German baron in 1865, "Guerrilla warfare is not known in Europe, nor have they any idea how useful it is. The events in Spain at the beginning of this century have been forgotten . . . In countries like Mexico, mountainous and dry, with a mild climate, where horses abound, and inclemency of weather never prevents out-door movements; where food is found everywhere to supply the necessaries of life, guerrillas always exercise a deciding influence . . . Mexico gained its independence of Spain by a series of sudden victories by guerrillas."[34] Such boasts did little to endear Mexico to the outside world, and indeed France claimed a civilizing influence as part of its avowed mission to Mexico.

⊷⇒ ⇐⊷

If we turn to more public sources, we find that there is no bibliography of English-language works on this subject, and a survey of readily available books, magazine articles, and pamphlets turns up only a few works. Among these, however, there appears to be the same surprising presence of arguments on Maximilian's side. Vine Wright Kingsley (perhaps a pen name playing on "divine right of kings") opposed monarchy in Mexico, and George E. Church, who had accompanied Juárez in Mexico for a time, insisted that "Mexico is to-day fighting the great battle of republicanism against imperialism."[35] But F. J. Parker's pamphlet regarded the possibility of defeat of Maximilian as a "calamity."[36] The only full-length book on the subject, published contemporaneously in the United States, was written by the Democrat Henry M. Flint. He whitewashed Maximilian in a sharply partisan anti–Radical Republican work. Frederic Hall's adulatory biography of Maximilian, published shortly after his execution, was colored by the author's having acted as a lawyer for the emperor's defense at the final court martial.[37]

⊷⇒ ⇐⊷

Ironically, it required a dedicated Mexican statesman, Matías Romero, to remind doubters in the United States of the importance of the republican example to the world. And along the way, he discovered the utility of reminding them as well of their fealty to the international laws and customs of war and their ingrained revulsion at their violation. One of the keys to Romero's case against the French and Maximilian was to point to violations of the laws and customs of war on the part of the Old World's regime in countering Mexican guerrillas.

Romero, the Mexican minister to Washington for much of the period of the French incursion, deliberately, skillfully, and persistently stoked the fires of republican zeal in the United States to see the French and Maximilian leave Mexico. He met and talked with as many of the powerful people in the North as he could, but Romero probably had his greatest effect through influencing the content of the publications of the official diplomatic correspondence of the U.S. State Department. It may be difficult for modern readers to understand the impact of these volumes. They have the thick and uninteresting look of official records—just the sort of source that modern historians tend to look behind, around, and under in order to locate the real story. But the United States remained book-starved in the 1860s, and those who were lucky and well-connected recipients of the free copies of the volumes franked by the department or by members of Congress were grateful and often actually read in the volumes. Newspaper editors scanned them for material to grind in their daily and weekly mills of political agitation. It would be cynical to ignore their republican significance too: the United States in general and this administration in particular prided themselves on running on principles of foreign policy distinguishable from those of the old European world by their spurning of secret diplomacy. Readers more or less actually expected the documents to reveal truths about America's dealings with the greater world.

The case of Sylvester Mowry presents a prime example of the effect of publication of such documents. An entrepreneur in Arizona who had built the Mowry Silver Mines in 1862, only to have trade obstructed by the war in Mexico caused by the French incursion, Mowry fended off Apache raiders and awaited a decision in Mexico.[38]

How this Democratic loyalist got his copies of the diplomatic correspondence is not known, but he had good reason to read them. What he saw he did not like, and in response he wrote a long and lecturing letter to the great Democratic newspaper in New York, the *World,* which published it.

Mowry thought that his experience in Arizona and the Mexican state to the south, Sonora, qualified him to combat the illusions of American public opinion on the nature of Mexico under Maximilian. "The wide-spread idea," he wrote, "of 'liberal institutions,' 'republican government,' 'civil and religious liberty,' in Mexico, is not to be accepted without very great qualification." There could "be no nation founded on republican principles" without "a people a fair proportion of whom possess, if not intelligence and average virtue, at least a respect for laws, the observance of which are necessary for a national existence in some form." "There is no population in Mexico which is capable of maintaining any form of representative government," he pointed out flatly.

Such a low opinion of the people did not lead inexorably to imperialist designs on Mexico. Mowry had mixed feelings:

> If we drive out Maximilian, we must replace his government by one equally strong and repressive, or consign Mexico to anarchy, unless, indeed, it is proposed to annex all Mexico, and admit her various provinces as States. In view of such a contingency, the question of negro suffrage sinks into insignificance. The half-breed population—of mixed Indian, negro, and Spanish blood, with all the worst qualities of either race and the good of none; steeped in ignorance and superstition, loyal to nothing, lapsing into barbarism—would hardly add much by their senators and representatives to the glory or well-being of the "model republic."

Mowry had designs only on Sonora, necessary for the security of Arizona and for a railroad route in which he was interested.

Mowry noticed the effects of Romero's propaganda efforts in the State Department correspondence and mentioned him by name in the part of his letter defending the Black Decree:

> The outcry against Maximilian's order to put to death guerrillas is as just as it would be against the United States for putting to death guerrillas in the Southern States. The men who fight under the banner of Juárez are worse if possible than those who would now fight under the banner of the C.S.A. This may be unpleasant truth for Señor Don Matías Romero, but it is truth nevertheless; and if to-day we drive out Maximilian, it will become our duty to put to death these guerrillas, or we shall be recreant to the cause of law and order which we take from Maximilian's hands to fulfill.

Thus yet another American had become, as the cynical *World* expressed it, "a converted imperialist."[39]

Mowry's response was proof, in a negative way, of the effectiveness of Romero's propaganda. The young diplomat worked tirelessly for the cause of the Mexican republic. Romero was only twenty-four years old when the American Civil War began, but his subsequent career in Washington and New York showed skill well beyond his years. From 1861 to 1863 he was the chargé d'affaires, and after some months spent in Mexico, he returned as minister to the United States.[40]

The generally overlooked fruits of his labors are on display in House Executive Document 73, from the first session of the Thirty-ninth Congress, the two-volume set of diplomatic correspondence for the period of the French intervention in Mexico.[41] Much of the correspondence from Mexico and many other documents selected for inclusion in the volumes came from Romero. The State Department must have ultimately determined what was published in the series, and nearly everything printed there was favorable to the republicans and unfavorable to the empire. At bottom, the specific content of that favorable image of the republican cause was attributable to Romero.

Romero had many arrows in his quiver. He depicted the French regime as pro-Confederate, antirepublican, and alien to the Mexican nation. Romero also brought to the attention of the Americans in the North the violations of the laws and customs of war committed by the French and imperial forces in Mexico. This strategy was obviously grounded in the assumption that the people in the United States would be outraged by revelations of such practices. The strategy had the further advantage, under the peculiar circumstances of the French intervention, of exposing the hypocrisy of French claims to be acting as a civilizing force against the barbarism of the Mexicans. And it helped to counter the image of the Mexicans as bloodthirsty and cruel guerrillas.

Even as General William T. Sherman was marching through Georgia, Romero was supplying information to the State Department about French campaigns in Mexico and their attendant military depredations. Some of these revelations gained valuable exposure in the American press while the Civil War was still going on, but it was difficult to direct the attention of American editors and readers to such foreign events at the expense of coverage of the spectacular war at home. Most editors and many other readers would learn about them for the first time in the later publication of the diplomatic correspondence, well after the end of the Civil War. What follows is a description and analysis of the case against Maximilian found in the diplomatic correspondence.

As early as 1864 Romero sent a report from a republican source in Mexico that equated French court-martials with "assassinations." Already, Romero saw need to debunk the surprisingly good press that Maximilian was often able to generate: "Abandoning his apparent mildness and clemency . . . [he] has proclaimed as bandits and malefactors and condemned to death all the defenders of Mexican independence, recommending their extermination to the French court-martial."[42] Indeed, many events prefigured the Black Decree. In a report from the special correspondent for *Le Messager Franco-Americain* of December 10, 1864, readers learned: "At Puebla they have already commenced to put in execution the new measures of 'protection' ordered by the emperor. On the 5th instant six liberal prisoners were shot, and the military commander of the district, wishing no doubt to give evidence of his zeal, has decided that henceforward all prisoners should be executed within the twenty-four hours succeeding their capture."[43] Romero forwarded to Seward the decree of the French General Armand Alexandre Castagny of January 25, 1865, establishing a court-martial in Mazatlán, "from which there is no appeal, to pronounce, at discretion, sentences which are to be executed within twenty-four hours, against every republican guerrilla, and even against any prisoner made from the regular forces who defend the independence of their country, for it is known that the former, and even in many cases the latter, are called by the invaders of Mexico, 'armed malefactors,' against whom apparently the decree . . . is levelled. This barbarous system of trying by foreign courts-martial . . . has already carried to the gallows hundreds of victims, among them many such as Señor Chávez, the constitutional governor of Aguas Calientes and general Ghilardi, the companion in arms of Garibaldi."[44]

Romero's enterprise was aided by the bold denunciations of the Mexican venture by the political opposition to Napoleon III in France. Jules Favre, for example, in a debate in the French Chamber of Deputies denounced the burning of San Sebastián by General Castagny and added: "That is not all, gentlemen; these acts have been committed contrary to the law of nations, contrary to the laws of war, which require that neutrals should be respected; that private property should not wantonly and without cause be destroyed; that the sacking of cities should not be made a means of coercion in order to intimidate the mind of a people and inspire a salutary terror to insure the success of a pretender. Such are the principles laid down by all moralists and all who have written on the law of nations."[45] The official French government reply to Favre's speech was also printed in the American diplomatic record. In essence, the French government admitted the facts of summary executions and, incidentally, shared the universal obeisance to the laws of war and even chivalry:

> What, then, has General Castagny done? . . . Whence comes it that for the benefit of those who are called the soldiers of Juárez, who are but miserable wretches, assassins, who disembowel women, who slay children, who commit nothing but pillages and conflagrations, whence comes it that for the benefit of such men an insult is offered to a brave French general who nobly commands his men? . . . He is conducting his men against a ferocious enemy that flies before him; that always flies unless he be ten to one. He finds him committing atrocities and outrages, and yet you wish him to be treated as a soldier! How! Must we respect men who have committed such massacres; must we treat them as gallant men, as brave soldiers?
>
> No; General Castagny has them shot, because he sees in them only wretches, bandits, all steeped in crime . . . And here, gentlemen, General Castagny has certainly done his duty; he has acted as anyone ought to act under such circumstances . . . Not, indeed, as honor and the dignity of the flag demand when we fight with true soldiers, but as the security of men demands when they are opposed to a set of bandits.[46]

There was no escaping the ironies of the situation, however. A report of the burning and pillaging of sugar plantations along the Mexican coast under the guns of a French steamship included this stinging comment from Alejandro García: "This barbarous act . . . is an instance of what the people on the leeward coast must expect from those who, contrary to common sense, proclaim themselves the propagandists of civilization, and calls for the most summary vengeance on our part."[47]

Conversely, the diplomatic correspondence included anecdotes documenting the adherence of the republican forces to the standards of the laws of war, despite the Mexican nation's willingness to embrace guerrilla warfare as the national way of fighting. The republican general José María Arteaga thus wrote the French commander General Achille Bazaine in the spring of 1865, "By special request of the Belgian lieutenant, M. Guallo, who was taken prisoner on the 11th instant, I . . . remit to you . . . a gold watch belonging to Baron Chazal, son of the minister of war of Belgium, who was killed in the said assault."[48]

In a little-noticed highlight of the early Reconstruction period in the United States, Romero did more damage to the reputation of the enemy by featuring another major blow to humanitarianism dealt by the imperial regime. He saw to it that the Andrew Johnson administration was supplied with Maximilian's notorious order on laborers of color. Desperate for men to protect his throne, Maximilian attempted to attract former Confederates to Mexico by weakening Mexico's historic abolition of slavery. President Johnson submitted the new laws to the attorney general of the United States for a determination whether the code constituted slavery. The attorney general's opinion was that Maximilian had in effect, though not in name, reestablished slavery based on color in Mexico. That determination led in turn to the extraordinary statement by Secretary of State William H. Seward in an official dispatch to Paris, printed in the official correspondence and thus freighted with great weight in American policy if not law: "The establishment of the perfect equality of men of the African race with men of other races throughout the whole continent is a policy which the United States may hereafter be expected to cultivate with constancy and assiduity."[49]

The ultimate outrage, of course, was the Black Decree, and Romero played a major role in publicizing its importance to the American people through the official correspondence. He was one of two people to bring the decree to the attention of the U.S. Department of State. He supplied the text with an English translation on October 25, 1865. The subsequent treatment of the decree in the diplomatic correspondence shows that the volumes were less a published archive than an artfully constructed narrative or a moral fable. The section devoted to the Black Decree was entitled "Raising of the Black Flag by Maximilian in Mexico."[50] The practical effect of the decree was seared into public memory by the execution of two republican generals, four colonels, and other officers taken prisoner only ten days after Maximilian issued the decree.

The execution of General José María Arteaga proved particularly damaging to the imperial cause, for Arteaga had appeared in earlier pages of the diplomatic correspondence as a chivalric officer. He not only had returned the watch of the slain son of the Belgian foreign minister but also had offered an articulate defense of the laws of war in a long letter published in the volumes. "It is Mexico," he wrote in response to the hypocrisies of French claims to civilization, "who by her example gives them lessons of gentlemanliness." "Women and children are always respected in war," he reminded the invaders, as he pointed out that "neither a loyal nor chivalrous war is waged against Mexico." Arteaga even received a letter of thanks from French officers taken prisoner for his policy of taking prisoners despite great provocation by the actions and official decrees of the imperial government and the French army in Mexico.[51]

"Raising of the Black Flag by Maximilian in Mexico" included as its central drama the martyrdom of Arteaga. Readers could see the letter from General Arteaga to his mother written on October 20, 1865, the "evening of the day before his sacrifice," as well as letters in protest against the treatment of Arteaga drafted by Belgian officers held as prisoners of war by the republicans.[52] William H. Seward's letter about Arteaga's execution stated that the United States "fully deprecates the practice of a system of warfare so little in consonance with the usages of enlightened states."[53]

The fact of the matter is that Romero had much to choose from when it came to the record of infamy of the French forces in Mexico. The towns of Ajusco and Tlacolulán were burned in retaliation for guerrilla attacks. General Castagny burned Concordia, a town of some 4,000 inhabitants, to the ground and bombarded Guaymas after the Liberals had left the town. The infamous French court-martials of Mexicans often took the attitude expressed by one president of such a court. "Bah!" he said. "Every Mexican is a *guerrillero;* either he has been or he will be. You don't take any risk of being wrong when you shoot the ones you catch."[54]

Romero apparently understood that these outrages were best epitomized by a dramatic martyrdom under the Black Decree. The damage to Maximilian's reputation was severe. Maximilian was much and feelingly criticized for the Black Decree despite the rather weak identification of the United States with Mexican republicanism. The decree played a major role in bringing about his execution and in decreasing the natural outpouring of human sympathy for this courageous autocrat who refused to become the merest tool of aristocratic and ecclesiastical reactionaries in Mexico. The Black Decree formed part of the specific indictment against Maximilian drawn up for his military trial. The decree had made him essentially a war criminal, and Maximilian may have been the first major leader in history to suffer capital punishment for war crimes.

Newspaper opinion in the United States on the execution of Maximilian was surprisingly diverse. The *New York Herald* surveyed newspaper opinion across the country on the event, and, if its sample is representative, a majority of papers followed the State Department line in hoping that the republicans would not execute Maximilian. The Department of State took the view that execution would itself be a blot on the reputation of republicanism and make it appear vengeful and inhumane. The *Herald* itself, when Maximilian's fall began to look inevitable in the spring of 1867, focused on Mexico's incapacity for republican self-rule and stated that "Mexico's only hope is to shelter herself under the eagle of the republic of the United States." In other words, the prospect of the inevitable fall of the Austrian emperor led not to celebration of the survival of another republican example in a dangerous world of monarchical nation states but to a renewed faith in "Our Manifest Destiny." The North American continent, crowed the *Herald,* is the future map of the United States.[55] The newspaper position was arrived at without excusing the inexcusable, however. "The probability," the paper predicted while Maximilian's life hung in the balance, "is that his life will be spared—not so much in justice as in policy, for if justice were meted out the barbarous decrees of Maximilian, which disgrace the civilization of this century, would, in a trial, tell very heavily against him; not to mention the carrying out of these decrees, which has resulted in the wholesale massacre of thousands of the leading liberals of Mexico and the desolation of their country."[56]

Among the newspapers surveyed by the *Herald,* only the *Albany Argus* advocated Maximilian's execution. The others (three from New Orleans, a Brownsville, Texas, paper, and five Northern newspapers) urged mercy, but the reasons varied.[57] None took the occasion, apparently, to celebrate the survival of a republic, the resilience and determination of Mexican republicanism and nationalism, or the perseverance of Benito Juárez. But some did take notice of the Black Decree. The Brownsville newspaper noted that mercy would come despite the fact that the "bloody order issued in the name of Maximilian, directing that guerrillas and unauthorized bands of armed men should be summarily shot, will not be forgotten." And the *New Haven Courier* acknowledged that the republicans had "the right to summarily execute" him because of the executions of "republican patriots" and the burning of towns.[58]

The only newspapers vigorously supportive of the execution of the emperor were the *New York Evening Post* and *Wilkes's Spirit of the Times*.[59] The *New York Tribune,* the *New York Times,* the *Washington National Intelligencer,* and the *Chicago Tribune* criticized the execution but acknowledged the very great irritant of the "Sanguinary Decree" of October 3, 1865.[60] The *Richmond Dispatch* and the *New Orleans Bee* characterized Maximilian's execution as "cold blooded murder" and called for the annexation of Mexico.[61]

In Congress, by contrast, Radical Republicans expressed uncompromising support for the execution. Zachariah Chandler and Jacob Howard of Michigan brought the subject up more than once. In these debates they justified the Radical Republican reputation for vindictiveness. Howard was seeking to correct "a sort of childish sentimentalism . . . on the subject of the execution." He called Maximilian an "adventurer," and Chandler characterized him as leading another "filibuster." The focus of the debate proved to be the Black Decree, and the whole of the infamous document was read into the record, producing more than a long column of dense prose.[62] Divisions were roughly partisan, but the focus of both Maximilian's detractors and his defenders was mainly on the Black Decree and its effects on Mexico. Chandler noted the deaths of Arteaga and other officers and estimated that 2,000 other "Mexican patriots" had been executed under the decree.[63] Senator Joseph Fowler of Tennessee, a moderate Republican, put the number executed under the decree at 10,000–12,000.[64] James W. Nye of Nevada also weighed in in Mexico's favor. But Reverdy Johnson of Maryland, a Democrat, said that he had heard that "not even hundreds" had been executed and insisted that Maximilian would have provided Mexico with "a better government than it had ever had in the past."[65]

The October 3, 1865, decree played a role in almost all expressions of opinion on the subject of Maximilian's execution, and, though Senator Howard was right to say that there was considerable sentimentalism expressed over Maximilian's execution, only the fiery *New Orleans Bee* and Democrat Reverdy Johnson of Maryland in the Senate made any attempt to excuse the decree itself.[66]

For the most part, then, people in the United States regarded the October 3, 1865, decree as an infamous measure, whatever they thought of the Mexicans as a people. For a revealing and extensive discussion of the issue, we can return to Henry Shelton Sanford, who provides the viewpoint of an interested and informed source, but not one sentimentally attached to the cause of Mexican republicanism. In June 1867, before news of Maximilian's execution reached France, Sanford had dinner in Paris with Marshal Bazaine, the former French military commander in Mexico. The conversation got quickly around to atrocities. According to Sanford, Bazaine himself raised the subject: "He insisted that the enormities in the way of destroying towns &c laid to their [the French army's] charge were not true—when I suggested that giving no quarter to Mexicans whose only crime was defending their homes, might fall within that designation he insisted that they were Brigands & deserved no better treatment."[67] Sanford also had a conversation with the duc d'Echlingen, the French officer who commanded a notorious French regiment called the Contra-guerrillas after the removal of their original and feared commander Colonel Charles-Louis Dupin. There could scarcely have been a better source for knowledge of French violations of the laws of war in Mexico, for the reputation of the Contra-guerrillas was that they more than matched the Mexican guerrillas in cruel disregard for humanity and international law.[68] The duke, reported Sanford, "confirmed to me a fact which I have before mentioned to you, that they gave no quarter—his orders he said were to shoot all persons taken with arms in their hands, and as it was very *enn[u]yeux* to have to do it, his orders were to take no prisoners & he punished those who did." Prince Murat told Sanford that "Maximilian deserved to be shot & would be in any other country—but he hoped as a matter of humanity his life would be spared & he repeated to me that Mexican soldiers were shot by his orders."[69]

After Maximilian's execution, Sanford had breakfast with the Prince of Wales in Paris. The prince, as well he might, "spoke with some feeling of the horrible Execution of Maximilian." Sanford, however, "could not help telling him that while I deplored it, it was doubtless justified by the laws of war—that for two years past Mexicans taken prisoner while defending their homes & a flag which we recognized had been by his orders shot by hundreds." Sanford tried to convince Seward that liberal opinion in Europe was heading in the same direction. The "cry about 'murder' & 'assassination' which governmental journals throughout Europe have set up over the execution of Maximilian in defence of the theory of the infallibility of Princes, & in France as a shield for the responsibility of the Emperor—is causing a reaction in public sentiment." "The Liberal press," Sanford reported, "are republishing details of atrocities committed under orders of Maximilian—officers shot when taken prisoners, for having

defended their flag & country, & public opinion is settling down to
the opinion that however cruel & impolitic the act, it was perhaps
justified as reprisal & is what would have been meted out in any
country in Europe under similar circumstances."[70]

Sanford would not let the subject drop. In Brussels he had a conversation with the former commander of the Belgian legion in Mexico about casualties in the war. "His estimate of prisoners shot under the orders of Maximilian (Proclamation of Octr 1865) was 2000
about—I told him in so far as I could get data for a judgment, I
thought 5000 was nearer the truth—he admitted the possibility of
that number."[71]

⋯⟹ ⟸⋯

Republicanism mattered less, and the laws of nations and rules of
civilized warfare mattered more, in determining American opinion
on the French intervention in Mexico than we might be led to think
from reading the current literature on the Civil War era. One thing is
certain: nothing that Americans saw in Mexico made them think that
anything had changed in the way civilized nations ought to go about
fighting wars. I have never been able to find anyone, in private or in
the press, State Department sophisticate or frontier soldier, Mexican-
phobe or republican apologist, who made an observation like this
about the notoriously unorthodox conflict in Mexico: we know from
our own recent experience in our civil war that the rules of warfare
naturally break down and that this business of not taking prisoners
and raising the black flag and burning towns and making war on civilians and slaughtering innocents is what war is fast coming to in
our modern age.

It is testimony to the reckless racism of Mexico's enemies in the
middle of the nineteenth century that they showed so little interest in
totaling enemy casualties. Civilian losses are even more difficult to
calculate. By any measure available, however, the destructive war

waged in North America in the middle of the nineteenth century was the one the French waged in Mexico. At Maximilian's trial prosecutors asserted 11,000 prisoners had been killed in cold blood by French and imperial forces. Even Belgians and Frenchmen admitted there were considerable atrocities under the order of October 3, 1865, alone, and considered 2,000–5,000 deaths viable estimates. Other estimates run much higher than any of these figures, even to 40,000.

These are not figures for unfortunate civilians caught in the line of fire. These are deliberate killings. The figures are shocking in the extreme. The population of Mexico did not equal that of the Confederacy, though it was nearly equal to the white population of the Confederate states.

There exists no systematic estimate of civilian casualties in the American Civil War based on documentary records—or of deaths of partisans and guerrillas as distinguished from regularly enlisted men.[72] No one would put the number of prisoners killed by Union forces in the Civil War at any magnitude near 11,000 to 40,000. Even the Confederates, whose acute racial consciousness and desperate military circumstances drove them to infamous atrocities, did not come close to matching the French and imperial Mexican record statistically. The murder of about 100 African American soldiers who had surrendered along with some East Tennessee white Unionists at Fort Pillow, Tennessee, on April 12, 1864, caused a crisis of response in the Lincoln administration and was widely reported. It would be unimaginable that there be 100 or 400 Fort Pillows more in the American Civil War, but it would require that to equal the terrible record of the French and their allies in Mexico. When the Chicago chromolithographers depicted a Confederate atrocity late in the nineteenth century, Fort Pillow was surely an easy choice of subject. They did not have hundreds more from which to choose.

It is noticeable too that the most famous atrocities, the Fort Pillow

9. *Mexican Gendarmerie, Escolting* [*sic*] *Prisoners,* Mexico, 1863–1864. The Mexican troops in Maximilian's service were not numerous or potent in battle. This lithograph, with its depiction of the ragtag opposition to the empire and its glorification of the native mounted police, probably had little trouble passing the censors of Maximilian's regime.

Massacre and the Lawrence Massacre, were caused by Confederate forces and that the most lurid terrorist plot, the one to burn New York City after the election of 1864, was a plan concocted by Confederate agents. Yet "terror" is a term that has somehow attached to the work of the Union army. The specter of bodies hanging upside down from trees, apparently a common sight in Mexico's war, was virtually unknown in the American Civil War.[73] The total number of trials by military commission instituted by the Union during the American Civil War was 4,271, and death sentences were seldom the outcome of these.

Indeed, the armies of republics, and especially of the United States, enjoyed a much more creditable record than the armies fielded by the vaunted "civilizations" of Europe. The record of the U.S. army in Mexico in 1846–1848, volunteers and regulars alike, does not come close in brutality to the record of the French and imperialists in Mexico twenty years later. Degradation of the laws of war proved central to the conflict in Mexico in the 1860s and embarrassingly reversed one of the major rationalizations for French invasion: the French were supposed to be a "civilizing" force.

To be sure, Napoleon III attempted to identify Mexicans as part of a common "Latin race," but the French soldiers on the ground in Mexico acted as though they regarded the enemy as a different and despicable race. U.S. forces might have imitated French severity against the same Mexican enemy identified as a degraded race. But happily for the reputation of the United States in the world, the United States was not put to that test in the 1860s, and France must bear the shame alone for their soldiers' truly terrible Mexican adventure.

The American Civil War was, if anything, remarkable for its traditional restraint. Unlike the French, who in Mexico brutally displaced the chivalric conventions of warfare associated with Europe, the republicans in the United States did not take steps that might lead the country to the wholesale slaughters of the twentieth century.

## 4

# THE SHENANDOAH VALLEY
## Sheridan and Scorched Earth

OF THE TWO legendarily destructive military campaigns of the Civil War—William T. Sherman's march to the sea and Philip H. Sheridan's march through the Shenandoah Valley—Sherman's has garnered a great deal more attention from historians. The result has been a decisive turnaround in its reputation. The military historian Joseph Glatthaar scrutinized Sherman's march through Georgia over twenty years ago and quietly debunked the idea that Sherman attacked the civilian population of the Confederacy. "In general, Sherman's army treated Southern civilians well. The fact that three prominent Confederates—Lt. Gen. William J. Hardee, Maj. Gen. Gustavus W. Smith, and Col. Edward C. Anderson—left their wives to the care of Sherman's occupation forces in Savannah indicated that the soldiers opposing the march had no reason to doubt that Sherman's men would treat civilians properly." Likewise Glatthaar carefully established that the destruction of civilian property has been exaggerated. "If Georgians did not bushwhack or impede the march or attempt to conceal cotton inside," Glatthaar concluded, "Sherman's troops did not set fire to their homes, except in the case of prominent Confederates, whose homes universally received the torch."[1]

Sheridan's campaign, however, has not enjoyed a similar revisionist treatment.

The myth persists that General Sheridan "burned" the Shenandoah Valley in the late summer and early autumn of 1864. A recent book on the subject is entitled, simply, *The Burning*.[2] A Civil War textbook published in 2003 declares that "Sheridan's men systematically burned out both military and civilian targets, destroying thousands of farms and their crops. The great breadbasket of Virginia was no more."[3]

But Gary Gallagher's distinguished series "Military Campaigns of the Civil War" has chosen to focus a second time on the Shenandoah Valley campaign, and with William G. Thomas's essay in the volume interpretations of Sheridan's campaign are at last beginning to come into line with what we know about Sherman's campaign and about guerrilla warfare in the Civil War. "Heavy as these losses were," writes Thomas of the Union destruction of agriculture during the campaign, "Sheridan's forces had inflicted limited and targeted damage that neither destroyed the entire Valley nor subjugated its population." Yet Thomas also rendered "The Burning" with capital letters, as though it were a mystical milestone, and elsewhere in the essay emphasized destruction.[4]

Change is coming, obviously, in interpreting Sheridan's Shenandoah Valley campaign, but no true reversal of opinion has yet occurred.

The documentary record of destruction uncovered by the diligent work of William G. Thomas leaves us with a curious anomaly. He discovered an official survey of destruction in Rockingham County undertaken for the governor of Virginia. When the losses are compared with the figures for production in the county reported in the U.S. Census of 1860, it appears that a bit less than one third of the wheat and hay were destroyed. The striking disparity, however, comes in the figures reported for corn: 50,000 bushels destroyed compared to 684,239 bushels produced in 1860. Why was there such a disparity in the types of crops destroyed?[5]

The loose expression "the burning" has served too long to obscure a more controlled and less complete series of acts in need of more precise description. It is not clear why an indiscriminate "Burning" would devastate the wheat crop and do only minor damage to the corn.

→▭ ▭←

Any deliberate use of fire as a weapon of war in the middle of the nineteenth century was frightening to all concerned. Its use in the Shenandoah Valley of Virginia in 1864 conjured up apocalyptic images in the biblical imaginations of the residents. Thus a terrified woman from Berryville described what she had witnessed in August of that year:

> Fires of barns, stockyards, etc. soon burst forth and by eleven, from high elevation, fifty could be seen blazing forth. The sky was lurid and but for the green trees one might have imagined the shades of Hades had suddenly descended. The shouts, ribald jokes, awful oaths, demoniacal laughter of the fiends added to the horrors of the day . . . In almost every instance every head of stock was driven off. Those young animals that refused to go were shot down . . . large families of children were left without one cow. In many of the barns were stowed . . . wagons, plows, etc., and in no instance did they allow anything to be saved.[6]

Such scenes of destruction, as it turns out, were not appealing to the arsonists either. The Michigan cavalryman J. H. Kidd, in his postwar recollections, described burning a grist mill, and then went on:

> It was a disagreeable business and—we can be frank now—I did not relish it. One incident made a lasting impression on the mind of every

man who was there. The mill in the little hamlet of Port Republic contained the means of livelihood—the food of the women and children whom the exigencies of war had bereft of their natural providers and, when they found that it was the intention to destroy that on which their very existence seemed to depend, their appeals to be permitted to have some of the flour before the mill was burned, were heartrending. Worse than all else, in spite of the most urgent precautions, enjoined upon the officers in charge, the flames extended. The mill stood in the midst of a group of wooden houses and some of them took fire. Seeing the danger, I rode across and ordered every man to fall in and assist in preventing the further spread of the flames, an effort which was, happily, successful. What I saw there is burned into my memory. Women with children in their arms, stood in the street and gazed frantically upon the threatened ruin of their homes, while the tears rained down their cheeks. The anguish pictured in their faces would have melted any heart not seared by the horrors and "necessities" of war. It was too much for me and at the first moment that duty would permit, I hurried away from the scene.[7]

The anecdote is striking not only for its revelation of fundamental humanity in the firebrand cavalryman but also for its perspective. "We can be frank now," he said forty years after the war. During it, he had sometimes to conceal his humanitarian feelings under a veil of soldierly fierceness. Such cultural forces worked on the battle reports, orders, and letters of Civil War soldiers to leave us a record of the war more terrible perhaps than it really was.

The historian Michael G. Mahon, who has called attention to these two valuable quotations from eyewitnesses to the so-called burning of the Shenandoah Valley in 1864, has also provided a logistical context in which to understand them. Above all, he has shrewdly questioned the accepted wisdom of taking Sheridan at his word, backed up by the hostile and hysterical accounts of some of the victims. Did Philip H. Sheridan really do what he said he did: destroy the Shenandoah Valley as a breadbasket for the Confederacy?

Sheridan assigned to his three divisions of cavalry the task of destroying some crops and livestock when they did not have other more important things to do. General Alfred T. A. Torbert headed the cavalry. His subordinates were Wesley Merritt, who commanded the first division; William W. Averell, who commanded the second until Sheridan removed him in favor of William Powell; and James Wilson, who commanded the third division until he left to head the cavalry in Sherman's army and was succeeded by George Armstrong Custer. These men, all West Point graduates, clearly did not "destroy" the valley, as Mahon painstakingly proved. They did not devote enough men to the task or spend enough time on the project. Sheridan's statistics of destruction do not account for anything like the production of the valley counties in the 1860 census.

Mahon also contends, after examining quartermaster and commissary records, that the Confederacy had long since looked elsewhere for its major military food supplies.[8] Is it possible that Sheridan was working under an erroneous assumption? It is important to get clear what exactly Sheridan did do to the valley. Mahon's view is that Sheridan did destroy something, and since the valley was largely depleted of supplies by the end of 1862, then Sheridan must have destroyed what the people would have used for local consumption. That, of course, constitutes a truly drastic view of the destruction in the Shenandoah Valley.

⋯⊨○ ◐⊨⋯

The destruction visited on the Shenandoah Valley in 1864 was a secondary consideration for Sheridan and his army. On that point, at least, Mahon is accurate. Theirs was not a raid, after all. It was a military campaign, the major purpose of which was to defeat and destroy if possible Jubal A. Early's Confederate army, which had retreated to the valley after a raid that reached the very suburbs of Washington, D.C., and brought the president of the United States under enemy fire. The rage Early inspired in the North spilled over to the very valley in which his army operated, but the first objective of Sheridan's campaign was to destroy the Confederate army. When not engaged in combat with Early's army, the Union soldiers might occupy themselves with destroying grain and forage and running off livestock. In truth, they sometimes did neither and merely encamped.

When they were not fighting the enemy's army but were engaged in destroying what could be found on farms in the valley, it is not crystal clear what Sheridan thought he was to do and what his subordinates thought they were to do on his orders. Kidd, the Michigan cavalryman, for example, said in his recollections: "The fiat had gone forth from General Grant himself, that everything in the valley that might contribute to the support of the [Confederate] army must be destroyed before the country was abandoned."[9] Sheridan's purposes seem perhaps a little less clear because he made several statements on the subject and they are not all exactly alike, but his aim seems reasonably close to what Kidd said it was. For example, on October 7, 1864, Sheridan told Grant about his retrograde movement from Port Republic to Harrisonburg: "In moving back to this point the whole country from the Blue Ridge to the North Mountains has been made untenable for a rebel army."[10]

Sheridan was under the impression that "all the grain, forage, &c., in the vicinity of Staunton was retained for the use of [Jubal A.] Early's army [operating in the valley]; all in the lower part of the Valley was shipped to Richmond for the use of Lee's army."[11] But he repeatedly said in orders that he was attempting to eliminate the grain and forage used by Confederate raiders *in* the valley. Whatever the case, the Union soldiers conceived of their mission as destroying what would sustain Confederate armies. What sustained armies was never spelled out, but the practical effect, from the agricultural producers' perspective, was to see the destruction of their surplus and not their subsistence, the commercial crops and not the garden, what was stored in the barns or being processed in mills before going to market, not what sat in pickle jars and small kegs in the pantry. Whether Sheridan and his cavalry subordinates operated under a mistaken assumption about the role of the valley's agriculture in the Confederate military supply chain or not, they never intended to bother ripping up the gardens and stealing the kitchen's vegetables and fruits.

And indeed, such a plan meshes perfectly with the image of the valley rendered by eyewitnesses during Sheridan's campaign. They saw barns and mills burning, discrete points emitting smoke here and there across the landscape. The valley was not scorched.

It probably could not have been "burned" without application of some potent fire accelerant, with which the army, trained and fitted for combat rather than terror and sabotage, was not equipped. The reference to green trees as an incongruous part of the Berryville diarist's vision of hell in the valley serves to remind us that the roads, hedges, orchards, and forests of late summer, not to mention the brooks and streams, would act as impediments to scorching the earth in any literal sense. The conditions were otherwise ripe, since the valley had endured its second summer of drought, but the fires were controlled.[12] They had to be, because Sheridan had put another limit on the destruction that was to be meted out to the valley's farms: dwellings were not to be burned.

He knew that generals were given to extreme statements that could not be taken literally and that Grant had gone too far in his orders about destroying the provender in the Shenandoah Valley. The orders are famous in the lexicon of Civil War literature that emphasizes the destructiveness of the war's later phases. James M. McPherson renders them this way: Sheridan was to make "the Shenandoah Valley [into] a barren waste . . . so that crows flying over it for the balance of this season will have to carry their provender with them."[13] In truth, those were not the orders Sheridan received. On August 26, 1864, Grant told Sheridan to damage railroads and crops and to drive off slaves so that there would be no planting. He concluded: "If the war is to last another year we want the Shenandoah Valley to remain a barren waste."[14] The other, more vivid part of the Grant quotation, came from a different letter altogether. Grant had written General Henry W. Halleck on July 14, 1864, updating him on Early's raid on Washington, D.C., which had been turned back only two days previously. "If the enemy has left Maryland," General Grant said with high irritation, "as I suppose he has, he should have upon his heels veterans, militiamen, men on horseback, and everything that can be got to follow to eat out Virginia clear and clean as far as they go, so that crows flying over it for the balance of this season will have to carry their provender with them."[15] Grant might well have given Sheridan such an order as we saw at the beginning of this paragraph, but in fact he did not. What Grant actually had in mind, once he had calmed down from his rage over Early's raid on Washington, was the disruption of the planting of commercial crops for the next season— in case the war lasted another year. We will look at Grant's orders to Sheridan more closely later in this chapter.

In his final report on the brilliant Shenandoah Valley campaign, General Sheridan said he had given his cavalry "directions to burn all forage and drive off all stock, &c., as they moved to the rear, fully coinciding in the views and instructions of the lieutenant-general [Grant], that the Valley should be made a barren waste." He added immediately: "The most positive orders were given, however, not to burn dwellings."[16] Indeed, Grant himself had told Sheridan, "It is not desirable that buildings should be destroyed."[17] In other words, no one was serious about making the valley literally a "barren waste," though Grant tried to sound as fierce as possible and did sound more so than Sheridan or his subordinates.

Such fierce language was used out of spleen and for the sake of public consumption, especially for the ears of the enemy. And the enemy did hear what the generals wanted them to hear. General Early told Robert E. Lee that "Sheridan's purpose, under Grant's orders, has been to render the Valley untenable by our troops by destroying the supplies."[18] Just two days before, Sheridan himself had reported to Grant that his army made "the whole country from the Blue Ridge to the North Mountains . . . untenable for a rebel army."[19] Early's use of the very term "untenable," a favorite of Sheridan's, might have been a coincidence, but it seems likely that some of the language of military orders had uses meant for the enemy more than the friends of the Union.

Avoiding setting fire to dwellings while burning nearby mills, barns, and piles of hay and grain was not easy. A house could catch fire accidentally when arson was employed for war, as the recollection of the Michigan cavalryman shows. The cavalrymen had to be careful and restrained even when their consciences did not bother them as Kidd's did. Confederate soldiers operating in the Shenandoah Valley confirmed the reports of the Union soldiers. The topographical engineer Jedediah Hotchkiss, for example, who must have had a good eye for landscape, since making maps was his principal function in the war, said in his final report of the campaign only, "The enemy retreated, burning barns and hay and grain ricks as they went."[20]

The Union cavalrymen did not, apparently, set fire to whole fields of crops in something like a prairie fire. They burned what was gathered in "ricks," as Hotchkiss put it. Harvest time had come, of course, by the end of the campaign, and much of what had been raised would have been gathered already. Almost twenty-five years later, in describing the field of the Battle of Opequon, of September 19, 1864, in his *Memoirs* General Sheridan recalled, "Clumps of woods and patches of underbrush occurred here and there, but the undulating ground consisted mainly of open fields, many of which were covered with standing corn that had already ripened."[21] Fields of crops were available, but they were not regularly set afire, apparently. In all likelihood, the Union army conceived of its purpose as burning or capturing the surplus agricultural production of the valley, the commercial crops and livestock that might otherwise have been sold to the Confederates.

They did not conceive of their mission as destroying the subsistence of the inhabitants. In the case of livestock, the difference would hardly be clear: they were not going to distinguish the milk cows for the children from the other animals, perhaps. Corn presents a different and clearer case. It played a major part in subsistence for the Southerners living in the Shenandoah Valley, and the Union cavalry apparently made little point of destroying it.[22] General Merritt, reporting what he destroyed and captured through October 5, noted only 515 acres of corn. This was the only produce accounted for in acres rather than by weight or volume, but it simply was not very much. With 640 acres in a square mile, Merritt surely had not destroyed many of those fields of ripened corn Sheridan reported as features of the valley landscape.[23] The Union cavalrymen were selective—or, as they said themselves, "delicate."

Reporting destruction in acres was unusual. Sheridan reported the results mostly in tons, bushels, and pounds of produce, but surely the produce was not everywhere waiting for the Union soldiers in weighed lots, and the cavalry did not carry commercial scales with them. Doubtless, captured goods, rather than destroyed goods, were measured by the Union provost marshals, quartermasters, and commissary officers who must have received such captured goods, but the process is not spelled out in the documents printed in the official records of the campaign.[24] The general impression given by the reports is that the grain and produce were mostly destroyed rather than carried off by the cavalry. The estimates of destruction were made to impress a general, Grant, who had issued sweeping and terrible-sounding orders impossible to carry out. In other words, the measurement of the destruction was surely imprecise and probably exaggerated.

The commander of the Second Cavalry Division in Sheridan's army made a crucial distinction, not made with adequate precision in the histories of the campaign written since that time: "The country through which I have passed and in which I have operated has been left in such a condition as to barely leave subsistence for the inhabitants. The property destroyed, viz, grain, forage, flouring mills, tanneries, blast furnaces, &c., and stock driven off, has inflicted a severe blow on the enemy. The money value of this property could not have been less than $3,000,000."[25] The Union cavalry destroyed much of value but not the "subsistence for the inhabitants."

Kidd confirmed the picture we see here, verifying the anomalous crop statistics. Writing to his father on December 5, 1864, Kidd reported, "Nothing is left where we have been but corn and not much of that. Barns and mills are destroyed. Hay and grain has been given to the flames. A relentless war this we are now waging but it may be the speediest way."[26] Corn in the Yankees' estimation was for subsistence, but hay and grain were commercial crops sold as surplus—to the Confederate armies.

General Wesley Merritt's recollection was similar. He said that the cavalry "did not shrink from the duty" of "destruction," and he characterized the work this way: "It is greatly to their credit that no personal violence on any inhabitant was ever reported, even by their enemies. The Valley from Staunton to Winchester was completely devastated, and the armies thereafter occupying that country had to look elsewhere for their supplies. There is little doubt, however, that enough was left in the country for the subsistence of the people, for this, besides being contemplated by orders, resulted of necessity from the fact that, while the work was done hurriedly, the citizens had ample time to secrete supplies, and did so."[27] Sheridan's final report on the campaign does not sustain the image of the destruction of the valley now blazoned forth in most modern histories or in his own *Memoirs* decades later. He mentioned the destruction of grain and forage as part of the task he had to carry out in obedience to Grant's orders. But when he summed up the brilliant campaign, after his (very modest) description of the Battle of Cedar Creek, where he personally saved the day for the Union and rallied his demoralized troops to final victory, Sheridan said:

> This battle practically ended the campaign in the Shenandoah Valley. When it opened we found our enemy boastful and confident, unwilling to acknowledge that the soldiers of the Union were their equal in courage and manliness; when it closed with Cedar Creek this impression had been removed from his mind, and gave place to good sense and a strong desire to quit fighting. The very best troops of the Confederacy had not only been defeated, but had been routed in successive engagements, until their spirit and esprit were destroyed . . . Practically all territory north of the James River now belonged to me, and the holding of the lines about Petersburg and Richmond by the enemy must have been embarrassing, and invited the question of good military judgment.[28]

Although Sheridan had begun his report with a description of the abundance produced by the Shenandoah Valley and its ability to sustain Confederate armies marching up and down it, "billeting on the inhabitants," he made little of the accomplishment of destroying the supplies of the Confederacy in the conclusion to his report.[29] The report made nothing of the alleged effects of that destruction on the morale of the people in the valley.[30]

Sheridan might have pointed out that ultimately his famous battlefield victory was attributable to the destruction of food in the Shenandoah Valley. At Cedar Creek, the decisive battle of the campaign, Early's troops at first surprised the Union army in its camps and achieved a rout of at least one corps. But then the Confederates stopped to loot the Union supplies. Were they simply too hungry to keep their minds on fighting? No one has said so. While they paused, Sheridan came riding back, rallied the Union forces, and made a decisive counterattack. Early attributed the reversal to a lack of good junior officers who could maintain discipline. Sheridan never commented on these matters.[31]

Instead, Sheridan described what were for him the important results of the campaign in traditional gendered moral terms: the campaign had proven the manliness and courage of the Union army to the scoffing Confederate army. He also explained the situation in traditional military terms of battle-map strategy, not in terms of economics and supplies. He never used the term "scorched earth" in his reports.[32]

⊷⊨◉ ◉⊨⊶

The traditional nature of the ideals and goals exemplified in General Sheridan's report was perhaps even more pronounced for the cavalrymen assigned the task of destroying supplies in the Shenandoah Valley. It has escaped notice that assigning the job to that particular arm of the service probably made a difference in its execution. The cavalry was more traditional in its outlook on warfare and had more to prove by way of equaling the manliness of the Confederates than the infantry or the artillery or any of the technical branches.

The Union cavalry in the East had heretofore been the goat of Civil War military reputation. It had often been relegated to performing inglorious duty: guarding wagons, for example, or preventing the desertion of the infantry on the march or escorting generals or standing on picket guard. Sheridan thought such uses frittered the

10. *Battle of Cedar Creek,* 1890. General Philip Henry Sheridan did not himself lead the famous Union cavalry charges of the Shenandoah Valley campaign of 1864, as this image, with Sheridan on his famous black horse, Rienzi, at the center, suggests. He did, however, invigorate the Union cavalry by massing it in a mounted corps and giving it prominent combat roles in the campaign.

cavalry away, and he had longed to see it bunched together in a great corps, where it could negate the feared Confederate cavalry.[33] The inglorious role of the Union cavalry had even caused the mounted men to suffer the sting of sarcasm from a previous commander of the Army of the Potomac. General Joseph Hooker was reported as having said once: "Who ever saw a dead cavalryman?"[34] According to Sheridan, President Lincoln himself used the dead cavalryman query in his personal interview with Sheridan before the general left to head the cavalry of the Army of the Potomac.[35] Public opinion had been merciless. At least since the time of Confederate General J. E. B. Stuart's famous ride around the Army of the Potomac in early 1862, the Northern press commonly criticized the Union cavalry as inferior to its Confederate counterpart. And the cavalry operating in Virginia suffered its share of general humiliation for the Northern defeats in 1862. Northern soldiers fighting in Virginia, mounted and dismounted alike, all felt the shame of defeat by Stonewall Jackson in the famous Shenandoah Valley campaigns of 1862. There were many psychological scores to be settled in the valley in 1864.

To read the reports of the cavalrymen after the 1864 campaign is to realize that settling those old scores by proving their mettle as horse soldiers may have been uppermost in their minds. General Torbert, whose report was largely a dry presentation of operational movements, did at one point stop to comment on a cavalry action early in the campaign: "The First Division (Brigadier-General Merritt) moved out in the direction of Leetown, Va., where it met the enemy's cavalry in force and gallantly drove them with the saber through Smithfield and across the Opequon Creek."[36] What is noticeable, of course, is the mention of "the saber." In describing other actions, Torbert did not say what weapons proved most useful to the cavalrymen.

General Wesley Merritt, who was commander of the First Cavalry Division of Sheridan's army, saw in the glorious military feats of the army in the campaign "a theme for the poet; a scene for the painter." In characteristic vein, he concluded, "The battle of Opequon was truly a glorious occasion for the First Cavalry Division, and there is not a man nor officer in the command who does not take a just pride in what was done by the division toward winning the victory and trailing the rebel banners in the dust in the Valley of the Shenandoah, the former valley of humiliation to Union armies."[37] Erasing memories of previous humiliations by defeating the Confederate cavalry in charges on horseback with the saber drawn was the dream of the Union cavalry in 1864.

Union cavalry commanders in the Shenandoah Valley in 1864 took particular pride in the use of the most traditional shock tactics. They wanted to be remembered by history in the chivalric tradition of the sword and not as a mounted scavenging horde. Merritt, whose reports on the campaign were flowery by the standards of after-battle reports, described an attack by General Thomas C. Devin's Second Brigade of the First Division on Confederate cavalry this way: "Although outnumbering the Second Brigade it could not stand before the keen steel and resistless force of the sturdy troopers of the 'Ole War Horse.'" Opequon offered a "field . . . open for cavalry operations such as the war has not seen, such as all good cavalry officers long to engage in; nor was the division slow to take an active part in the grand theater of battle which was being enacted at our feet."[38]

George Armstrong Custer, who began the campaign in command of the First Brigade of the First Cavalry Division, carefully noted that when the "First, Fifth, Sixth, and Seventh Michigan, with a portion of the twenty-fifth New York," charged the enemy near Winchester on September 19, 1864, "most of the command" was "using the saber alone."[39] The commander of the Second Brigade of the same division, Thomas C. Devin, expressed an equally traditional outlook on cavalry warfare. He described proudly to his superiors a cavalry charge at Opequon: "The wild cheer and gleaming sabers of the gallant ninth [New York Cavalry], as they dashed at the 'chivalry,' so dismayed them that, barely meeting the shock, they whirled and broke for the woods on their left, leaving a lieutenant-colonel and a number of prisoners in our hands."[40] Devin had officers of even more traditional outlook as subordinates. At the Battle of Cedar Creek about a month later, he ordered a brigade commander "to dismount his command and seize and hold the stone walls crossing the road." The officer "protested that his men had great objections to fighting dismounted, and declined to accede to my request."[41]

Such views were not universal, and one encounters some contrary evidence. One of Kidd's favorite anecdotes from the campaign recalled the words of a Captain Brittain of the First New York Dragoons, who had replied when ordered to form up for battle, "I have no cartridges. We have shot them all away." To which Kidd answered, "You have sabers." "Yes, and by ___ they are loaded," replied Brittain. In other words, it seemed unthinkable at first to Captain Brittain to go into battle as a cavalryman without a carbine, and his saber was so little used as to be forgotten in circumstances of battle.[42]

But the highest-ranking cavalry officers were all but unanimous in their reports. Thus James H. Wilson, who commanded the Third Division, proudly described the charge of the Second New York Cavalry at Opequon: "Captain Hull formed his regiment by platoon, at a trot, and with sabers drawn dashed gallantly forward, riding through and scattering the rebels in all directions."[43]

General Powell, whose report dwelt to an extraordinary degree with incidents of retaliation for guerrilla activities and who devoted more space than his fellow cavalry commanders to describing the destruction of civilian property in the valley, did recall the use of sabers in a charge once. Late in the campaign, in November, he said, "I moved my whole line forward . . . with drawn sabers (having the lines well supported on each flank and the center), charged the enemy, broke his lines, and drove him in great confusion beyond Front Royal."[44]

Everyone in the Union cavalry under Sheridan was happiest when reporting saber charges on their former nemeses. We have heard here from Torbert, Merritt, Wilson, Custer, Devin, and Powell. Only Averell among the Union cavalry commanders failed to call to mind at least one such saber charge, and his report was especially preoccupied with protesting his removal from command in the midst of the campaign and offered less in the way of description of actions in the field.

Subordinate cavalry commanders took their keynote from Sheridan himself, long a commander of cavalry. Despite his association by modern historians with the advent of a decidedly unromantic style of warfare, Sheridan retained a traditional view of the uses of cavalry, massed into a corps and employed on the battlefield against the enemy's cavalry. He reported to General Henry Halleck, for example, "The cavalry made some handsome saber charges."[45]

The psychological drama of the Union cavalry in the Shenandoah Valley in 1864 has been obscured by the strained emphasis on destructive "modernity" in the writing on the Civil War. The image of cavalry charges on horseback with the saber does not seem to point toward the warfare of the twentieth century. Typical of the modern treatment of these late campaigns is James McPherson's description of the Union cavalry in the valley campaign: "Northern cavalry with their rapid-firing carbines played a conspicuous role; two divisions of horsemen even thundered down on Early's left in an old-fashioned saber charge and captured the bulk of the 2,000 rebels who surrendered."[46] Such a description departs the world of the Civil War cavalryman to view the valley campaign from the eyes of a twentieth-century observer. The cavalrymen did not call saber tactics old-fashioned in their reports. Their reports did not mention new technology in carbine design. In fact, they seldom mentioned carbines at all and never praised their use or explained the damage they did to the enemy. Fond descriptions were left for the use of the saber only. Pistols were never mentioned.

Destroying civilian crops was not fully compatible with the recovery of the glory and reputation of the mounted arm of the Union army. The cavalrymen dutifully described their work of destruction in their reports, but it is certainly instructive to hear General Merritt's description of this work: "On the 17th the division marched at 8 A.M. in compliance with orders, destroying the grain and forage, and driving off the cattle in the Valley from Cedar Creek to Berryville. This duty, not among the most agreeable assigned to soldiers, was thoroughly though delicately done; no private property, save that mentioned, being injured; nor family molested by any soldier in the command to my knowledge."[47] The tone of embarrassed reluctance aside, Merritt did carry out his orders exactly as General Sheridan wanted, apparently. Sheridan had explained to his chief of cavalry, Torbert, in mid-August, that in destroying "wheat and hay" and seizing "mules, horses, and cattle" "no houses will be burned, and officers in charge of this delicate, but necessary, duty must inform people that the object is to make this Valley untenable for the raiding parties of the rebel army."[48] The "burning" and "destruction" of the Shenandoah Valley were somehow also "delicate."

The cavalrymen's concerns with redeeming the reputation of their arm of the service and avenging previous humiliations inflicted on the Army of the Potomac were echoed by their superiors. Secretary of War Edwin M. Stanton commended Sheridan for the work of the mounted arm, saying, "Under gallant leaders your cavalry has become the efficient arm in this war that it has proved in other countries."[49] General Grant himself, if he did not mention cavalry specifically, was none the less mindful of the motivation of erasing previous humiliation. He congratulated Sheridan for the victory at Opequon in a letter written on September 22, 1864, and added, "Better still, it wipes out much of the stain upon our arms by previous disasters in that locality."[50]

In assessing the tactics used in fighting against Confederate cavalry in the Shenandoah Valley, I think the truth probably lies somewhere in the middle—between the glorious reports of the cavalrymen and the modern historians' emphasis on advanced firearm technology. A combination of weapons was used. According to one authority, those Union cavalry units armed with breech-loading carbines would establish a skirmish line that drew the Confederates' fire. But the Confederate cavalry, without sabers at this point in the war, was soon faced with resisting a saber charge holding muzzle-loading weapons in need of reloading.[51] Merritt recalled "making charges on foot or mounted according to the nature of the country."[52] Whether in mounted charges or dismounted skirmishing, the desire to redeem the reputation of the mounted arm was at stake for Sheridan's cavalry, and destruction of food and supplies was not their highest priority.

Both Sheridan and Merritt described the task of destroying the property of civilians as "delicate." The explanation insisted on by Sheridan in his orders to Torbert to be offered to the residents of the valley who would become the victims of the policy is doubly interesting. First, the generals felt the need to explain. Second, the explanation was exactly consistent with the usual statement of the policy: it was meant to keep the Confederate armies from having the supplies. The officers were not instructed to tell the civilians that the destruction of their crops would teach them a lesson and that they should not in future support the Confederacy or its armies. Kidd, one of those who actually set the fires, by no means did that. He attempted to put out a spreading fire, and then fled the scene in remorse and avoidance. If the civilians suffered a blow to their morale, as no doubt many of them did, the Union army left them to draw the moral lesson on their own: they did not help the process along with propaganda. Instead, they attempted to explain their unacceptable behavior away.

⤞≈ ≈⤝

Although it says nothing for certain about the actual extent of damage done to enemy civilians' property, attitude surely must have mattered some. The cynically humorous description of the work of General William T. Sherman's foragers, or "bummers," in Georgia was quite different from the atmosphere of the grim work in the Shenandoah Valley. Sherman and President Lincoln kidded about foraging on board the *River Queen* when, along with General Grant, they met for a "social visit" on March 27, 1865. Lincoln, Sherman recalled, "was full of curiosity about the many incidents of our great march, which had reached him officially and through the newspapers, and seemed to enjoy very much the more ludicrous parts—about the 'bummers,' and their devices to collect food and forage when the outside world supposed us to be starving."[53]

Notes of levity about Sheridan's campaign of destruction of supplies in the Shenandoah Valley were not common at the time.[54] The cavalry's desire to recover its lost glory was matched, in its effect of restraining destruction on civilians, by the ordinary soldiers' habitual and internalized restraint. I examined the letters, diaries, and memoirs, some published and some unpublished, of ten soldiers who campaigned under Sheridan in an attempt to see destruction close up. In fact, it is not easy to do. J. H. Kidd's admission that he himself set fires is quite unusual, and he was in a position to say that he attempted to restrain the fires once they proved threatening to civilians' houses.

More typical is the view of the destruction glimpsed by William Thompson, attached to the headquarters of the Third Division, Second Army Corps. Writing on August 22, 1864, he said, "The war is becoming desperate on both sides[.] Our forces are burning every thing they pass in the Valley[.] I suppose most of the houses occupied by southern sympathizers will be burned up[.] I do not like this mode of warfare by either side but tis gradually coming to that point."[55] First, Thompson testified to very widespread destruction (in this instance, not carefully described but said to be based on distinguishing between Unionists and Confederate sympathizers). Second, he said nothing of his own agency or activities. Third, he expressed disapproval.[56]

John P. Suter, a recently married captain, as an infantryman saw the cavalry's work only at a distance. Writing on October 2, 1864, from a camp near Harrisonburg, Suter said, "During the week our cavalry have been destroying all the granaries & mills they could find between this & Staunton. They are now stationed about six miles in front of us."[57] Commenting on General Early's surprise attack at Cedar Creek, Suter wrote, "Finally after it was thought the campaign had ended in a general conflagration of wheat stacks barns & houses he suddenly reappears." As a Pennsylvanian, Suter had especially sober thoughts about the destruction. "There is one thing that is certain as fate," he declared, "whether our people know it or not. If ever a rebel army gets into Penna they will make that portion they pass over a desert waste . . . this valley has been made almost uninhabitable within the last month."[58] Conscious consideration of the unpleasant possibilities of retribution for destruction was rare.

John W. Elwood of the Ringgold Cavalry, though he admitted being "called upon to help lay waste this valley," did not feel called upon to describe precisely his personal role in applying a torch to this or that. The orders were "carried out with unsparing severity," he said.[59]

John F. L. Hartwell of the 121st New York Infantry described the overall destruction, as most soldiers did, within the terms of the orders from headquarters: "A large force of Cavelry dashed on to Staunton finding but slight opposition. Thare [*sic*] they destroyed a large amount of Military Stores and Railroad material blowing up culverts burning bridges, barns Grain and in fact distoyed everything that could be used to subsist an army." Hartwell himself described eating green corn, apples, and grapes that grew near the roads the army marched on.[60]

Some soldiers made only passing comment or none at all.[61] On the whole, Union soldiers testified to being shocked at the destruction in the valley, but they did not elaborate more specifically than did Sheridan and the other general officers whose reports and correspondence appeared in the official records of the campaign. They generally seemed uneasy with destruction. But taking food for their own use was obviously commonplace and regarded as rough-and-tumble justice. That practice was nearly universal in the war, early and late, and far and wide. It is testified to by the willing and often cynical confessions of the men themselves and by the many orders issued by officers to try to get their men to stop doing it. Colonel J. M. Campbell, commander of Captain Suter's regiment, for example, a year earlier had issued general orders to end the "vicious practice" of soldiers leaving the line of march to raid gardens, grain fields, orchards, and houses. "Our duty as Soldiers," he pointed out, apparently in vain, "does not require us to commit depredations upon private citizens and we should not forget that each soldier should be a gentleman."[62]

⇥⇤

Philip H. Sheridan and the soldiers under his command made another crucial distinction in their behavior. Like the officers and soldiers operating against General Price in Missouri at the same time, Sheridan and his men fought guerrillas in a different way and by different rules, though they were unwritten, than they fought the regularly constituted army of Jubal Early. The difference was simple: The Union soldiers might destroy the subsistence and dwellings of the guerrillas and their families and abettors. They did not destroy the subsistence and dwellings of the other residents of the valley.

The Shenandoah Valley campaign offered many examples of adherence to this bedrock distinction made by most Civil War soldiers. Two of the most vivid will be described here. General William H.

Powell, the commander of the Second Division of cavalry, was more preoccupied in his reports with actions against guerrillas than the other cavalrymen described here. He noted carefully: "October 4, had two bushwhackers shot to death in retaliation for the murder of a soldier belonging to my command by a bushwhacker, the soldier having been found by my command with his throat cut from ear to ear." A little over a week later, Powell faced another and more trying incident:

> October 13, having learned of the willful and cold-blooded murder of a U.S. soldier by two men (Chancellor and Myers, members of [John S.] Mosby's gang of cut-throats and robbers), some two miles from my camp a few days previous, I ordered the execution of one of Mosby's gang whom I had captured the day previous at Gaines' Cross-Roads, and placing the placard on his breast with the following inscription: "A. C. Willis, member of Company C, Mosby's command, hanged by the neck in retaliation for the murder of a U.S. soldier by Messrs. Chancellor and Myers." I also sent a detachment, under command of Captain Howe, First West Virginia Cavalry, with orders to destroy the residence, barn, and all buildings and forage, on the premises of Mr. Chancellor, and to drive off all stock of every description, which orders were promptly carried out.

Powell included destruction of the rebel partisan's "residence."

The rest of Powell's report followed the customary form, ending with acknowledgment of the services of his subordinate officers and their soldiers. Then he returned to the subject of the guerrilla incidents:

> On the 5th and 13th instant it became my duty, though painful and repugnant to my own feelings, to order the execution of three Confederate bushwhackers, in retaliation for two union soldiers murdered by guerrillas, believing it to be the only means of protection to our soldiers against the operations of all such illegal and outlawed bands of

horse-thieves and murderers, recognized and supported by rebel authorities, for which I have been threatened by the Richmond press. But
by this I cannot be intimidated in the discharge of my duties under orders. And I wish it distinctly understood by the rebel authorities that if
two to one is not sufficient I will increase it to twenty-two to one, and
leave the consequences in the hands of my Government.[63]

Powell left a publicly hanging body, a rare sight in the Civil War.
General Powell in Virginia in 1864 sounded a defiant note reminiscent of General McNeil in Missouri in 1862, and the statement seems
to be meant for reading by the enemy as much as by Powell's superiors. Such fierceness was reserved, east and west, for guerrillas.

In a more famous incident of the Shenandoah Valley campaign,
General Sheridan himself retaliated for the murder of his engineer-
ing staff officer, Lieutenant John R. Meigs, by ordering "all the houses
within an area of five miles . . . burned." Custer drew the duty, but
he was apparently pulled off the job before finishing. In his *Memoirs,* years later, Sheridan recalled, "The prescribed area included the
little village of Dayton, but when a few houses in the immediate
neighborhood of the scene of the murder had been burned, Custer
was directed to cease his desolating work, but to fetch away all the
able-bodied males as prisoners."[64] No further explanation is given.
It sounds as though Sheridan did not realize at first that a village was
included in the five-mile area and the burning of whole villages
was not what Sheridan had in mind. Indeed, his earlier orders to
Merritt—aimed only at innocent citizens of the valley, to be sure,
and not written for a situation of retaliation or guerrilla warfare—
excluded from destruction both "villages" and "private houses."[65]

It may also have been the case that Custer had to be pulled off that
retaliatory duty for what was regarded as the more important one of
the active military campaign against the Confederate army. Confederate cavalry had been irritating the rear of Sheridan's columns, and

he ordered both the First and Third Divisions of cavalry to turn and attack. Custer commanded the Third at the time. "I deemed it best to make this delay of one day here and settle this new [Confederate] cavalry general," Sheridan reported.[66] Settling scores with the Confederate cavalry was at least as important as destruction of private dwellings.

Though more drastic measures were assumed to be legitimate in dealing with guerrillas, such measures did not always reach to the dwellings of the people who lived in areas in which the guerrillas operated. Before the Battle of Cedar Creek, Sheridan complained that the "refugees from Early's army, cavalry and infantry, are organizing guerrilla parties and are becoming very formidable and are annoying me very much. I know of no way to exterminate them except to burn out the whole country and let the people go North or South."[67] This letter expressed exasperation but not a real plan; such a drastic strategy Sheridan never employed in the Shenandoah Valley. But over a month later, Sheridan ordered the most drastic campaign of his Civil War career, not against the Shenandoah Valley's inhabitants but against those who lived in the Luray Valley and Loudoun County, where John Singleton Mosby usually operated. "In retaliation for the assistance and sympathy" given by the residents there to Mosby's forces, Sheridan, late in November, ordered General Merritt to "consume and destroy all forage and subsistence, burn all barns and mills and their contents, and drive off all stock in the region." "This order must be literally executed," he added, "bearing in mind, however, that no dwellings are to be burned, and that no personal violence be offered the citizens."[68] Even in this extreme order, Sheridan exempted dwellings, but he did specify "subsistence," as he had never done in orders touching the residents of the Shenandoah Valley.

The campaign in the Shenandoah Valley, like Price's Raid in Missouri, affords the Civil War historian opportunity to watch the Union army at work against legitimate Confederate armies and major partisan forces at the same time, because John Singleton Mosby, and a few other small groups, operated in the area as well. Sheridan fought Early hard, but he resorted to the sorts of measures regularly used against guerrillas in Missouri only when dealing with assassination or effective partisan warfare. The one form of warfare was more severely limited than the other and both were employed at the same time. As always, the choice was determined by the situation and the perception of the sort of enemy he faced. The distinction seems time-honored and culturally ingrained.

Whether in the East or the West, the Union armies operated, even in the latest campaigns of the Civil War, on compartmentalized principles. The more unrestrained form of warfare never supplanted the restrained.

⊷⟢ ⟣⊷

By the late 1880s, when Sheridan wrote his *Memoirs,* he had managed to bring together thoughts about the nature of his campaign that had not completely jelled in the heat of the action in 1864. At last, he knew, he had to provide a "reason for the destruction." Sheridan first described Grant's assigning him to command in the Shenandoah Valley. In the beginning, General David Hunter was to retain nominal command of the geographical district, and General Grant therefore gave Sheridan the orders pertaining to the enemy's supplies that he had given Hunter on August 5, 1864. There the expression Grant had used was, "In pushing up the Shenandoah Valley, it is desirable that nothing should be left to invite the enemy to return." He told Hunter to "take all provisions, forage, and stock wanted for the use of your command." He was to "destroy" what "cannot be consumed." He cautioned, however, that it was "not desirable that the buildings should be destroyed—they should, rather, be protected; but the people should be informed that so long as an army can subsist among them recurrences of these raids must be expected, and we are deter-mined to stop them at all hazards."[69] Sheridan excerpted Grant's lan-guage precisely in giving orders to his cavalry commander, General Torbert, on August 16. These were the orders whose execution caused Jedidiah Hotchkiss to make his observation about destruction of farms in the valley.

In his memoirs years later, Sheridan recalled that "Grant's in-structions to destroy the valley began with the letter of August 5 to Hunter, which was turned over to me, and this was followed at inter-vals by more specific directions, all showing the earnestness of his purpose." Sheridan then lined up five orders in chronological order and reproduced them carefully. In fact, they showed nothing of the kind. Instead of demonstrating Grant's "earnestness," they revealed his second thoughts and doubts about the policy. They constituted a whittling down of the original sweeping intent. And they were con-cerned mostly with the problem of the Confederate guerrillas led by John Singleton Mosby and not with the overall supply problem of the Confederacy, let alone general civilian morale.

Grant's orders reproduced in Sheridan's memoirs were dated Au-gust 16, 21, and 26, September 4, and November 9, 1864. The first re-ferred to Loudoun County, the area where Mosby operated, and con-tained the new instruction to arrest all men there under the age of fifty capable of bearing arms. The next qualified that danger-ously sweeping order by noting that the Quakers who lived in the area were friendly to the Union and should be exempted from arrest and promised payment for provisions destroyed. Only the order of August 26 dealt principally with the Shenandoah Valley. "Do all the damage to railroads and crops you can," Grant wrote. "Carry off stock of all descriptions and negroes, so as to prevent further plant-ing. If the war is to last another year we want the Shenandoah Valley to remain a barren waste." On September 4, Grant returned to the subject of Loudoun County and its arms-bearing population and told Sheridan to exercise his "own judgment as to who should be exempt from arrest, and as to who should receive pay for their stock, grain, &c. It is our interest that that county should not be capable of subsisting a hostile army, and at the same time we want to inflict as little hardship upon Union men as possible."[70]

Grant's final order, of November 9, when he was considering the winter to come, was not an order at all, but a question asked of Sheridan: "Do you think it advisable to notify all citizens living east of the Blue Ridge to move out north of the Potomac, all their stock, grain, and provisions of every description? There is no doubt about the necessity of clearing out that country so that it will not support Mosby's gang. And the question is whether it is not better that the people should save what they can. So long as the war lasts they must be prevented from making another crop, both there and as high up the valley as we can control."[71] Grant said nothing in the entire series of orders about inflicting suffering on the people of the Shenandoah Valley in order to terrorize them or to weaken their morale to sustain the war. When he dealt with the question of suffering, it was with an eye to limiting suffering, first for the Unionists of the area and then for *all* the people of the Shenandoah Valley. Grant did not want them to plant next year's crop and feed Confederate armies in the valley, but he considered having the people take what they had to subsist on and leave the area for a time.

It was Philip H. Sheridan in his memoirs some twenty years afterward and not Grant at the time of the campaign who came up with the rationale for a strategy of inflicting economic deprivation on the Confederate people of the valley. Grant's orders, examined carefully, did not absolve Sheridan of guilt. They proved it.

Surely Sheridan did not himself misread the orders, but he seems to have thought his readers would. And in anticipating the tone of rash severity to be attributed to Grant's orders by historians later, Sheridan proved correct in his assumption. With that misleading evidence laid out before the reader, meant to absolve Sheridan of blame, he launched into what has become a famous description of the rationale for the form of warfare waged late in the Civil War:

> He [Grant] had rightly concluded that it was time to bring the war home to a people engaged in raising crops from a prolific soil to feed the country's enemies, and devoting to the Confederacy its best youth. I endorsed the programme in all its parts, for the stores of meat and grain that the valley provided, and the men it furnished for Lee's depleted regiments, were the strongest auxiliaries he possessed in the whole insurgent section. In war a territory like this is a factor of great importance, and whichever adversary controls it permanently reaps all the advantages of its prosperity. Hence, as I have said, I endorsed Grant's programme, for I do not hold war to mean simply that lines of men shall engage each other in battle, and material interests be ignored. This is but a duel, in which one combatant seeks the other's life; war means much more, and is far worse than this. Those who rest at home in peace and plenty see but little of the horrors attending such a duel, and even grow indifferent to them as the struggle goes on, contenting themselves with encouraging all who are able-bodied to enlist in the cause, to fill up the shattered ranks as death thins them. It is another matter, however, when deprivation and suffering are brought to their own doors. Then the case appears much graver, for the loss of property weighs heavy with the most of mankind; heavier often, than the sacrifices made on the field of battle. Death is popularly considered the maximum of punishment in war; but it is not; reduction to poverty brings prayers for peace more surely and more quickly than does the destruction of human life, as the selfishness of man has demonstrated in more than one great conflict.[72]

"I endorsed the programme in all its parts," Sheridan said in one sentence, and in the next one, "I endorsed Grant's programme." He did more than that. He put it in place with as much severity as he could lend to the purpose while fighting a real army, and then he later supplied a new rationale for the "programme." Sheridan had learned in the intervening years since the Civil War, many of them spent fighting grim contests against the Plains Indians in the West, a new language of cynicism, somewhat at odds with his earlier values. We can learn from this passage that the original idea was Grant's and not Sheridan's. We can learn from the determination with which he seized on orders from Grant, most of them applying to Mosby and not to the Shenandoah Valley at all, that he wanted to make it clear that it was Grant's idea. We can also see him at work trying to make sense of it all, looking back over the years, lining up the orders from Grant, examining them all in one place and trying to piece together a philosophy or strategy. We can now see a new element of strategy emerging, barely mentioned in Sheridan's writing on the campaign in the 1860s: the effect on the willingness of the people to send their sons and husbands to battle while they were being personally impoverished by war. We can see Sheridan's considerable powers as a writer, comparing the less cynical conception of warfare to a "duel." But we do not recapture the attitude of 1864, when the open and gently rolling countryside of the Shenandoah Valley invited the Union army under Sheridan to redeem itself from previous failures of manliness by riding down the Confederate army with the saber.

# 5

# THE SAND CREEK MASSACRE
## The Grand Burning of the Prairie

INTEGRATING INDIAN AFFAIRS into the overall history of the Civil War has not proven easy. James M. McPherson's magisterial survey, *Battle Cry of Freedom: The Civil War Era,* for example, does not mention the Sand Creek Massacre of 1864, a landmark event in the confrontation between the United States and the Plains Indians. Neither does *This Terrible War: The Civil War and Its Aftermath,* though the emphasis in that book is definitely on the most terrible events of the period. Paradoxically, excluding truly terrible warfare, such as that fought against the Plains Indians during the Civil War, eases the historian's task of making the Civil War itself seem terrible and destructive, for everyone knows there simply was nothing to match the Indian wars for unrestrained ferocity and destructiveness.

As was the case with reinterpreting Sheridan's Shenandoah Valley campaign, however, Civil War history is turning a corner in regard to Indians. Historians owe a debt to Michael Fellman and Mark Grimsley for this inclusive turnaround. In a brief article entitled "At the Nihilist Edge," Fellman urged historians to explain the varying intensities of warfare across the ages by considering culture: "the treatment accorded by warriors to those whom they consider to fall inside their culture as opposed to the treatment that they apply to those whom they consider to be cultural outsiders. Consciously or unconsciously, warriors of all nations apply their cultural standards while at war." Fellman noted specifically that the "guerrilla war in Missouri, of whites against whites, never crossed" the barriers to slaughter and mutilation of women and children perpetrated at Sand Creek.[1]

Focusing less on psychology and "nihilism" and more on internalized values, the historian Mark Grimsley has also worked to integrate Indian wars into Civil War history. Grimsley disagrees with the view that "nineteenth-century America had two experiences with 'total war': the first against the Southern Confederacy, the second against the Western Plains Indians." To believe that similar methods applied in those two conflicts, he points out, is to believe that "the role of race in the final military contest with Native Americans was not central." The contrasts between the Civil War and the Plains Indian wars, he insisted, "are compelling."[2] Both Fellman and Grimsley properly and vividly remind us of the centrality of conceptions of race to warfare on the American borders.

Civil War historians need to expand these insights beyond article-length confines and out to the warfare of the era as a whole. They need to consider the horrors of war waged against those perceived as racially different—and the inhibitions and restraints of war waged against those perceived as racially the same. The internalized sense of racial identity operated quietly but powerfully in all theaters of the war and at all times. In a war fought mostly against other Americans perceived as coming from the same racial stock, the primitive perception of racial similarity generally restrained the Union soldiers.

Mark Grimsley shows us the way in his brief 24-page essay about "Rebels" and "Redskins." He properly emphasizes "the persistence of restraint among Union soldiers during the Civil War" and "the qualitative difference between the Civil War and the Indian Wars [that] can be laid at the door of racial antagonism."[3] His insights in this regard need to be applied more generally to the outlines of the history of the Civil War. When Grimsley attempted that himself, in his earlier history of Union strategy in the Civil War, he put too sunny a face on a reality that at bottom was rooted in perceptions of race. After pointing out as one "explanatory feature" of the persistence of restraint "the similarity of white Southerners to their Northern counterparts," Grimsley eventually concluded:

> If the Union's hard war effort displayed a novel element, it lay primarily in the linkage with a democratic society. That made it possible to blame Southerners for the outbreak and continuation of the war, and so justify the destruction. But it also made possible a politically and morally aware citizen-soldiery capable of discrimination and restraint as well as destruction. The Union volunteer who marched under Grant, Sherman, and Sheridan was a very different instrument than the *ancien regime* soldier under . . . Frederick the Great; for that matter, a different instrument even than contemporary European soldiers. It was the peculiar nature of the Federal citizen-soldier—his civic mindedness, his continued sense of connection with community and public morality—that made possible the "directed severity." The Federal rank-and-file were neither barbarians, brutalized by war, nor "realists" unleashing indiscriminate violence. Their example thus holds out hope that the effective conduct of war need not extinguish the light of moral reason.[4]

Somehow, by the end of that passage the visceral and subconscious matter of racial perception has disappeared from the final appraisal of the soldiers' work, and the "light of moral reason" prevails. There is yet room for reconsidering the ideas of terror and war in the nineteenth century, and we can begin here by comparing the uses and abuses of fire in the Civil War and in the contemporaneous Plains Indian wars.

⤙═◎ ◎═⤚

The burning of cities was at the time of the Civil War and has been ever since a subject of great controversy, the underlying issue animating the debate being the indiscriminately destructive inhumanity of conflagrations. From different causes, Columbia, Atlanta, Richmond, and Chambersburg did famously burn. But in 1867, when the U.S. Senate debated a resolution about the execution of Maximilian in Mexico, one of the senators pointed out by way of justification of Mexico's act that the emperor "burnt down whole towns."[5]

Fire was not a controllable agent of destruction, as the recollections of the cavalryman Kidd from the Shenandoah Valley remind us. The uncontrollably destructive potential of fire was subject matter for propaganda during the Civil War. When the Union army employed primitive incendiary artillery shells in 1863 during the long siege of Charleston, South Carolina, the flamboyant Confederate general Pierre Gustave Toutant Beauregard, famous for his melodramatic public appeals, issued a protest against their inhumane use on the city. Obviously, the appeal was heard around the world, as the *Punch* cartoon in Chapter 2 showed.

Some, of course, would use fire for their purposes anyway. In November 1864 Confederate agents tried to set fire to New York City, in the Civil War's only true attempt at terrorism on a vast scale. For the political end of Confederate national independence, the saboteurs, some of them escaped Confederate prisoners of war from John Hunt Morgan's cavalry raiders, targeted thousands of innocent people—many more than the number who were killed in the attacks of September 11, 2001—in thirteen hotels, in popular night spots such as Niblo's Theater and the Winter Garden, and at Barnum's Museum.

The agents deliberately aimed at the innocent, even the frivolous; they ignored the city's shipbuilding yards and arms factories and other military suppliers. The untrained former cavalrymen and invalid soldiers assigned to the task employed the favored but wholly inadequate incendiary compound of the era, the dreaded "Greek Fire," a compound containing phosphorous in which they soaked rags that would ignite upon contact with air.[6]

Greek Fire was no such thing, really. The actual recipe for the incendiary substance, made famous in the early Middle Ages in sieges of Constantinople, was long since lost. The Civil War generation merely borrowed the name from the earlier era to apply to incendiary compounds that raised great fears. The composition and alleged fiery results of Greek Fire varied, depending on the inventor and saboteur. Critics of the use of Greek Fire as a "barbarous" practice argued that the British army had studied its use before the time of the American Civil War and rejected it as too terrible.[7] Critics and promoters alike agreed on only one thing: Greek Fire inspired terror.

The experimental incendiary shells lobbed into Charleston had an interesting history, vividly narrated by the historian of Civil War science and technology Robert V. Bruce. President Abraham Lincoln, who had been an inventor himself and possessed a characteristic Yankee fascination with technological innovation, grew interested in the possibilities of such a "very destructive missile" and arranged for a test.[8] In two demonstrations early in 1862 the shells failed to live up to the inventor's promise. Bruce laconically notes something very curious about the aftermath of the failed test: "Next day, seconded by the two Senators from Kansas, Short offered [ordnance chief James W.] Ripley two thousand shells at $12 each, for use in plains warfare." The closed-minded army turned the inventor down as usual, and therefore Bruce did not pause to explain the term "plains warfare" or why incendiary shells would be thought particularly well adapted to it.[9]

Incendiary shells, as we know, went on to have a brief and inglorious history in the siege of Charleston, but Short had also tried to peddle his terrible invention for use, apparently, on the plains of Kansas. There they were likely to be used, not against besieged Confederates, but against Indians. The mythical dimension can never be separated from a discussion of the subject of Greek Fire. Because its use was mentioned in Gibbon's *Decline and Fall of the Roman Empire,* Greek Fire was a part of the cultural learning of the age. It had been used by Crusaders against Muslims, and thus even writers for the sober *Scientific American* referred to its having frightened "the brave and warlike Saracens."[10] Its possible use fired the imagination with images of terrorizing a terrible foe, one as demon-like as Muslims. Perhaps it is little wonder that the shells appealed to the men from Kansas.

⋯⋙◉◉⋘⋯

On the Great Plains "scorched earth" had genuine possibilities even early in 1862. By 1864, the army was indeed setting the prairies on fire.

Union soldiers looked upon warfare waged against the Indians of the Plains in an entirely different way from how they viewed the war on the Confederacy. Cultural assumptions about the enemy were crucial in both cases.[11] It is also true that the assessment of the enemy's economy made a difference to military strategy. The differences added up to an entirely different arsenal of tactics and even weapons.

The Euro-American cultural assumption of Indian barbarism played a crucial role.[12] To their white foes the Indians also seemed poverty stricken. Sheridan made the point simply, in describing his experiences as a campaigner against Indians in the West in the 1850s: "Indians are always hungry."[13]

The American government learned—to its very great surprise— that it was not really possible to destroy the economy of an advanced agricultural nation such as the Confederacy. The antebellum anti-slavery critique of the South had led Northerners, one and all, to believe the Southern economy was weak and pitiful and that the Confederacy would therefore be no match for the North. They also thought the poor yeomen of the South would not unite with the planters to defend slavery and their land. Both assumptions proved wrong, and the North spent perhaps the first year and a half learning those lessons. The economic lesson was epitomized in William T. Sherman's observation to his brother, written from camp near Vicksburg early in 1863 as the general reflected on nearly two years of war with the Confederacy: "The South abounds in corn, cattle, and provisions and the progress in manufacturing shoes and cloth for the soldiers is wonderful. They are as well supplied as we."[14] Sheridan himself repeatedly stated—even as he dutifully carried out Grant's orders to lay waste to the Shenandoah Valley's forage and stock—that the destruction of the Confederate armies was the key to military success in the war. In the context, that was tantamount to saying that destroying the economy was not the key to military success.

Besides, for traditional moral reasons, Southern society, except for seaborne international trade and eventually the slave labor base, lay essentially off limits for the whole war. The powerful symbol of this was Sheridan's self-conscious and noisy insistence that homes were not to be burned. Civil War soldiers did not like to put down on paper what they would *not* do to the enemy, for fear that the enemy would somehow exploit the knowledge of such limits. Soldiers thought it best to sound, within enemy hearing, uncontrollably fierce and as though their willingness to destroy had no limit. But the uncontrollable nature of fire forced them to express the limits of their wrath: both Sheridan and Grant spelled out in their orders for destroying crops and driving off livestock in the Shenandoah Valley that dwellings were to be exempted from destruction. I have never seen a similar exemption spelled out for Indians.

The American soldiers on the Plains knew full well by the time of the Civil War that the laws and customs of war need not apply to barbarous enemies. They assumed that the economies of the Indians were perilously shaky and fragile, and that Indian society had for some time been as much a target of military action as the warriors. The situation could not have been more different from that of the war against the Confederacy. The Union learned its lesson about the Confederate economy. It never changed its mind about the Indians of the Plains.

On the prairies, a "scorched-earth" strategy had genuine possibilities. Robert R. Livingston, who commanded the eastern subdistrict of Nebraska with headquarters at Fort Kearney and who was colonel of the First Nebraska Cavalry, reported to the War Department in 1864, "On the 22d of October last, the wind being from the north and favorable, I caused the prairie south of Platte River Valley to be simultaneously fired from a point twenty miles west of Julesburg continuously to a point ten miles east of this post, burning the grass in a continuous line of 200 miles as far south as the Republican River."[15] Colonel Livingston's measurements seem rough, but if they are plotted on a map, he burned an area perhaps as great as 7,500 square miles.[16] Recalling General Merritt's 515 acres of cornfields scorched in the Shenandoah Valley—less than a square mile—makes for a vivid sense of the difference in warriors' worlds. The distance from Winchester to Staunton in the Shenandoah Valley is about 100 miles, and the whole valley is less than 200 miles long. Union forces never laid claim to destruction beyond Staunton.

Although the prairie grass proved too sparse to burn everywhere, the Nebraska soldiers' work was systematic. Livingston sent other detachments later with the result that "every cañon and all the valley of stream along this line have been thoroughly burned, thus depriving hostile Indians of forage for their animals in their hiding-places and driving all the game beyond the Republican River." Livingston maintained that the fires were a controllable weapon of war, surgically applied to foes and kept away from friends. "From a point ten miles east of this post to Little Blue Station I have burned only the creek valleys and cañons, compelling the Indians to graze their stock on the high prairie if they remain in that part of the country, and leaving the game in that section undisturbed for the use of the Pawnees [allies of the U.S. troops against the Cheyennes]."

Livingston waged a continuing campaign of conflagration:

The firing of the prairie has been commenced on the north side of Platte Valley from Mullahla's Station to a point twenty-five miles west of Julesburg, Colo. Ter., extending north in some instances 150 miles. Universal consternation has spread among the Indians, to whom this mode of warfare is apparently new, and their presence along the road through this sub-district need not be apprehended during the winter. Officers from Fort Laramie tell me that already the effect of this grand burning of the prairie is manifest among the Indians, and that they are anxious to make peace, but whether their propositions are induced by fear of starvation, the game being driven off by fires, or only to check the process of burning until they can renew hostilities in the spring, I am not prepared to say, and would simply suggest a continuance of the work as a punishment for past misdeeds and a warning to them of what may occur in the future should they persist in their unfriendly conduct. One thing is certain, this burning of the prairie has produced a marked effect on the Indian tribes along the road, and they begin to dread the white man's power. It will be borne in mind that the Platte Valley proper—that is, the country lying each side of the river up to the bluffs on either side—had been protected from fire by express orders, and carefully preserved for the use of the immense amount of stock used in transporting merchandise over the road to the States and Territories west of Missouri River, and no suffering can possibly occur to the numberless teams traveling to and from the west.[17]

The degree of control Colonel Livingston could exert is surely exaggerated, and a precise measure of the destruction seems nowhere available from contemporary sources. But it was vast by any measure.

To those on the ground at the time, it seemed even greater than it was. Captain Eugene Ware, who has left us perhaps the single best account of the Indian wars of 1864 from the side of the U.S. forces, witnessed "this grand burning of the prairie." So great was its extent, and so grandiose the plans of the soldiers who set it, that Ware imagined that the fire extended over most of the Great Plains. Ware attributed the strategy to General Robert B. Mitchell rather than to Livingston, but he provided valuable details of the project, though he vastly exaggerated its scope:

He cleared the telegraph line early in the forenoon, and wired instructions up and down the river, and also requests to the officers in command of Colorado stations. The orders and requests were that fire details be sent up and down so as to connect, and that at sundown the prairies be simultaneously fired from Fort Kearney west to Denver. Instructions were sent to every ranch and post along the line. Each was to use its own method to accomplish the purpose, but the whole country was to be set in a blaze at sunset. The order was fully carried out. The country was fired for three hundred miles. At Julesburg the method used was to make light bales of hay, bound with chains and pulled, while blazing, over the prairie and with a dragging lariat-rope. The bale would skip and set fire once in a while as the horses ran with it. The fire details had their horses loaded with hay, and each man had several boxes of matches. The wind took up the scattered beginnings;

they were soon united, and they rolled a vast confluent sheet of flame to the south. At Cottonwood Springs we rode out onto the plateau to see and watch it. The fire rolled on and on, leaving in its train only blackness and desolation. All night the sky was lighted up. The fire swept the country clean; three days afterwards it was burning along the banks of the Arkansas River, far to the south, over which river it passed in places and ran out down in the Panhandle of Texas. There were some islands of grass left in some places far apart, here and there, but not many. The Indians back-fired against it in places, and managed to save themselves, but the game was driven out of the country before the fire. It did much damage to some portions of the Kansas frontier, which was then far east of the middle of the State.[18]

The modern editor of Ware's book duly notes the author's exaggeration of the extent of the conflagration, though he does not supply its actual extent. But that seems to miss an important point. Ware's willingness to imagine that a fire extended all the way from what today is southern Nebraska, consuming over half the state of Kansas, piercing the Oklahoma Panhandle, and dying out somewhere in the Texas Panhandle offers a suggestion of the limitless destruction the western soldiers were willing to contemplate in their struggle with the Plains Indians.

This astonishing application of prairie fires in warfare against the Indians and the equally astonishing exaggerations of it in the imagination of at least one western soldier match, as nothing in the conflict with the Confederacy does, the image of Civil War destruction so memorably conjured up by the historian Charles Royster in his book *Destructive War: William Tecumseh Sherman, Stonewall Jackson, and the Americans:* "Experience of war was partly a flight into unreason: into visions of purgation and redemption, into anticipation and intuition and spiritual apotheosis, into bloodshed that was not only intentional pursuit of interests of state but was also sacramental, erotic, mystical and strangely gratifying. This process of taking the war to heart, believing that it would change everyone, worked as strongly as any other influence toward making it more inclusive and more destructive."[19] Had Royster applied this image to the Plains Indian wars, it might have been on the mark; as a description of the Civil War it flies very wide of the mark.

If Ware was accurate, then the Indians also employed fire, or at least were familiar enough with prairie fires to know how to fight them: with backfires. Unlike Sheridan in the Shenandoah Valley, Colonel Livingston and General Mitchell did not submit to their superiors even a rough accounting of the plants and animals destroyed by their military campaign on the Republican River.

Such profligate burning of the prairie may not have been equaled elsewhere, but fire was apparently widely used in Indian warfare on the Plains. On a summer expedition against the Sioux in Dakota Territory in 1864, Colonel Robert N. McLaren of the Second Minnesota Cavalry attacked an Indian camp, kept the Indians in the woods with skirmish fire, and set about his task: "to destroy with the least delay the vast quantities of goods left in the timber and ravines adjacent to the camp. The men gathered into heaps and burned tons of dried buffalo meat packed in buffalo skin cases, great quantities of dried berries, buffalo robes, tanned buffalo, elk, and antelope skins, household utensils, such as brass and copper kettles, mess pans, &c., riding saddles, dray poles for ponies and dogs." He could not "make the destruction complete" in one day's time, so Colonel McLaren "fired the woods in every direction."[20]

The methods of warfare fell to the lowest common denominator of competition. The Indians, who had a long tradition of hunting by setting hunting grounds afire, fought back with the same fearsome and ultimately uncontrollable weapon.[21] Lieutenant Colonel William O. Collins reported after an action in western Nebraska early in 1865 that "in each engagement the Indians fired everything around them that would burn."[22]

If we compare the actual use of fire with the feeble attempt at Charleston, South Carolina, in this regard, too, the comparison is instructive. Before General Gillmore fired his shells harmlessly into Charleston, the city fathers had contemplated fighting fire with fire. On August 21, 1863, they issued "Report of Special Committee No. 2," on a proposal to set fire to the city voluntarily. In the end the five committeemen decided that the enemy had not much to lose by the reduction of the city to ashes and that noncombatants would inevitably be hurt.[23] Before the month was out, Gillmore's incendiary shells fell on the city. The fire department chief recommended keeping on hand a supply of water in case of a lucky hit.[24] The housekeepers of Charleston with characteristic sang-froid apparently dutifully kept buckets of water on hand and survived the bombardment with ease. The Greek Fire shells soon fouled the barrel of the cannon placed to fire into the city and the experiment in terror was over. As far as is known, Greek Fire did not cause a single casualty in the Civil War.

To make war on the Plains Indians, some soldiers made war on nature itself. It would be difficult to say that the soldiers had an ecological understanding of warfare, but they had, after over a decade of fighting Plains Indians, learned to look beyond the warriors to the society and economy that sustained them. And some were willing and able to destroy it all to keep the enemy from having any.

Moreover, when the soldiers on the Plains talked of wars of extermination, they meant what they said because they believed they could realistically hope to bring about such a complete conclusion to their work. Those historians who posit that after the Civil War the soldiers came west and applied the techniques of a total and terrible warfare learned in the Civil War to the Indians could not have reached a more erroneous conclusion.[25] Soldiers had learned the lessons in Indian conflicts preceding the Civil War and did not have the ability or inclination to apply them to the Confederacy. In other words, the true story is this: U.S. soldiers decided not to apply the lessons learned in the Indian wars to the enemy in the Civil War largely because the enemy in the Civil War appeared to be of the same race.

In those rare instances where the destruction of civilian agriculture was accorded trophy status in civilized warfare, as in General Sheridan's campaign in the Shenandoah Valley of Virginia late in 1864, the ultimate purpose was different from that of the Indian wars occurring simultaneously. The Shenandoah was thought to be the breadbasket for Robert E. Lee's army or at least for those raiders he detached to operate up and down the valley. The Great Plains were the food, clothing, and shelter source of the Cheyenne people. Lee's army might be driven to surrender by successful application of the strategy in the valley. The Cheyenne, as Colonel Livingston's report said directly, faced starvation. The one plan was strategic. The other was apocalyptic.

⋆⟾ ⟾⋆

As we have already seen in the case of the State Department's official correspondence, government reports did not have a primarily informational or archival purpose: they usually told a story. Certainly that was true of the various reports that emerged in the aftermath of the notorious Sand Creek Massacre, the most famous event of all the Indian wars of the Civil War era and among the most famous battles between Indians and whites in all of American history. But the story these reports told was new.

The historian Edmund S. Morgan pointed out years ago that Indian victories in American history are "generally known as massacres."[26] From Deerfield, Massachusetts, in the colonial era to the Custer battlefield in Montana in the late nineteenth century, that was true. But there was a famous exception: Sand Creek, Colorado. As the historian Michael Smith has pointed out, it was not the event itself but the reporting of it that was unusual. There had been many an atrocity committed against Indians before 1864, but the reporting, or what we might call the "memory," of this Civil War event was different: in this case the action of the whites earned the name usually reserved for Indian atrocities.[27] By and large, then, in the remainder of this chapter I will focus not so much on the attack by Colorado volunteers on a Cheyenne and Arapaho camp at Sand Creek in eastern Colorado as upon the image of the event that quickly emerged.

It would be careless to leave the impression that the battle, if it may be called that, was typical: it was a particularly egregious example of venting of white wrath against Indians. The Cheyennes and Arapahos, led by Black Kettle, had come to an American fort but proved too numerous to be fed continuously on government rations. Eventually they were sent away and some of their arms returned to them so that they could support themselves at the designated camp by hunting. The Indians apparently understood themselves to be essentially wards of the soldiers.

Such was not the understanding of the Colorado volunteers raised in Denver and led by Colonel John L. Chivington. Bent on revenge for a reported "massacre" of a white family, the Colorado volunteers surrounded and surprised the camp, consisting of perhaps 130 lodges, 8 of them Arapaho, on November 29, 1864. Chivington greatly exaggerated the number of Indians engaged and killed and failed to mention altogether that the majority of the casualties must have been women and children. Scalping and mutilation, especially of women's corpses, were rampant. The aftermath, it must be said, was as important for the reputation of the needless raid as the raid itself. The volunteers paraded through the streets of Denver, brandishing as trophies of their campaign scalps and the private parts of female Indians.

The grisly story as it is told here emerged immediately in the press—it did not wait investigation and debate. The first person to call the action a "massacre" may well have been one of the officers present at the raid, Major Scott J. Anthony, in his report of December 15, 1864. He bore a peculiar relationship to the action, as participant and critic. His first report, which he said he did not write himself, sounded as triumphant and exaggerated as Chivington's own. In the later report, of December 15, Anthony said, "The massacre was a terrible one" but went on to finish the sentence this way, "and such a one as each of the hostile tribes on the plains richly deserve." The problem was that the band massacred at Sand Creek was not hostile, as Anthony pointed out.[28] Likewise Major Edward W. Wynkoop, who bitterly disagreed on the treatment of this peaceful band and had been removed from command just before the Chivington campaign, called it a "massacre."[29] In this instance, then, unusual disagreements among white officers in the West on how to deal with the Indians led to divulging the truth of the story.

Perhaps the heightened hunger for news and increased skills of the press in reporting it induced by the Civil War had something to do with the immediate and substantially truthful emergence of the story of Sand Creek as a massacre rather than a triumph. That was the phenomenon on which historian Michael T. Smith remarked in his article on the subject: it did not require the reports and months of investigation and interrogations of legions of witnesses after the event to bring about a version of the truth to dispute some official report of victory. It was a "massacre" from the start. Debates and reports did ensue, but they did not uncover a hidden story: they simply verified and amplified it.

The brief debate in the U.S. Senate on the massacre of Cheyenne Indians, as it was called, has been somewhat neglected, but it is revealing. True, it came, as congressional debates often did, on a point oblique to the issue. The Senate resolution in question called for the suspension of pay of the soldiers involved in the attack at Sand Creek pending the outcome of proper investigation by Washington authorities. Thus the senators were able to take sides on whether such action constituted a presumption of the soldiers' guilt or whether it called for discussion of the question of the inhumanity and illegality of the attack at Sand Creek. Moreover, most of the senators proved content to leave the debate to Westerners.

The debate gave a picture of what senators deemed unacceptable in warfare, all the same. They made it clear that the deliberate killing of women and children in warfare was uncivilized and illegal. To be sure, women and children did occasionally get killed in war, but such deaths were usually accidental. They were tolerable as a likely outcome of deliberate strategy only in two circumstances. First, such casualties might occur legitimately as an accidental outcome of the tactics necessary to get at elusive enemies who would stand and fight only when they had to protect their women and children. Second, such casualties were acceptable as the result of a deliberate tactic—or at least understandable given the emotional nature of men—if they came about as retaliation for the enemy's having adopted the strategy and tactics of a war of extermination first.

Otherwise, killing women and children except by random accident was beyond the pale for military forces in war. It was unthinkable as a positive, explicit, and articulated goal of military action. As an official government policy it would be "inhuman." It was so wrong that there was no requirement that a common soldier obey an order deliberately to kill women and children. Military law did not demand that. These assumptions came out fully in the debate.

Senator James Nesmith of Oregon, who gave the only long speech on the subject, strove to excuse the alleged actions of Colonel Chivington. He speculated that the Colorado volunteers must have been motivated by a desire for retaliation for previous Indian atrocities committed against white families. Rather than cover up the atrocities, in other words, Nesmith, as a self-conscious Westerner and former Indian fighter, was inclined to plead their commonplace nature in the long history of Indian warfare. Nesmith did not himself say that the country should wage a war of extermination against the Cheyennes, but he did readily identify a tradition of U.S. massacres of Indians:

> I would not recommend extermination under ordinary circumstances; but when men whose families have suffered barbarities and cruelties at the hands of the Indians have a chance to retaliate, I am not prepared to blame them altogether when they attack the Indian village and put them to the fire and sword. This is an old complaint. Miles Standish attacked the Pequods, and it was said that he did so, and that was about the earliest complaint of the butchery of women and children in this country. We heard of it again in [Andrew] Jackson's wars in the Southwest. I believe that at Horseshoe Bend and in some other places in Alabama, he was accused of butchering women and children in indiscriminate warfare. Some time subsequent to that, and it is within the memory of every person here, general Harney attacked the Sioux villages at Ash Hollow, and he was accused of there putting men, women, and children to death indiscriminately.[30]

Near Ash Hollow, Nebraska Territory, General William S. Harney had attacked a Lakota Sioux village on September 3, 1855. He killed over a third of the inhabitants and took some seventy women and children prisoners, with few losses on his own side. Apparently, Harney's troops also killed women and children.[31]

Nesmith brought the ugly history right up to Civil War times. He referred to General Patrick E. Connor's campaign in Utah and Idaho. Well north of Salt Lake City, at a place called Bear River, Connor and his California cavalry in the cold of winter early in 1863, attacked a Shoshoni camp. Nesmith said that "doubtless, some women and children were killed." The senator argued that attacking villages was the only strategy that would work against such elusive enemies, and admitted of the Civil War itself: "Women and children have been killed in this war. There is scarcely a town or city which has been shelled during this war where more or less of them have been sacrificed by the missiles that have been hurled at their residences. It is not properly a cause of complaint, because it is a thing that happens unintentionally and unavoidably under the circumstances."[32]

A myopic ethnocentrism underlay the whole debate, even though senators spoke both against and for excusing the Chivington massacre.[33] The common practices of Indians in making war were denounced but never analyzed. Later and more sympathetic observers described the practices of Cheyenne warfare and tried to understand them. If we translate their findings into the terms of the debate in this book, we might well say that the Cheyenne too had their customs of war that limited their destructiveness. Ordinarily, they did not kill women and children. Perhaps because of their chronically low population numbers or because of religious or cultural values, they preferred to take them prisoner. They resorted to killing them only when desperate combat circumstances meant that their withdrawal from action could not be encumbered by prisoners. Warfare for them was similarly not necessarily as destructive of human life as it might have been. Some famed warriors went to war only to steal horses and had no interest in harming the men who rode them. Displays of courage were more important in these warrior cultures than actual destruction visited on the enemy.[34] In other words, one might imagine that if the Euro-Americans had known as much about their Indian enemies as others they faced, they might have engaged in a warfare in which it was mutually assumed that women and children would not be harmed by weaponry but might be taken prisoner. Exchanges of such prisoners could be brought about and could be fruitful of peaceful results even under the assumptions that actually prevailed in the West. The fragile peace that brought Black Kettle and his Cheyenne group to the American fort to live on rations and without weapons in 1864 was brought about by a deal in which the Cheyenne showed their peaceful intentions by bringing some white women and children captives to the soldiers, to be exchanged for Cheyenne prisoners held in Denver.[35]

Nevertheless, fundamental values in regard to warfare were certainly in conflict. Although nomadic Indian societies were incapable of waging warfare as Euro-American ones did, steadily over time (as the historian Robert L. Monkres has pointed out), the male part of the Cheyenne society still constituted a culture always ready for war, and individuals or groups or the whole nation were likely always to resume war.[36]

⊸⧥⊙ ⊙⧥⊶

Soldiers tended to drag their feet when asked by politicians and generals in Washington to investigate and punish soldiers fighting Indians. General Samuel Curtis apparently had genuine reservations of conscience about the direction Indian warfare was taking on the Great Plains. When asked to investigate Colonel Chivington, he told Henry W. Halleck, the general in chief in Washington, that the Colorado officer had surely violated Curtis's own orders in regard to the conduct of warfare against the Indians, but he refused to say that indiscriminate killing of Indians only made matters worse on the frontier. Curtis believed that such were the views of the Indian agents and traders with the Indians, whom soldiers despised as a general rule, but that in fact harsh warfare reduced the Indians' numbers and brought them "to terms." He promised to seek to destroy the hostile bands too and then relented, a little: "I will be glad to save the few honest and kindly disposed, and protest against the slaughter of women and children; although since general Harney's attack of the Sioux, many years ago at Ash Hollow, the popular cry of settlers and soldiers on the frontier favors an indiscriminate slaughter, which is very difficult to restrain. I abhor the style, but so it goes from Minnesota to Texas."[37]

It is difficult to know how sincere General Curtis was in his declarations of conscience about the Indians. He had expressed concern about the Indians' plight before Halleck raised the issue of the Sand Creek Massacre. As a Civil War general, Curtis, of course, had to think in terms of loyal and disloyal Indians. Curtis had an obligation to protect those Indians who declared their loyalty to the United States and spurned the Confederacy. He was particularly moved by an injunction, now apparently lost, that President Lincoln gave him, urging caution and respect for the loyal Indians in the territories west of Arkansas. He told the president more than six months before the Sand Creek Massacre:

> When in 1861 I had penetrated western Arkansas so as to command the Indian Country on my right flank, you telegraphed me to give such protection to the loyal portion as I could.—Knowing the attitude taken soon after my movement by [Cherokee chief] John Ross and the Pinn Society, I carefully avoided entering the Indian Country because I knew my troops were exasperated after some barbarities committed by the Indians at Pea Ridge and because I could not remain and protect them from want of supplies which I soon exhausted in the country.—
>
> But I have always borne your injunction in memory, and in subsequent movements of troops through the Indian Country and beyond, favored by every means in my power the wisdom and humanity of your prescribed policy.[38]

Curtis went on to describe the pitiful condition of the Indians. They had abandoned their farms out of fear and necessity and were now crowded together in miserable hovels, living off government rations. Some were slaveholders, apparently, and thus some 15,000–20,000

Indians and African Americans stood in need of government protection.

The history of Plains Indian warfare Curtis supplied Halleck with in 1864 is arresting. He knew that the landmark event in the history of Plains Indian warfare was the Ash Hollow fight of 1855, and he knew its significance: it was regarded as the wave of the future, the modern example of exterminating Indian societies by killing men, women, and children alike. If we regard Nesmith's ability to call to mind immediately a tradition of attacking whole Indian societies, in which Ash Hollow figured prominently, along with Curtis's similar ability to date Western lack of restraint in exterminating Indian societies from the same Ash Hollow action, we can see that from the point of view of the era, properly recovered, Sand Creek was different not in kind, but in reputation. Ash Hollow was a green light; Sand Creek proved—at least for a moment—to be a red one.

But why? It is true that the Sand Creek action may well have exceeded in gruesome practices and in extent any similar event since the Gnadehutten massacre of 1782, the murder of ninety Moravian-convert Delaware Indians by Pennsylvania militia, who took them in small groups and systematically dashed out their brains while the remainder prayed and sang and awaited their inevitable fate.[39] Sand Creek was a matter of extent rather than kind. Reporting was fuller and scrutiny more intense, and that factor too must be weighed in the balance in order to understand the memory of Sand Creek.

The image of the massacre was certainly more pronounced because a powerful congressional committee with practiced methods of publicity and accustomed to badgering the army was in place and issued a special report on it. The famous Joint Committee on the Conduct of the War was misnamed. It should more properly have been called the Committee for the Vigorous Prosecution of the War. The committee for three years said little about the conduct of troops in the field and denounced atrocities only if they were allegedly committed by the enemy. They did not appear to care much about soldiers' conduct on their own side. So minimal was Congress's interest in the subject that the new regulations of soldiers' conduct, General Orders No. 100, were drafted and circulated by the executive branch, though the Constitution gave the legislative branch power to "make Rules for the Government and Regulation of land and naval Forces."

Some of the atrocities attributed to the Confederates did in fact occur, and one of these was the notorious Fort Pillow Massacre of April 12, 1864. Two committee members went to Tennessee to take testimony in this case of slaughter of African American soldiers and white Tennessee Unionist soldiers after they surrendered to Confederate forces under General Nathan Bedford Forrest. The members of Congress interviewed victims of the massacre, wounded men who had escaped death. After returning to Washington, they helped put together a report that, in the end, was published with the committee's investigation of abuse of Northern prisoners of war in Confederate military prisons. They called the Fort Pillow incident a "massacre."[40]

Their investigation of the Sand Creek Massacre proved scalding. Perhaps the most important action of the committee was naming the event "The Massacre of the Cheyenne Indians." The House of Representatives, in requesting the investigation, had sought an inquiry not into a "massacre" but "into . . . all facts connected with the late attack of the third regiment of Colorado volunteers, under Colonel Chivington, on a village of the Cheyenne tribe of Indians, near Fort Lyon."[41]

The committee's description of the preliminaries to the Sand Creek attack was important. The peaceful Cheyennes, the committee maintained, had been sent to the fort by Colorado Governor John Evans and Chivington: there they "were treated somewhat as prisoners of war, receiving rations, and being obliged to remain within certain bounds."[42] A new commander of the fort sent the Indians to Sand Creek to hunt and subsist on their own, the rations being cut off and some of their arms being restored to them. On November 29, 1864, Chivington attacked the village. Black Kettle ran an American flag up over his lodge when the troops were in sight. The committee made note of this. The committee had now constructed a powerful scene: virtual prisoners of war under the U.S. flag ambushed in their camp by U.S. soldiers.[43] The creation of the image of the attack came at a time of congressional concern over treatment of the U.S. prisoners of war in Confederate camps.

The polite rules, written and unwritten, of congressional debate did not apply to interrogation of witnesses before committees or to the reports based on it. Evans and Chivington were baldly accused of "prevarication." The testimony of the Colorado governor, a Republican and therefore not a target of partisan animosity, was singled out as being "characterized by such prevarication and shuffling as has been shown by no witness they have examined during the four years they have been engaged in their investigations."[44]

The term "massacre" and the viewpoint that the whites massacred the Indians in this event stuck to Sand Creek like glue. A special committee appointed in March 1865 to investigate the condition of all the Indian tribes in the end devoted some seventy pages of its report to "The Chivington Massacre."[45] Ironically, the War Department gave the battle the name that would last in history. The annual report of the secretary of war of February 1867 included the testimony of the seventy-six-day-long military commission investigation of the "Sand Creek Massacre."[46]

Describing the action at Sand Creek as a "massacre" preceded by some fifteen years the revolution in elite opinion on Indian affairs marked by the publication in 1881 of Helen Hunt Jackson's *A Century of Dishonor: A Sketch of the United States Government's Dealings with Some of the Indian Tribes.* Chapter 9 of her book consisted of an innovative enumeration of "Massacres of Indians by Whites." Even at that late date, after many more Indian wars fought after the embittering experience of Sand Creek, Jackson could list only three items in her chapter: the Conestoga massacre, the Gnadehutten massacre, and recent massacres of Apache Indians. She included as an appendix an exchange of correspondence from the *New York Tribune,* published in 1879, about the Sand Creek Massacre.[47] The other key work of the period for revolutionizing attitudes toward Indians, George Manypenny's *Our Indian Wards,* published in 1880, quoted the description of the Sand Creek battle from the government report of 1867. Manypenny, who had been superintendent of Indian affairs in the Pierce administration and during the time of the Ash Hollow battle, struggled constantly to keep Indian affairs out of the War Department and under the aegis of the Interior Department. He took care to point out that General Harney had neglected to say in his report that he had killed women and children, not merely captured them, at Ash Hollow, and Manypenny treated Ash Hollow and Sand Creek as a sort of tradition.[48]

Manypenny's ability to understand massacres of Indians was peculiar and reflected his unusually close attention to Indian affairs and his long conflict with the War Department over Indian policy. For other Americans it required something more than Ash Hollow to understand the nature of the Indian wars. It required something more than mere publicity and investigative enthusiasm. The investigations merely seared into memory an altered point of view. The very fact of investigation stemmed from a changed point of view in the first place. The event was investigated because it was obviously a massacre; the main idea was to fix responsibility for it. Somehow, many members of Congress had to be brought to the different point of view that George Manypenny arrived at.

The American Civil War probably played a key role in that transformation. The change in point of view may well have stemmed from the heightened consciousness of the laws and usages of war brought about by the Civil War. The occurrence of major Indian wars in the midst of the Civil War begged for contrasts. If the one was a contest between civilized belligerents, then the others were contests between civilization and savagery. It was now more important than ever and clearer in the imagination how to distinguish the work of civilized belligerents from that of savages. Making warfare against women and children had become the mark of savagery—even if practiced by armies thought to be civilized belligerents. To make war in that style was to reduce one's own vaunted civilization to the level of savagery. The effect, then, of the American Civil War on attitudes toward Plains Indian warfare was probably opposite to what has customarily been posited. The United States did not, as a result of the Civil War, apply newly discovered cruel methods of "total war" to the Plains Indians. Instead, some people in the United States now realized for the first time that the time-honored cruelties indulged in fighting "barbarians" and "savages" were hardly acceptable to humanity. Now whites and Indians alike were deemed capable of massacring their enemies. A massacre of Indians, the Sand Creek battle, for the first time was widely recognized as such during the American Civil War. The effect of the Civil War on behavior toward Indians was brief if it had any, but it left its mark on history and memory in the name "Sand Creek Massacre" forever.

⊶⟩⟨⊷

Examining the Indian wars that occurred during the Civil War and the Civil War itself simultaneously yields insights that are difficult to arrive at if we look at them alone—as separate subjects in separate specialties of American historical writing and scholarship. To be sure, these specializations are important, and I obviously feel in writing this chapter my own lack of familiarity with Western history. But a start must be made. In the case of the Civil War, this simultaneous examination permits us to realize the restraints that assumptions about civilization and barbarism placed on behavior. The Union army set fire to barns here and mills there, but they could not and would not actually set the Shenandoah Valley, or any other troublesome expanse of the Confederacy, ablaze. By contrast, the army set much of Nebraska on fire and was quite willing in its imagination to let the blaze extend over western Kansas into the Texas Panhandle in their struggles with Plains Indians.

When army officers spoke of extermination in the case of the Indians they meant it and thought they were capable of bringing it about. When Senator James R. Doolittle of Wisconsin learned in 1865 of the military policy of rounding up the entire Navajo nation and bringing it to a small reservation called Bosque Redondo in New Mexico Territory, he was irritated beyond measure. It angered him that an officer on the spot could initiate policies toward whole Indians nations without any authorization or consideration by government authorities in Washington. He noted that "the Navajoes, as a nation, consisting of about ten thousand men, were captured in the mountains in New Mexico and brought over and placed upon the Pecos river."[49] The entire nation could be captured and put in a concentration camp. That could not be done to the Confederacy. The Confederacy could not actually be exterminated. When people in the North spoke of wars of extermination or scorched-earth campaigns waged against the Confederacy, they were not serious. They could not scorch the earth there, and they could not exterminate the Confederacy, a numerous people living in a vast region with plenty of rainfall and a vast commercial economy. Talk along those lines about the Confederacy was bluster indicative only of the intensity of national feeling in the North. It had nothing to do with realizable strategy and tactics.

More important, the United States did not really want to do such things to white people. It becomes clear that the United States could do dire things to the Indians and it did. Senator Doolittle, from a critical point of view, like Senator Nesmith from an apologetic one, suddenly realized this. "The indiscriminate slaughter of men, women, and children has frequently occurred in the history of Indian wars," Doolittle noted in 1867.[50] But the effect of the Civil War was not to harden policy or attitudes. If anything, its indirect influence—briefly and too often in areas remote from the Plains—ran the other way, suggesting the application of the laws and customs of war not only to "civilized" belligerents but to all peoples. Its effect on actual policy was brief, for harsh Plains Indian wars ensued in the wake of the Sand Creek Massacre and lasted, off and on, to the end of the century. We must not lose sight of the actual occurrences on the ground that were more important than the formal act of naming afterward. But a similar transformation shaped attitudes toward Benito Juárez. French violations of the laws and customs of war caused some people, despite their racial perceptions, to sympathize with the liberal Mexicans.

The slow change in cultural attitudes that is marked by the appearance of Helen Hunt Jackson's and George Manypenny's works at the beginning of the 1880s might be seen as a culmination of a Civil War sensibility. From the Declaration of Independence to the Civil War, Americans had conceived of two modes of warfare. Thomas Jefferson, in the Declaration of Independence itself, had condemned George III because, among other things, "he . . . endeavoured to bring on the Inhabitants of our Frontiers, the merciless Indian Savages, whose known Rule of Warfare, is an undistinguished Destruction, of all Ages, Sexes and Conditions." Euro-Americans fought by other rules, restraining mere destruction in war, when fighting people who were not regarded as savages. Northerners did not have much trouble maintaining that distinction throughout the Civil War and some people emerged from it, indeed, only with doubts in regard to the propriety of fighting "savages" without the same restraints.

·→≡◎ ◎≡←·

Naturally the same restraints applied to the Confederates. The Fort Pillow Massacre was the result of fighting African American soldiers. We can understand the emotional restraints, driven by racial beliefs, not by democracy, community, and literacy, when we read the diary of one Judge Brown of Arkansas. Brown had opposed secession, and though he closed ranks with the Confederates to defend Arkansas, he was little affected by the enthusiasm of early volunteering for the war, which he thought should have been avoided. Brown was an old man and destined to spend his time with the women left behind. This was his dyspeptic view of knitting socks for the soldiers in early 1861: "And the busy bustle at the social circle of mothers and sisters, in hastily making the uniforms which are destined no doubt to be the shrouds of their beloved sons, without even the comfort of feeling that the sacrifice was making in resistance of a foreign foe or savage fierce invader."[51] It was not common for Confederates to view the white enemy as savages worth fighting mercilessly. Confederate generals often strained to demonize the enemy. In Arkansas, General Thomas Hindman issued a bombastic proclamation to his troops on the eve of the Battle of Prairie Grove in late 1862: "Remember that the enemy you engage has no feeling of mercy or kindness toward you. His ranks are made up of Pin Indians, free negroes, Southern tories, Kansas jayhawkers, and hired Dutch cut-throats."[52] What is conspicuous in this appeal is the necessity of describing the enemy as people quite different from the people the Confederates really faced

*The Sand Creek Massacre*

11. *The Fort Pillow Massacre,* 1892. Northern memory of rebel atrocity in the Civil War was still alive in the 1890s, as this searing chromolithograph reveals. The print depicted the murder of women and children as well as prisoners of war, but only soldiers died in the 1863 massacre.

in hopes of arousing hatred on the eve of battle. The truth was that some Confederate soldiers probably felt that the enemy, sharing common racial bonds, did harbor feelings of mercy and kindness toward them.

It was not common on either side to regard the white enemy as savages to be fought mercilessly. Sand Creek belonged to the Plains Indian wars, not to the American Civil War.

## 6

# AVENGING ANDERSONVILLE

## Retaliation and the Political Uses of Hatred

IN RECENT YEARS the gap between the sentimental popular image of Abraham Lincoln and the more hard-boiled image of him held by professional historians seems to have widened. It is best symbolized by the view of Lincoln taken by the editor of a widely used anthology of Lincoln's letters and speeches. Andrew Delbanco's *Portable Abraham Lincoln* introduces the section containing documents relating to Lincoln's role as commander-in-chief in the Civil War with a powerful line: "He directed the war without relish, but also, in his way, without mercy."[1] Delbanco's statement represents the triumph of the anti-sentimentalist campaign begun in 1966 by Edmund Wilson in *Patriotic Gore,* who insisted that Lincoln's "writings do not give the impression of a folksy and jocular countryman swapping yarns at the village store or making his way to the White House by uncertain and awkward steps or presiding like a father, with a tear in his eye, over the tragedy of the Civil War."[2] Sentimentalism in serious writing on the Civil War may have died a slow death, but it is at last dead. We can now discuss frankly the restraints placed on war in the era without risk of glorifying it.

Congress was certainly more unforgiving than the president, and at no time was that more obvious than in late 1864 and early 1865. As for describing Lincoln as "merciless," that is surely wrongheaded. On December 20, 1864, Senator Morton S. Wilkinson of Minnesota, a sharp-tongued and unforgiving Radical Republican, offered a resolution that "in the opinion of Congress it would be wise and proper for the Secretary of War to direct that the rations, clothing, and supplies to be furnished to the rebel prisoners in our hands be limited in amount and kind to those furnished by the rebel authorities to Union troops held by them as prisoners of war, and that they be treated in all respects as the Union prisoners are treated by the rebel authorities."[3] Mild though it may sound in this guise, the resolution was in fact a directive to starve and freeze Confederate prisoners of war to death as a deliberate government policy.

S.R. 95, as this resolution came to be called, was referred to the Committee on Military Affairs, after Wilkinson gave a brief speech. He relied upon an eyewitness account of the suffering of Union officers held as prisoners of war in Columbia, South Carolina. The same eyewitness officer, from George A. Custer's staff, had told Wilkinson of the shocking death rate from starvation and suffering at Andersonville, Georgia. The power of "Andersonville," even in times of peace after the war was over, to arouse popular passions on sectional issues proved enduring and great, and here was this powerful engine for generating hatred introduced while the war still raged and hundreds of thousands of angry armed men marched over the land.[4]

It was widely known that the president, if not the Congress, possessed a generally forgiving nature, but the country early in 1865 saw Lincoln in perhaps his least charitable public posture. The Second Inaugural Address, with its plea for "malice toward none and charity for all," lay two months in the future. What the people and the press recalled in January 1865 was the president's most recent public statement on retaliation, given in the spring of 1864. Lincoln was then considering a retaliatory response for the slaughter of African American prisoners of war at Fort Pillow. In a rare public appearance, at the Baltimore Sanitary Fair on April 18, 1864, Lincoln referred to the "painful rumor," and attempted to address the problem:

> There seems to be some anxiety in the public mind whether the government is doing it's duty to the colored soldier, and to the service, at this point . . . Having determined to use the negro as a soldier, there is no way but to give him all the protection given to any other soldier. The difficulty is not in stating the principle, but in practically applying it . . . To take the life of one of their prisoners, on the assumption that they murder ours, when it is short of certainty that they do murder ours, might be too serious, too cruel a mistake. We are having the Fort-Pillow affair thoroughly investigated . . . If there has been the massacre of three hundred there, or even the tenth part of three hundred, it will be conclusively proved; and being so proved, the retribution shall as surely come.[5]

Though the administration did not follow up with action, the president was on record and the press remembered well. "Retaliation," recalled the *New York Evening Post* in January 1865, "was announced by the President, in his Baltimore speech, as a sound and justifiable policy."[6]

Moreover, the most recent revision of the laws of war as interpreted by the Lincoln administration retained retaliation as an essential principle. Article 27 of General Orders No. 100, the code drafted by Columbia University law professor Francis Lieber in 1863, asserted that the "law of war can no more wholly dispense with retaliation than can the law of nations, of which it is a branch. Yet civilized nations acknowledge retaliation as the sternest feature of war. A reckless enemy often leaves to his opponent no other means of securing himself against the repetition of barbarous outrage." And article 59 specifically asserted that "all prisoners of war are liable to the in-fliction of retaliatory measures."[7]

Fewer obstacles than ever lay in place early in 1865 to prevent Con-gress from causing the war to degenerate into retaliatory atrocities. The presidential election was behind them, and the Democrats could now see that they had nothing to gain by appearing to be soft on the Confederacy. Little wonder the issue spilled onto the floor of the Sen-ate on January 16, 1865. By that time irate citizens of Fort Wayne, In-diana, had petitioned their senator to put former prisoners of war, who had returned from the notorious Confederate prisons, in charge of Union camps holding Southern prisoners. That would guarantee that the retaliation would be in kind—that the government not only would kill its prisoners but do so by starving Confederate prisoners to death. At the same time Benjamin F. Wade of Ohio introduced his own set of resolutions on the subject. They resembled Wilkinson's set introduced a month before but contained more forceful and less ad-visory language, stating that it was the president's duty to follow the retaliatory policy. And Senator Wade added that "if any officer . . . shall fail to comply with and rigidly carry out the provisions . . . such officer . . . shall be immediately dismissed the service and subject to such further punishment as a court-martial shall . . . inflict."[8] Wade seemed as much interested in testing the radicalism of Northerners as in protecting the prisoners of war, until he realized the wrathful potential that lay in the Fort Wayne petition. He stated immediately that he would like to see his resolutions amended in committee to embody the mechanism suggested in that petition.

Such a vengeful device was too delicious to be ignored by the most enthusiastic members of Congress, and when a recommendation emerged from the military affairs committee, it contained the knife-twisting Fort Wayne proposition. S.R. No. 97 combined the various retaliatory proposals that the committee members liked best. Senator

Henry Wilson of Massachusetts introduced the resolution on the floor.[9]

The resolution was lengthy, beginning with a denunciation of treatment of prisoners of war in insurgent hands "unexampled for cruelty in the history of civil war, and finding its parallels only in the conduct of savage tribes." The deaths of "multitudes," it argued, stemmed from "the slow but designed process of starvation and by mortal diseases occasioned by insufficient and unhealthy food by wanton exposure . . . to the inclemency of the weather, and by a deliberate assassination of innocent and unoffending men, and the murder in cold blood of prisoners after surrender" (doubtless a reminder of the unavenged Fort Pillow Massacre). The Confederate practices were likened to barbarism three times and said to be "in contempt of the laws of war."

Congress now recommended retaliation only against Confederate officers. They should receive, "in respect to quantity and quality of food, clothing, fuel, medicine, medical attendance, personal exposure," and other ways, treatment similar to that Northern prisoners had received at Confederate hands. To ensure the brutal treatment, they were "to be placed under the control and in the keeping of officers and men who have themselves been prisoners in the hands of the insurgents, and have thus acquired a knowledge of their mode of treating Union prisoners." The policy was to continue until the president received proof that the Confederates had ceased to treat Union prisoners harshly. "Congress do not, however," the resolutions finally stated, "intend by this resolution to limit or restrict the power of the president to the modes or principles of retaliation herein mentioned, but only to advise a resort to them as demanded by the occasion."[10]

Senator Howard introduced the resolutions in the Senate. The debate on retaliation had a strikingly modern trigger for its sensational emotions. Senators found placed on each member's desk copies of

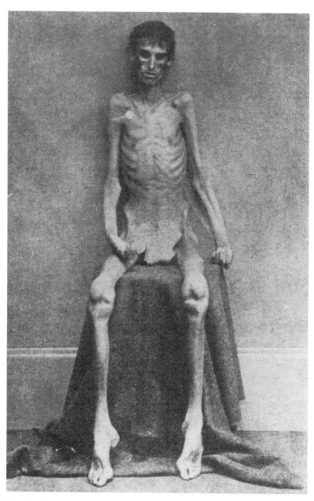

12. A Federal prisoner, returned from prison. It is little wonder that the shocking images of returned Federal soldiers who had been prisoners of war in the Confederacy
outraged Northerners. Yet there was nothing visceral about the delayed reaction of
the U.S. Congress, which initiated its bloodthirsty campaign for revenge on Confederate prisoners months after the poor soldier depicted here returned to the North
and was photographed.

the photographs taken of Union prisoners of war, returned in April 1864 from southern camps, and in skeletal condition, with their skin literally rotting. Debate ensued, two long weeks of it, off and on, and from it we could construct as destructive a doctrine of war as was ever devised during the American conflict.[11]

No fewer than thirty Senators spoke. Several expressed shocking extremes of sentiment. Henry Lane of Indiana introduced the retaliatory petition from his constituents in Fort Wayne, and despite his reputation as a moderate, he set the scene for extreme positions. "Now, sir," he said, "if this is to be a war of extermination, let not the extermination be all upon one side." He literally demonized the enemy as "those felons, and traitors, and demons in human shape." The idea of a war of "extermination," as we know from the chapter on Sand Creek, was usually reserved for Indian warfare, and the language of "demons in human shape," as we know from the chapter on Price's Raid, had most often been applied to guerrillas in Missouri such as "Bloody Bill" Anderson. These words were now creeping into congressional debate to refer to the legitimate Confederate enemy.

Benjamin Wade afterward led the charge in debate, as was often the case with radical measures. Jacob Howard provided much assistance. Between them, they assumed snarlingly tough positions. When admonished by reminders of Christian restraint in war, Wade scoffed that he did "not understand that there is very much Christianity in war."[12] Howard told the senators that he wanted to "drive from their hearts that sentimentalism which would refuse the protection of a just retaliation."[13] The Southern prisons, he said, were worse than Dartmoor, the Black Hole of Calcutta, and the British hulks in which French Napoleonic prisoners were said to have rotted. He blamed failures in Union recruiting on the specter that now hung over the potential volunteer of being starved to death if he should be taken prisoner.[14]

James Harlan of Iowa was not only a senator but also a prominent Methodist leader, and yet he saw reasons not only for retaliation but also opportunity for urging a calculated cessation of exchanges of prisoners of war: "The rebels are no longer able to meet us in the open field. Their armed soldiers fight us now almost exclusively behind their works and in fortifications. Military men tell us that it requires at least four men outside to take one inside of a fort . . . an exchange man for man will make the rebels relatively stronger."[15] Thus immediately upon entering into debate on the subject, the U.S. Senate had witnessed the formulation of shocking doctrine: the war might become one of "extermination"; the enemy was literally demonized; and compelling reasons were being found for ending, if not the practice of taking prisoners altogether, at least any further exchanges of prisoners once taken.

Democrats and conservative Republicans rose to oppose retaliation in the debate. Senator Thomas A. Hendricks, a Democrat from Indiana, had a brother-in-law who had languished in Confederate military prisons since June 1864, but Hendricks's solution to the problem was to resume prisoner of war exchanges rather than to retaliate on Confederate prisoners now in Union hands. Throughout the war and earlier, during the political antislavery controversies of the late 1850s, the Democrats had argued against dragging the pulpit into the political quagmire, but now Hendricks argued that war was "Christianized."[16] On the whole, however, Democrats opted for silence while they watched the Republicans disagree with each other and, most important, with the policy and direction of military affairs of the Republican president and commander-in-chief.

Resumption of prisoner of war exchanges was the conservative position because it most directly criticized the liberal president and his Radical allies, and because it raised the race issue, something the Democrats had proved increasingly eager to do. The great accumulation of Union prisoners in Confederate camps was caused by ceasing to exchange prisoners under the cartel agreement of 1862 to exchange prisoners equally, by formula, as in any international war. What ostensibly caused the North to halt exchanges under the old cartel was the Confederates' refusal to treat African American soldiers and their officers taken as prisoners the same way white prisoners and their officer were treated. Some of the opposition politicians could bait the race question on account of this policy. Garrett Davis of Kentucky, for example, declared that "all the negroes in America should never have been one iota in the way of or an obstacle to the free and prompt deliverance of our unfortunate white soldiers in captivity."[17]

Reverdy Johnson of Maryland gave the sort of measured but obstructionist speech for which he was famous. A Democrat who took a moderate and resigned stance on the Thirteenth Amendment, Johnson nevertheless made trouble for the Republicans on the prisoner of war question. He noted that the exposé of Confederate practices that caused malnutrition, disease, and death in the prison camps had come before the Senate from Wade's Joint Committee on the Conduct of the War back in May 1864. The question now, Johnson maintained, should be whether there was evidence that "the barbarities have continued." If punitive action was taken against Confederate prisoners in Union hands now and those practices in the camps had actually ceased, it would merely constitute revenge. Retaliation would be legitimate only if its intention was to cause the Confederates to cease ongoing abuses. Johnson also used the word "torture" to describe the form of retaliation recommended by the Senate resolution, a word scrupulously avoided by the advocates of retaliation.[18]

Pennsylvania Senator Edgar Cowan, a conservative Republican, likewise refused to jump aboard the Wade-Howard bandwagon of retaliation. Cowan argued, among other things, the constitutional point that decisions about prisoners of war were matters for the commander-in-chief and not for the legislative branch.[19] That point drew an admission from Howard that the resolution was merely "advisory" to the president and "not mandatory."[20] Wisconsin conservative Republican James R. Doolittle raised the constitutional point also, but saw it another way. He doubted the president's authority to retaliate against Confederate prisoners, citing the clause of the U.S. Constitution stating that "Congress shall have power to define and punish . . . offenses against the law of nations."[21]

The politicians in opposition naturally had to handle such an issue, touching so sensationally on the welfare of the common Union soldier, very gingerly. Cowan made it clear, for example, that he would support any "manly" policy in substitution for the retributive eye-for-an-eye resolutions originally laid before the senators.

⊷⊷◉⊶⊶

Opposition to the Radicals' crusade for retaliation thus drew the predictably partisan and factional responses, but some resistance had deeper roots. Perhaps the most important opposition came from Radical Republican Senator Charles Sumner of Massachusetts.[22]

Sumner's stance in the debate on retaliation runs contrary to his conventional image and, in truth, remarkably contrary to much that he stood for up to 1865. The allegations of Confederate atrocities against prisoners of war only confirmed what Sumner had been saying for years. After his brutal caning at the hands of the South Carolinian Preston Brooks in 1856, Sumner's seat in the Senate remained shamingly vacant, but when he returned, he did so with a vengeance. His major campaign thereafter—to depict slave society as a barbarism—began on the eve of the Civil War with his maiden speech after his return to Congress: "The Barbarism of Slavery."

It proved to be an uphill struggle, before the war, to convince even Republicans of the point. Only a minority of Northerners, despite the region's long indoctrination about the arrogant violence of the

Slave Power, were quite ready for this. Republican leaders in 1860, smelling political victory and uncomfortable with allegations by Democrats that they were fanatics, wanted to avoid appearances of extremism.[23]

In April 1862 Sumner introduced a resolution asking the Joint Committee on the Conduct of the War to investigate "the barbarous treatment by the rebels, at Manassas, of the remains of officers and soldiers of the United States killed there." The revelations were necessary, he said, so that "the country and mankind may see how Slavery in all its influences is barbarous,—barbarous in peace, barbarous in war, barbarous always, and nothing but barbarism." The United States, he concluded, was "now in conflict with beings who belong to a different plane of civilization."[24] In the summer of 1863, Sumner sensed the time was right to renew the effort, and he chose then to reissue the speech, with as much fanfare and distribution as he could muster. He boasted in the new introduction to the pamphlet that the term "barbarism of slavery" was "new" three years earlier when he introduced the idea, but was "common now." And he reminded the nation that the "question . . . presented" by the war lay "between Barbarism and Civilization,—not merely between two different forms of Civilization, but between Barbarism on the one side and Civilization on the other side."[25]

In 1865 Sumner halted his carefully constructed campaign to prove the South barbarous and refused to add impetus to the crusade for retaliation for what was being routinely described by Radical Republicans as "barbarous" treatment of Union prisoners of war in Confederate camps. Instead, Sumner acknowledged rebel barbarism in passing and insisted now that it must be conquered and not imitated. He recommended amending the resolutions to forbid retaliation in kind. Sumner's amendment characterized retaliation as "harsh always" and permissible only when "it may reasonably be expected to effect its object, and where . . . it is consistent with the uses of civilized society." Otherwise, it constituted "useless barbarism, having no other end than vengeance, which is forbidden alike to nations and men." He pointed out that "any attempted imitation of rebel barbarism in the treatment of prisoners would be plainly impracticable, on account of its inconsistency in the prevailing sentiments of humanity among us; . . . would be injurious at home, for it would barbarize the whole community . . . and . . . must be rejected . . . precisely as the barbarism of roasting or eating prisoners is always rejected by civilized Powers."[26]

Sumner was thorough and produced the results of the farthest-reaching research into the law. He knew that Francis Lieber's code endorsed retaliation, and he produced a letter from Lieber himself saying, "I am unqualifiedly against the retaliation resolutions concerning prisoners of war . . . All retaliation has some limit." Lieber opposed retaliation in kind. Sumner cited Henry Halleck on prisoners of war, Emerich Vattel on the laws of nations, and Chancellor Kent on precedents: "Incidents of resolutions to retaliate on innocent prisoners of war occurred in this country during the revolutionary war, as well as during that of 1812; but there was no instance in which retaliation, beyond the measure of secure confinement, took place in respect to prisoners of war."[27]

It is fortunate for historians that Senator Sumner took the surprisingly contrary position he did in the debate in 1865, because he had a large and loyal following of eager and articulate correspondents who wrote to him and responded to the stimulus of his frequently franked congressional speeches. Moreover, these letter writers cannot adequately be described as Sumner's constituents, because he had a national reputation and many people outside Massachusetts wrote to him. He had a moral constituency, for his correspondents overwhelmingly derived from that group of Americans who were identified with evangelical antislavery reform.

Almost fifty people wrote Sumner about his stand on retaliation, and their response represents an unusual and valuable batch of historical evidence. It is certainly no longer accurate to say that religion has been neglected as a Civil War subject, but it is nearer the truth to say that religion still speaks largely with one voice in the pages of Civil War histories: "onward Christian soldiers."[28] No doubt that voice is accurately captured, and was the dominant religious voice for the Protestant denominations, and yet there must have been some rare religious voices that restrained the soldiers from retaliatory excess. It must have been an inner voice in many instances that held them back from atrocity and from retaliation. The historian Mark Grimsley has to some degree documented the effect of that voice on their behavior, in tempering the common soldiers' visceral tendency to rip up the rebels and their countryside out of sheer hunger and cold and to retaliate against them for pain and personal loss.[29]

The religiousness of the letters written to Sumner on the subject of retaliation is obvious. E. M. Furness identified herself "as a Christian mother." Another correspondent, Israel Washburn, of the famous Maine political family, was president of a Universalist association and a prominent layman in that faith, as well as a Republican politician. James Butler, a captain in the Thirtieth United States Colored Infantry, stationed in Baltimore, commended Sumner's "Christian speech." Orville N. Wilder cited the Golden Rule and quoted Christ's words in commending the speech on retaliation. Mary Howard Schoolcraft, the widow of the famous authority on American Indians Henry Schoolcraft, agreed with Sumner's position and doubted the feasibility of the hideous proposal made in the Senate. "No evidence short of direct revelation from heaven," she said, "could convince *my* heart, or judgment that any man in this Bible educated land could *willfully* starve a prisoner. War, between Christian peoples, I know, is the carnival season in Hell." Robert Anderson, the Union commander at the fall of Fort Sumter, said the speech marked Sumner as "a Christian and a patriot."[30]

Sumner's moral constituency transcended not only Massachusetts's borders but those of the United States. From London, England, came the praise of the dissenting clergyman F. W. Newman. James E. Harvey, who worked in the American legation in Lisbon, did not always agree with Sumner but in this instance noted that "the wisdom of statesmanship, the benevolence of philanthropy and the spirit of Christianity" were "the master chords of that discourse." Likewise, James H. Campbell, writing from the legation in Stockholm, knew the United States needed the "blessing of Divine Providence" and thought that Sumner's position made such aid possible. He thought the speech would resonate "so long as Christian civilization endures."[31]

We can surmise that this was the sort of morality that restrained some soldiers from extreme violence because more than one soldier responded favorably to Sumner's exhortation to restraint. John L. Maxwell of Ann Arbor, Michigan, saw himself as one of Sumner's national constituency. "When the fire eaters fired on Fort Sumter," Maxwell recalled in his letter to Sumner, "I was at my plow." He joined up and for three years marched with the Seventeenth Illinois Infantry. The plight of Union prisoners rankled any soldier, and Maxwell said that the "conscience of every Man is now aroused by the barbarity of the rebels toward those men." Even so, Maxwell still opposed retaliation. Instead, he thought there should be a draft and a subsequent military campaign to capture the military prison in Andersonville and liberate the prisoners.[32]

Captain James Butler likewise supported Sumner's position despite the peculiar risks of cruel treatment if he or the African American soldiers whom he led in the Thirtieth Colored Infantry were made prisoners.[33] And Orville N. Wilder of Battery I, Third United States Artillery, agreed with Sumner despite the fact that he had a brother who had been a prisoner in the hands of Confederate "fiends."[34] General J. S. Donaldson, who served on the staff of General George H. Thomas at Nashville, wrote to thank Sumner for the anti-retaliation resolutions as well.[35]

One soldier, also an officer in an African American regiment, disagreed vehemently. Charles Francis Adams, Jr., a descendant of John Adams and similarly independent in his thinking, wrote Sumner and enclosed a clipping of a letter he had written for the *Army & Navy Journal*, arguing for retaliation. The "fatal fallacy" in Sumner's argument, Adams contended, lay in characterizing the motive for starving Confederate prisoners of war as vindictiveness. On the contrary, the retaliatory measures were but a means to a practical end, to force the Confederates up to the Union level. It was not bringing the Union down to theirs, Adams argued cleverly. "I would not injure Mr Davis himself if I had the power, unless in so doing I could shorten the war," Adams maintained. He argued as well that to shoot the prisoners rather than to retaliate in kind would invite howls of indignation "from all civilized nations." After giving thirty days' notice of Union intentions, Adams would starve 30,000 men and provide commissioners to report on the conditions in the Confederacy's prisons when a response came.[36]

Other glimpses of sincere and intense popular feeling about retaliation appear in the private correspondence of other politicians. President Lincoln, for example, received three letters on the subject, two of them eloquent appeals from women.

Mrs. A. Moor of Greenwich, New York, began her letter to the president with the gender disclaimer common to the era: "You may not deem it in womans sphere to address you upon this subject, but today our little village has witnessed one of the heartrending results of this war." A soldier from the town who suffered imprisonment at Andersonville was buried that day. He apparently escaped after seven months in prison and came home to die. Shortly before his death he wrapped himself in a flag and declared that it was for that flag he died. He gave the banner to his mother as a parting gift. "This cry for retaliation," Mrs. Moor said, "comes from all loyal mothers wives sisters and daughters of the north not that we would add to the sufferings of mankind but we believe it to be the most effective and speediest means of relieving them. It is the plea of humanity." Thus in the few samples of women's opinions available on the subject here, it appears that the range of arguments was wide. Mrs. Moor made an appeal from female roles—of wife, mother, sister—ironically employed to call for retaliation against those who victimized husbands, sons, and brothers.

Mrs. Moor did not make her case without some consideration of the laws and customs of war. "True," she added, "we look upon it as a barbarous practice at the south and at the north would not be guilty of it. But when driven to it by this extremity humanity calls for it if not justice." She pointed out that shooting deserters was "sanctioned by all nations" and that "a law for capital punishment authorized by the divine word for the security of society" prevailed. Surgeons too were "allowed to cut and saw off limbs from a living man to save his life, all of which to the unaccustomed senses would seem barbarous." She had a son and she understood Lincoln did too, and that meshed with the crucial family-centered part of her appeal. Before closing she reaffirmed that she was "not one of the 'strong minded' women," but that she felt strongly on that issue.[37]

Mrs. C. Greene Brayton, a collateral descendant of the Revolutionary War general Nathaniel Greene and the wife of a Rhode Island Supreme Court justice, had a more political outlook on the question of retaliation. She shrewdly linked the debate over retaliation to the rumors of peace initiatives coming from Washington. She warned the president against being identified with Francis Preston Blair in seeking peace from the Confederates. The enemy was not conquered yet, she insisted, and the slaves were "not freed—they [the Confederates] hate the working people of [the] North, and the man who sits in the presidential Chair just as bitterly." "Listen to the agonized wail from the prison pens," she urged. "Dare you make any compact with these men who have so tortured your prisoners of war?" "Has this suffering been hidden from your eyes [?] Send for one from Belle Isle [Prison in Richmond]—from Andersonville ask what he thinks of receiving them except upon the condition of full and entire submission—tendering up their leader in this rebellion their Genls and visiting upon them the full penalty of high treason Lenity is misplaced here Clemency worse than meaningless." Brayton was willing to wait for a loyal generation in the South to arise and to "keep for many years a standing army" if necessary until that happened.[38]

⇥⇤

Presumably these evocative letters to Sumner and to Lincoln come as near the true feelings of these people as historians can get. As for the true feelings of the senators who debated retaliation, these are notoriously difficult to get at. There could not really have been anything truly emotional or visceral about the Senate's response to the plight of Union prisoners in early 1865. The issue was not new at all. It had been sensationally revealed well over six months earlier. It was, in fact, introduced in the grisliest and most sensational fashion to the American public just as the presidential campaign of 1864 moved into its heated summer. The well-practiced Joint Committee on the Conduct of the War had included a report on the prisoner atrocities with its report on the Fort Pillow Massacre in May 1864. Yet the same politicians had said little or nothing about the issue back then. And no one had done anything about it.

The chronology of the prisoners of war abuse issue is critical, and nothing is more revealing about it than the now famous images of starved Union prisoners of war that were circulated at the time of the debate in the Senate. These photographs had been taken long before the retaliation debate of January 1865. On May 2, 1864, under a flag of truce, a boat carried to the Union lines a hundred Union prisoners of war from Richmond who were being released, despite the end of prisoner of war exchanges, because of their diseased condition. Dr. B. A. VanderKieft of the United States General Hospital, Division 1, of Annapolis, Maryland, was shocked to find among the prisoners skeletal shadows of real men. One soldier had eaten so little food in some six months of imprisonment that his weight had fallen from 185 to 108 pounds. Another soldier's forearm was so thin between the bones that it was transparent when held up to the light. A Dr. Ellerslie Wallace sent photographs of the prisoners to *Harper's Weekly*, the great New York illustrated newspaper, and there they were reproduced as wood engravings in the issue of June 18, 1864.[39] Meanwhile the Joint Committee on the Conduct of the War sent members to Maryland to see and interview the prisoners and the doctors. They made a report distributed in some 60,000 copies.[40]

Historians of the presidential campaign of 1864 do not identify the prisoner of war issue as important.[41] A searching examination of the contemporary press naturally turns up an article here or there about the abuse of Union prisoners of war during that election summer, but the political parties did not systematically make it an issue. Doubtless, it was not to the Democrats' interest to enflame war hatred of the Confederacy, an emotion bound to play into the hands of the commander-in-chief, who was the Republican nominee for president. Likewise, it would have been a delicate and dicey issue for the Republicans, for these abuses had occurred on their president's watch, and continuing abuse, if there was any, would only underline the powerlessness of the Union after some three and one half years of war to do anything about it by military means. Moreover, the great accumulation of prisoners of war had come as a result of ending exchanges because the Confederacy refused to promise to treat African American soldiers and their officers by the accustomed rules for prisoners of war. The Republicans understood the necessity of protecting African American prisoners of war but did not want to raise an issue of putting white prisoners at risk for the sake of black ones.

The campaign debate on prisoner of war abuse in 1864 may have been surprisingly subdued, but, the fact remains that by January 1865 the issue was not news to anyone. Therefore, political historians smell partisan reasons for the Radical Republicans' resurrection of the issue after the presidential election. They link the Radicals' return to the issue with desires to undermine rumored peace negotiations with the Confederacy. And the terms of peace were inextricably linked to visions and terms of reconstruction after the war.[42]

The government, it must be said, did nothing about the prisoners. The active solution was so simple that it did not require a general or a U.S. senator to recognize it. John Maxwell, the Illinois soldier who wrote Sumner, understood it: he called for a special draft to raise an army to capture Andersonville. Well before January 1865, a man named Charles F. Mitchell, from Cincinnati, recognized the possibility too. As soon as he learned of William T. Sherman's victory at Atlanta at the beginning of September 1864, Mitchell took out a map and surveyed the situation. He saw the line of action to be taken. He discovered Andersonville to lie "about 110 Miles [away,] where the Rebels have some 20,000 Union Prisoners." Mitchell urged the government to "organize forthwith a present expedition to liberate these suffering Prisoners." The logistics seemed feasible: "Not counting any aid from R.R. to Athens the plan could be worked by forced march of infantry in 6 days & the men could carry 24 days cooked ration." The plan reached the highest ranks of the administration because Mitchell sent his idea to Secretary of State William H. Seward, but nothing came of it.[43]

No other explanation than the political one will fit the chronology, and William C. Harris's assertion that renewed focus on Andersonville was meant to blunt the peace initiatives known to exist in Washington must be correct. The failure to focus on the issue in the presidential campaign suggests strongly some new provocation to the Radicals. Francis Preston Blair, Sr., went to Richmond on his secret peace mission on January 12, 1865. There had been other peace missions and even more rumors of missions. The debate on the prisoner of war issue spanned the period from January 16 to February 1. The Hampton Roads Peace Conference, the ultimate fruit of the Blair Mexico initiative, occurred on February 3, 1865.

Such an explanation fits not only the chronology but also the political culture of the era. The true political style of the age was brinkmanship. Politicians, as many historians have noted, rallied voters in America's individualistic and pluralistic democracy by calling for crusades against imaginary conspiracies that threatened to subvert the republic.[44] Such an appeal often proved more effective than getting the multifarious electorate to agree on some positive program. The politicians' stock-in-trade was spreading fear of the imminent fall of the republic and identifying as monsters those who were conspiring to cause it. In the midst of civil war, such tactics constituted playing with fire. But in that age, to see an evil result, such as the emaciated Union prisoners of war, was to assume that some evil social force had brought it about deliberately. The politicians were fresh from a presidential campaign in which they spread allegations of secret organizations conspiring to bring about the secession of the Old

Northwest and other subversive activities. Attempting to rouse the passions of the American electorate to take bloodthirsty revenge on Confederate prisoners of war—for the sake of defeating administration initiatives looking toward a negotiated peace—was brinkmanship of the most callous and inhumane sort.[45]

It speaks well for press and people that the irresponsible Senate debate did not start a fire that could burn well out of control. The response of the Northern press was generally tepid, and few editors took up the cause of the starving prisoners as one on which to spill ink in repeated editorials. Those who did argued for retaliation but not in kind—give the rebel prisoners rations like a common soldier's in the North, allow no correspondence with family, and make them labor on public works. The *New York Evening Post*, for example, settled for recommending such mild measures.[46]

Naturally the Democrats were lukewarm. Although the *New York World* admitted without doubt "the barbarity and cruelty of the enemy," these influential Democrats shifted the blame onto Secretary of War Edwin M. Stanton for refusing to exchange prisoners.[47]

The debate also failed to ignite public opinion despite a context of public events that might have encouraged such a result. It is difficult for us today, given our knowledge of the proximate end of the great war, to recover the sense not that conflict was somehow winding down but that it continued, rather, to be waged with accustomed vigor. But if we put ourselves in the shoes of the people in the Civil War and ignore hindsight, 1865 was the likeliest time for the emergence of extreme measures of warfare. Maximilian's Black Decree, after all, was issued at the height of his power, when he thought he was winning, not out of desperation while he was surrounded at Querétaro. There is no analogous order issued in the Civil War North, of course, but such an order was perhaps more likely to have been issued in late 1864 or early 1865. In addition to the hardening effects that four years of fighting are alleged to have exerted on Northern society and leadership, there was the lure of specious humanitarian justification: shortening the war in the long run and ultimately saving lives by making it extremely unpleasant in the short run.

Thus, according to one well-placed source, rumors that an extreme policy of executing prisoners of war was in the works abounded in the North early in 1865. James Kelley, the postmaster in New York City, told Secretary of State William H. Seward on April 3, 1865, "It seems to be the impression here that the President should issue a proclamation that the Rebels must disband within a certain time, or all officers, above the grade of a Colonel will be considered as murderers and treated as such."[48]

For their part, the Confederates were definitely desperate, and the various schemes they attempted, at the instigation of their agents in Canada, in late 1864 and early 1865 could have enraged public opinion in the North. Northerners at the time of the congressional debate on retaliation read in their newspapers about the difficulties of pursuing justice against Confederate raiders from Canada who had attacked St. Albans, Vermont. The *New York Herald*, commenting on Canadian magistrates who prevented the return of the escaped Confederate raiders, asked, "Reprisals When [Are They] Justified by the Laws of Nations?"[49]

"Reprisal" might have seemed even more likely as a response to the recent attempt by Confederate agents from Canada to burn New York City. This scheme, discussed in the previous chapter, cannot escape the label of terrorism; in fact, no single scheme of the Civil War fits the definition better. The plot was still in the news at the time of the retaliation debate in Congress because of the pursuit of the Confederate agents into Canada.[50]

Such events might be said to have fallen ripely into Charles Sumner's hands for further shaping his case for the barbarism of slavery.

But Sumner was chairman of the Senate Foreign Relations Committee, had many contacts among liberals in Great Britain, and, as David Donald has shown in his biography of Sumner, took his role in diplomacy seriously.[51] Whatever the schemes abetted by the Confederate agents in Canada proved about barbarism, irresponsible agitation of the issue invited war with England if U.S. forces pursued the Confederate agents across the border. Sumner did not press these issues in Congress and in fact saw to it that a proposal to arm the northern border against Canada was referred to his committee to die.[52] The overall reaction to the Confederate plots planned in Canada proved to be subdued and was not linked in the public mind with the prisoner of war issue.

⇥⇤

Retaliation on prisoners of war was never a serious policy initiative in 1865.[53] Debate was confined to the Senate and did not arise in the House, though the resolutions were called "joint." The measure debated was regarded as only advisory to the president. The resolution that finally passed in the Senate was so watered down by compromise as to be unrecognizable as the bloodthirsty resolution that had first emerged from the Military Affairs Committee. The country and its leaders were no closer now to disregarding the laws and customs of war than they were in 1861, despite rumors to the contrary and four years of bloody conflict. The retaliation debate was but another example of the extremes bred by the political culture of the era. It had no deep roots and must be dismissed as a downright cynical political ploy.

Leadership should also be given its due, and there is no doubt that it made some difference that Abraham Lincoln was a man who carefully avoided retaliation and its likeliest effect—the actual collapse of the American Civil War into the merciless struggle so often mistakenly depicted in the history books today. Lincoln left a meager written record, but what exists is clear and uncontradicted by contrary texts. He affirmed adherence to the rules of "civilized" warfare in public. "Civilized belligerents," he said in a public letter in the summer of 1863, "do all in their power to help themselves, or hurt the enemy, except a few things regarded as barbarous or cruel. Among the exceptions are the massacre of vanquished foes, and non-combatants, male and female."[54]

Little-known documents that Lincoln wrote for specific and non-public purposes reveal a clear idea of the proper limits of destruction in war. Thus on August 14, 1864, he wrote a letter in cipher to General Ulysses S. Grant, saying that the president and the secretary of war concurred "that you better confer with Gen. [Robert E.] Lee and stipulate for a mutual discontinuance of house-burning and other destruction of private property."[55] Only the condition of mutuality, and the fact that the letter addressed a problem of burning that had already occurred, separated this letter from being a revelation to the enemy, Lee himself, of what limits Lincoln would adhere to. The president had to leave decisions on particular houses in particular situations up to the commander on the ground, and the letter in cipher did not constitute an order from the commander-in-chief. Lincoln knew that adherence to such laws and customs of war was ultimately dependent on the forbearance of opposing commanders. But he encouraged it when he could, and, more important, generally expected it to be adhered to on the battlefields and campaigns in the Confederacy.

In yet another instance, when Lincoln was called upon early in 1865 by an aggrieved Arkansas woman to review a case of confiscation of her property by a Federal provost marshal, he concluded his order on the case (restoring her property) by stating the general principles involved: "The true rule for the Military is to seize such property as is needed for Military uses and reasons, and let the rest alone. Cotton and other staple articles of commerce are seizable for military reasons. Dwelling-houses & furniture are seldom so."[56] But these were not general orders and were not meant for, nor did they reach, the general public.

As for retaliation, Lincoln never really believed in it, and that separated him from many other policy makers in the Civil War. Generals such as John McNeil swore by its positive results. Members of Congress in the retaliation debate could cite its effectiveness in case after case. When the Confederates put Union prisoners of war to work on the breastworks of Charleston, General Robert S. Foster's retaliation ended the practice. When Union prisoners of war were placed in front of a redoubt at Richmond, retaliation by putting Confederate prisoners of war in the Dutch Gap Canal works ended the practice. When the Confederates said they would execute prisoners of war in their hands in retaliation for actions by Union occupying forces in New Orleans, the United States seized a relative of Robert E. Lee's and the threats ended.[57]

President Lincoln could surely have brought the memory of the same incidents to bear on the case if he wanted to. Opposition to retaliation was a matter of faith and not facts with him. When in 1861 General John C. Frémont issued his emancipation proclamation for Missouri rebels, the general issued other orders as well, with which Lincoln also disagreed. Frémont had decreed the trying of rebels in arms by military commissions, to be followed by the prompt execution of the prisoners. The order came as close to Maximilian's Black Decree as anything issued by Union authorities during the Civil War. Lincoln told Frémont: "Should you shoot a man, according to the proclamation, the Confederates would very certainly shoot our best man in their hands in retaliation; and so, man for man, indefinitely."[58] He disallowed executions without presidential review, and on the way to doing that, he had offered in the simplest language the sovereign explanation for spurning retaliation. Lincoln's disbelief made so much difference that the entire Senate debate on retaliation can be said to have been premised on the knowledge that the president was not likely to retaliate. Indeed, the Radical Republican Zachariah Chandler said as much: "The committee on the conduct of the war has been laboring for years to induce the Administration to adopt the system of retaliation; but the labor has been fruitless."[59]

Of course, Lincoln was not going to issue public orders and admonitions *against* retaliation, lest they constitute an invitation to the enemy soldiers to take any license they wished. And indeed such a consideration militated against any statement of the principles of limitation of force by the commander-in-chief. He made that point clear in 1861 in a private letter to an old associate, Orville Hickman Browning, then a senator from Illinois. In explaining his revocation of Frémont's proclamations for Missouri, Lincoln dwelt mostly on the emancipation proclamation. But before closing, Lincoln dealt as well with the provision to execute military prisoners summarily: "You think I am inconsistent because I did not also forbid Gen. Fremont to shoot men under the proclamation. I understand that part to be within military law; but I also think, and so privately wrote Gen. Fremont, that it is impolitic in this, that our adversaries have the power, and will certainly exercise it, to shoot as many of our men as we shoot of theirs. I did not say this in the public letter, because it is a subject I prefer not to discuss in the hearing of our enemies."[60] Charles Sumner's Senate colleague from Massachusetts, Henry Wilson, made the same point in the debate on retaliation over three years later. Wilson pointed out the uncomfortable truth for those opposed to imitating rebel barbarism in the matter. He did not want to vote *for* retaliation, but he definitely could not vote for a resolution *against* retaliation. "I hope," Wilson said, ". . . we shall adopt a practical plan."[61]

Thus President Lincoln's only full statement of the position on the laws of war, quoted above, came as a defense of the emancipation proclamation and as a statement of latitude allowed by law: the president could do anything he wanted to harm the enemy in war except a few things, such as ordering the massacre of prisoners or targeting women and children. In other words, the statement affirmed the power to emancipate and seemed to minimize the restrictions on warfare. The explanation for the scarcity of affirmations of Lincoln's guiding principles along these lines lies precisely in that practical consideration, not in their lack of importance to him. It is significant, of course, that there are no statements from Lincoln to be weighed in the balance on the other side, statements in favor of massacres and vengeance.

Lincoln realized that he must risk the spiral of retaliation or leave African American soldiers in peril of execution or sale after capture, for the Confederates had spurned the laws and customs of war in the case of what they regarded as race war. On July 30, 1863, President Lincoln signed the following order for retaliation:

> It is the duty of every government to give protection to its citizens, of whatever class, color, or condition, and especially to those who are duly organized as soldiers in the public service. The law of nations and the usages and customs of war as carried on by civilized powers, permit no distinction as to color in the treatment of prisoners of war as public enemies. To sell or enslave any captured person, on account of his color, and for no offence against the laws of war, is a relapse into barbarism and a crime against the civilization of the age.
>
> The government of the United States will give the same protection to all its soldiers, and if the enemy shall sell or enslave anyone because of his color, the offense shall be punished by retaliation upon the enemy's prisoners in our possession.
>
> It is therefore ordered that for every soldier of the United States

killed in violation of the laws of war, a rebel soldier shall be executed; and for every one enslaved by the enemy or sold into slavery, a rebel soldier shall be placed at hard labor on the public works and continues at such labor until the other shall be released and receive the treatment due to a prisoner of war.[62]

The War Department wrote the draft and Lincoln signed it. He never really enforced it.[63]

When all was said and done, the president and the society he directed to victory in the Civil War came down on the side not of retaliating for atrocities but of avoiding atrocity. They came down on the side not of making war terrible but of making it no worse than necessary. The decades-long campaign to desentimentalize Lincoln's image has gone too far and blinded historians to the critical restraints he put on retaliation and other destructive policies and impulses. There were many notable exceptions, and the administration's refusal to embrace retaliation eagerly may have put African American soldiers and their officers at higher risk than others. Even so, we know that Senator Sumner's correspondent, Captain Maxwell of the Thirtieth United States Colored Infantry, opposed retaliation. And we know as well that the relative absence of atrocity from the Civil War remains to this day one of its most remarkable qualities. It is simply wrong to think that the war's destructiveness is what calls out to us for historical explanation and eager description. The opposite needs explanation and emphasis: the remarkable restraint of the people and the president who had organized and mobilized such vastly powerful and potentially destructive armies. War was all too well known in America, but terror remained a stranger to the country's shores.

# CONCLUSION

## The Cult of Violence in Civil War History

HATRED HAD its uses in public expression during the Civil War. Expressions of its opposite had none. That simple point goes a long way toward explaining what President Lincoln could say in public and what he could not. It explains the paucity of formal public statements of the restraints expected to be observed by soldiers in the field—from the president as commander-in-chief or from other responsible figures. It also helps explain the erroneous impression of the nature of the Civil War that now dominates the field. Extreme expressions embodying extravagant threats of violence ruled political debate, much military correspondence, and the journalism of the Civil War era. Their prevalence in the era has captured the imaginations of modern historians such as Charles Royster:

> In December 1860, while the southernmost states moved toward secession, Senator Benjamin F. Wade of Ohio was already talking about *"Making the south a desert."* Vehement public reactions to the fall of Fort Sumter and to the Federal defeat at Bull Run included visions of mayhem equal to anything the Federal army later enacted. Speaking in Philadelphia, Judge Levi Hubbell, a Democrat from Milwaukee, said in April 1861 that, if the war continued, the north must "restore New Or-

leans to its native marshes, then march across the country, burn Mont-gomery to ashes, and serve Charleston in the same way . . . We must starve, drown, burn, shoot the traitors." After the battle of Bull Run it was easy to see, Wendell Phillips said, that "General Scott might have burned over Virginia months ago, and left no weeds to conceal the masked batteries of Manassas."[1]

In fact the 1861 visions of mayhem *exceeded* "anything the Federal army later enacted," and therein lies the real tale of the Civil War. In recent times historians have too often taken the generals and politi-cians at their word. Their words were often fiercely expressed. But those words were shaped to ends short of universal truth. They were aimed at military victory.

The words might be seen as sincere barometers of the intensity of national feeling, but they cannot be interpreted as marching or-ders and policy papers. They were at most threats. More commonly, they were emotional, patriotic outbursts—truly sound and fury, sig-nifying nothing. We have to look at behavior rather than language to understand the nature of the Civil War.

That nature would seem obvious to anyone browsing the Civil War shelves at the local bookstore or public library. The recent titles of books written by academic professionals make the point: Royster's book, *The Destructive War: William T. Sherman, Stonewall Jackson, and the Americans* (1991), Mark Grimsley's *The Hard Hand of War: Union Military Policy toward Southern Civilians, 1861–1865* (1995) and a recent textbook on the period by Michael Fellman, Lesley Gordon, and Daniel Sutherland, *This Terrible War: The Civil War and Its Af-termath* (2002), embody the trend over the last fifteen years: histori-ans writing on the American Civil War have emphasized its hard, ter-rible, and destructive qualities.[2]

The road to this dominant interpretation has not been straight and narrow. It began in the shadow of World War II, when writers on the Civil War tended to see in the nineteenth-century conflict the beginnings of the economic production, technological innovation, and heartless doctrines of destruction that characterized the great "total wars" of the twentieth century. A certain hard-boiled cynicism marched hand in hand with this new view of the way the Civil War was won. T. Harry Williams's landmark essay in *Why the North Won the Civil War* (1960) depicted the American Civil War and the Northern strategy of victory as breaking the mold of a formalistic, static, and relatively bloodless eighteenth-century style of warfare. Williams famously characterized the Civil War as "the first of the world's modern wars," a mantle proudly placed on the conflict by American historians for over a generation afterward.

How Williams described its modernity was crucial: the war was "a rough, no-holds-barred affair, a bloody and brutal struggle."[3] He was at pains to contrast it with eighteenth-century warfare. War in the century previous to the nineteenth "was conducted with a measure of humanity," Williams wrote, "that caused Chesterfield to say: 'War is pusillanimously carried on in this degenerate age; quarter is given; towns are taken and people spared; even in a storm, a woman can hardly hope for the benefit of a rape.'"[4] The implied scorn for humanitarianism was no more important than the style of the passage in which it was communicated, decidedly smacking of barracks-room cynicism. Williams's viewpoint shared intellectual assumptions with Arthur M. Schlesinger's seminal post–World War II essay "The Causes of the Civil War: A Note on Historical Sentimentalism," published in 1949. Schlesinger was not really concerned with the nature of the fighting itself but with the war's political causes and consequences for slavery; still, he dismissed as mere sentimentalism the view that great social changes could be wrought in history without violence. Schlesinger's attitude bred tough-mindedness.[5]

Williams touted the importance in modern warfare of capitalizing on economic production, technology, and psychology; realizing their importance brought a new "destructiveness" to warfare. Williams used the term "destructiveness" at least twice in the course of a brief and brilliant essay that brought considerations of culture and intellectual history to military history and was destined to have broad influence.[6] The term has lingered ever since, and provided the intellectual rallying point for Charles Royster's book *The Destructive War,* published thirty-one years later. Royster argued: "Historians often have traced the changing character of the Civil War, starting as a conflict restricted to armies and increasingly becoming a war against Southern civilians as well. Extensive and successful use of invasion, devastation, and terror belonged to the Federal army. The conception belonged to civilians and soldiers of both the North and the South. Americans did not invent new methods of drastic war during the Civil War so much as they made real a version of conflict many of them had talked about from the start."[7] Other developments were crucial to sustaining this overwrought rhetoric of destruction among Civil War historians, and the advent of the word "terror," which makes a noticeable appearance in the passage above, was one of them.

Another landmark in the Civil War literature, like T. Harry Williams's essay in 1960 or Arthur M. Schlesinger's in 1949, appeared in 1973, when a historian named John B. Walters published a biography of William T. Sherman entitled *Merchant of Terror: General Sherman and Total War.*[8]

All of these terms connoting destruction, as Royster noted, aimed to comprehend the inclusion of civilians as legitimate military targets in wartime. At first the ideas were generally subsumed under the rubric of "total war," and a great synthesis of modern Civil War scholarship, James M. McPherson's *Battle Cry of Freedom: The Civil War Era,* served to fix the narrative of the Civil War as a progression from a war fought between armies for limited goals to a "total war." The most favored modern narrative structure for describing the war is simple and linear: the war grew more severe until the Union won by making a policy of severity. To put it another way, the war is generally seen as a crescendo of violence accompanied by a breakdown of initial Victorian or chivalric and traditional restraints. McPherson once stated it this way: President Lincoln "sanctioned this policy of 'being terrible' on the enemy," and the North thereby gained victory in a "total war."[9]

The fundamental problem for the historian attempting to understand and describe the grand strategy of the American Civil War is that it was nowhere written down at the time. In an era without military war "colleges" and a peacetime general staff, there were no contingency plans or white papers laying out strategic doctrine. There were only ad hoc responses to pressing military problems of war as it raged. As McPherson says of Confederate strategy in the war, "No one ever defined this strategy in a systematic, comprehensive fashion. Rather, it emerged from a series of major campaigns."[10] The same was substantially true of Union strategy. No one ever defined it in systematic language. Historians must discover Civil War grand strategy from events and from fugitive comments of generals and politicians in scattered letters, orders, and speeches. It is all too easy to overlook the context of the remarks, and the events themselves are notoriously open to multiple interpretations.

In other words, we simply do not know what the grand strategies of the Civil War were. We must infer them from events and from passing remarks left us here and there in the military and political record, official and unofficial. The absence of clear evidence on so important a point is obviously one of the major factors fueling the continuing controversy over the military history of the war. And it is important to maintain a humble attitude and realize that the policies are not clear and never will be. We should remain open to alternative viewpoints and not be committed to a single narrative.

To confuse matters still more, the events focused on in writing on the Civil War have broadened considerably. In the decades following the appearance of *Merchant of Terror*, the idea of destructiveness in the Civil War was transformed and given new and throbbing life. Obeying the impulse to transform military history and to give it a transfusion, historians took inspiration from John Keegan's brilliant book *The Face of Battle* (1976) and began to write military history more from the point of view of the common soldier in his trench than from that of the general in his headquarters.[11] The effect was naturally bloody, like touring a slaughterhouse rather than having a steak in the dining room of a meatpacking executive. But the war remained the same.

To the degree that such a viewpoint corrected the abstractly antiseptic military history written from the standpoint of the headquarters, it provided a valuable corrective. But where was military history to go from there?

One of the first and most innovative of these works of the New Military History, Gerald F. Linderman's *Embattled Courage: The Experience of Combat in the American Civil War* (1987), pointed the way to the future. A chapter near the conclusion, entitled "A Warfare of Terror," began with this sentence: "By 1864 the Civil War had expanded beyond the battlefield to encompass a warfare of terror directed primarily against the civilian population of the Confederacy."[12] Linderman himself did not examine the "warfare of terror" because he chose to exclude from his study "border state irregulars." But he did thus point the way to the next crucial development: the magnification of the importance of guerrilla warfare in the American Civil War.

At first, interest in the guerrilla fighting in the American Civil War was prompted by interest in the Vietnam War. No two Civil War books labor more in the atmosphere induced by the Vietnam War than Phillip S. Paludan's *Victims: A True Story of the Civil War* (1981) and Michael Fellman's *Inside War: The Guerrilla Conflict in Missouri during the American Civil War* (1989). Paludan derived important psychological insights into the Shelton Laurel Massacre in North Carolina in 1863 from writings on the Vietnam War.[13] Fellman drew gloomy conclusions from pioneering archival research. Missourians, as depicted in his book, were essentially average Americans, who, in the course of guerrilla warfare, became hardened killers and lovers of warfare as "blood sport." Fellman's book proved influential in at least two ways. First, he restored Missouri to the map of Civil War military history. Second, as the historian Edward Ayers noted at the time of its publication, he brought "the Civil War home front to life in a way no other book" had.[14]

The second point was far more important than the first. The concerns of the Vietnam War era faded, but the zeal for studying the guerrilla conflict in the Civil War persisted. And Ayres had hit upon the reason when he mentioned the "home front." What drove further studies toward the subject of guerrilla conflict in the Civil War was essentially a methodological imperative: the interests and methods of the New Social History. That great historical movement, which for the first time brought the common people and the whole pluralist community into the pages of academic history books, and conversely began to crowd the generals and politicians out of them, could continue to explore the Civil War if it focused on guerrilla conflict. Guerrilla warfare had the essential quality needed for social history: it involved whole communities, not soldiers alone, but men, women, children, slaves, and yeomen.

The growth of interest in guerrilla warfare in the Civil War proved critical for the health and well-being of the study of the Civil War itself, and, unconsciously, for the perpetuation of the old antisentimental view of the Civil War, concocted in the aftermath of World War II. So great a number of these studies accrued in a little over a decade that by the year 2000 the journal *Civil War History* published a long bibliographical article summing up the stunning reversal of historiographical fortune. The article was entitled "Sideshow No Longer." In addition to moving the guerrilla conflict to center stage in Civil War history the article also reflected the new vitality breathed into the old vocabulary of violence first made popular by the military historian T. Harry Williams. The language employed to characterize the recent works on guerrilla warfare in the Civil War was more sensitive to gender than Williams had been forty years earlier, but the modern historiographical article invoked a similar vocabulary of swaggering toughness: "hard-hitting," "brutality," "war is an ugly business," "grimly realistic," "raw, unregulated, no-holds-barred," "exposed the horrific guts of war," and "all of its darkest recesses fully exposed."[15] These are now terms of highest praise in evaluations of Civil War scholarship.

⟶⟹◉ ◈⟸⟵

The increasing importance of Missouri in writing on the Civil War played a role as well. The idea that the experience of war in Missouri hardened Union policy is now commonplace. James McPherson, for example, argued in 1992 that generals who later became famous for devising "total war" often had served in the Missouri theater early in their careers—U. S. Grant was a conspicuous example. "Events in that state," McPherson argued, "set the pace for the transformation from a limited to a total war, radiating outward and southward from Missouri." Indeed, Missouri has at times all but become the tail wagging the dog of Civil War military history. "Most of the Union commanders who subsequently became famous as practitioners of total war," McPherson added, "spent part of their early Civil War careers in Missouri—including Grant, Sherman, and Sheridan. This was more than coincidence."[16]

In fact, the effect of the guerrilla conflict in Missouri on overall Union policy and strategy is not so obvious. It had no discernible effect on generals in Missouri who fought regular Confederate armies at the same time, as in Price's Raid. Such men simply fought different enemies in different ways. The most obvious direct effect of the guerrilla war in Missouri had nothing to do with hardening policies and breaking down old-fashioned rules restraining violence in war. On the contrary, the principal direct effect of the Missouri experience was to cause the Northern high command to commission, codify, and publish rules to limit the destructiveness of war. The most important effect on overall policy was the creation of the first code of the laws of war in American history, Francis Lieber's famous General Orders No. 100.

These rules had their origins in reaction to the guerrilla violence of Civil War Missouri. General Henry W. Halleck, himself the author of a prewar volume on the laws of war, first asked Professor Lieber to draft a code of laws that would govern the novel situations Halleck had encountered in Missouri when he followed Frémont in command there. Lieber responded with a little pamphlet called *Guerrilla Parties Considered with Reference to the Laws and Usages of War*, first published in New York in 1862. General Orders No. 100 grew out of the original Missouri-inspired project the next year and was essentially an expanded version.[17]

The code consisted of 157 rules meant to govern and restrain the behavior of Union soldiers in the field. According to rule 72, for example, Union soldiers were not to steal the watches and jewelry of prisoners of war, the prisoners' private property. According to rule 35, works of art and scientific instruments were to be secured from all avoidable injury. The most important rules for comprehending the Civil War generation's own understanding of warfare were two that dealt with destructiveness directly. Rule 44 stated forthrightly: "All wanton violence committed against persons in the invaded country, all destruction of property not commanded by the authorized officer, all robbery, all pillage or sacking, even after taking a place by main force, all rape, wounding, maiming, or killing of such inhabitants, are prohibited under the penalty of death, or such other severe punishment as may seem adequate for the gravity of the offense." The philosophy underlying these prohibitions was laid out in rule 68: "Modern wars are not internecine wars, in which the killing of the enemy is the object. The destruction of the enemy in modern war, and, indeed, modern war itself, are means to obtain that object of the belligerent which lies beyond the war."[18] Put simply, for the Civil War generation as opposed to historians today, "modern" did not mean "destructive" in discussions of war.

To the degree that the experience in Missouri had direct effect on Civil War military doctrine, it was to codify and define and restrain. Missouri does not provide the missing link between new experiences of bloody conflict in guerrilla war and an overall hardened attitude toward civilians in war. In fact, the effect of guerrilla warfare in Missouri has been greatly exaggerated. It had little effect either way. Men at arms in America had always been prepared psychologically and philosophically to fight guerrillas with fewer self-imposed restraints than they felt in fighting the regular armies of "civilized belligerents."

→⊨◎ ◎⊨←

Throughout this book I have made a plea not only to understand the Civil War era as the people of that era did but also to search for behavioral standards of proof. We have seen already how imperfectly that era's understanding of destruction meshes with that of the twentieth and twenty-first centuries. Yet it may appear that those who would stress the war's violence and destructiveness have an ace in the hole when it comes to statistical evidence: the oft-repeated statement that the Civil War was America's bloodiest war.

The calculation that the Civil War constituted America's bloodiest war has played an important role in the modern transformation of the image of that conflict into a forerunner of terror and unrestrained violence. This claim to bloodiness now constitutes the standard introduction to the subject of the American Civil War.

The hand-me-down quality and imprecision of the casualty figures are seldom noticed. The statistical calculations underlying the modern assertions of the bloodiness of the Civil War are not themselves modern. In fact they are over a century old and have not been reevaluated in generations. They began with Frederick Phisterer, *Statistical Record of the Armies of the United States,* published in 1889 as a companion volume to Scribner's landmark Campaigns of the Civil War series. Phisterer dealt only with Union losses. William F. Fox followed in 1889 with *Regimental Losses in the American Civil War,* which aimed at definitive figures for deaths on both sides. Unlike Phisterer, Fox left us good clues as to the nature of his enterprise in compiling the statistics. He computed them by regiment. For him, the value of the figures lay in comparing the records of the regiments of the war. We can imagine the uses of the book in the veterans' organizations that thrived in the 1880s; old soldiers could point to its figures as proofs of the dangers they had survived. That was of real interest to Fox, apparently, for he wrote, by way of explanation: "To properly understand the relative importance of the various movements on a battlefield, the student must know the loss of life at the different points of the line. He will then see where the points of contact really were; where the pressure was greatest; where the scenes of valor and heroism occurred. There is no better way of doing this than by noting the place in the line held by the various regiments and ascertaining the loss of life in each."[19] Fox's enterprise was essentially to use the percentage of casualties as proof of valor, to valorize valor, and to validate old soldiers' claims to glory.

Thomas L. Livermore, who compiled the *Numbers and Losses in the Civil War in America, 1861–1865,* published in 1900, was skeptical of Fox's interpretation of the numbers. "Taken alone," he wrote, "the loss suffered by a routed army is not a measure of courage."[20] Livermore had his own way of valorizing valor, however, which served the very important purpose of national reunification. He calculated the losses on both sides, but he refused to make invidious comparisons between Union and Confederate forces. "The foregoing comparisons," he concluded, "do not give ground on which to award the display of superior courage or satisfaction to the armies as a whole on either side. The record on both sides places the people of the United States in the first rank of militant nations."[21] Naturally, these statistical historians did not escape the assumptions of their age about warfare. Someone might have compiled the appalling statistics of the Civil War in order to criticize war itself, but neither Fox nor Livermore did that, and indeed no one ever has. Instead, writing as the nineteenth century turned into the twentieth, the pioneering statistical historians of the Civil War affirmed the high value placed on "militant nations" in that age of imperialism and militarism.

More recently, the historian Drew Gilpin Faust, without recomputing any figures, has sought to explore the possible biases in them and to stress the importance of the computation for the people who lived through the war. The impulse, she suggests, came too late ever to sustain a reliable figure. The figures are all products of "postwar reconstruction," and the requirements for accurate recording of casualties were neither consistent nor stringent during the war itself. Even the figures available, as Faust points out, suffered from underlying biases, which she is at pains to point out. On the one hand, generals such as Robert E. Lee sought to minimize the casualties re-ported so that the enemy would overestimate Confederate strength. On the other, the prevailing attitudes toward courage probably led to maximizing casualty figures as an index of "valor" and, later, "sacri-fice."[22]

Faust is right to observe that, despite obvious reasons for inac-curacy, the "commonly accepted" total for deaths on both sides, 620,000, has become "iconic."[23] But icons are one thing and history quite another. Her searching analysis, published in 2002, serves most importantly to show how old and how little analyzed are figures so important to the modern understanding of the Civil War. To under-take the reconstruction of the basic calculations lies well beyond the scope of this book. But as the purpose of this book is not to define the Civil War but to provoke reconsideration of it, we can add to our "to-do" list a future sophisticated statistical assessment of the tradi-tional figures given for losses in the Civil War. For now, though, even taking them at face value, but realizing that they are only icons and not bedrock statistics, we can certainly begin to reassess their sig-nificance.

It seems unlikely that historians of the Civil War today are gov-erned by the same assumptions about war that drove Fox and Liver-more, but the statistics of bloodiness do serve purposes. They serve Civil War historians themselves, for example. The emphasis on un-equaled bloodiness has become a way for those of us who write on the war to impress our readers with the importance of our subject. The number of men killed, usually put at around 620,000, exceeded the number of American soldiers killed in all our other wars put to-gether, through World War I, World War II, Korea, and Vietnam. It is a horrifyingly impressive figure, but it is useful to remember the hid-den assumption that lies behind the eagerness to accept it as defining the nature of the conflict.

Oddly enough, another use often stems from strangely sentimental impulses disturbingly reminiscent of the purposes that drove Fox
and Livermore to the statistical records in the archives. Bloodiness
has abetted the idea of the importance of courage and dedication to
public causes in the individual Civil War soldier. It is important, also,
for demonstrating objectivity; it has the further advantage of not
making invidious distinction between the Union and Confederate
causes. Authors who emphasize the destructiveness of the war are
not likely these days to be labeled for their obvious bias toward either
North or South.

Altogether, the result has been to sensationalize Civil War history.
Emphasis on the relative bloodiness of the war has not served the
ends of analysis or statistical sophistication. The statistics are substantially unimproved from Livermore's era, more than a century
ago. More important, the usual number, 620,000 American dead,
lumps the dead from both sides together and calls them all "Americans," and this unique feature of reporting Civil War death statistics has gone without notice. Such a mixing of opponents is rarely
done in studying other American wars. It is not customary even
in other kinds of wars that pitted Americans against Americans, such
as the Plains Indian wars discussed in Chapter 5 of this book. If we
consider the Civil War casualties one "country" at a time, then the
360,000 Union dead do not equal even the 407,000 Americans killed
in World War II. The 260,000 Confederate dead constitute but 64
percent of the 407,000 Americans killed in World War II.[24]

The point is not to belittle the losses in the Civil War but to remind us to think hard about their meaning for the author using
them. If the casualty figures are meant as a measure of tragedy, then
they certainly are tragic. *But if they are meant as a measure of the intensity of fighting, destructiveness, mercilessness, and hardness, then to
combine the two is unfairly to have doubled the intensity, destructive-*

*ness, mercilessness, and hardness at the expense of American soldiers*
*who fought in other wars where such a combination of figures from both*
*sides is not possible.*

This problem is not one of chronology. It is not a problem of
sources or archives. It is not really a problem of historical interpretation. It is a simple statistical fallacy. No one would compare casualties
in wars by adding together the casualties incurred on both sides in
one war and then compare that figure to the casualties incurred on
one side in another war with any expectation of a meaningful result.
The assertion of the magnitude of bloodiness, then, rests on a simple
fallacy that ought to be discarded forever.

Other factors, weakly considered heretofore if at all, further com-
plicate the assertion of bloodiness as a function of numbers of deaths
reported. The 620,000 figure commonly used is an absolute number,
of course, and not validly interpreted without considering the population base from which the casualties came. Adjusted for population,
the death rate for the Civil War seems even more shockingly high.
Phillip S. Paludan reminded readers of the rate in his 1988 book on
the North in the Civil War by pointing out, "Had World War II produced the same proportion of casualties as did the Civil War, over 2.5
million men would have died."[25] By 2006 Drew Gilpin Faust could go
even further, saying that "an equivalent proportion of today's population would mean 5,500,000 dead."[26] That escalation of numbers
typifies the tendency of interpretation heretofore: ever upward toward sensationalizing results.

But the death rate also is no more a comparable figure than the absolute numbers. We need to know from what causes the soldiers
died. And we should remember that the Civil War deaths counted
those killed on both sides. In World War II the Americans would not
have been killing each other. And not all of those hypothetical American soldiers would have died in World War II because the causes of

death changed between the centuries. The most important defining fact of Civil War mortality was that the war was fought before the discovery of the germ theory of disease. That meant that a majority of those who died did not die from wounds inflicted by the enemy. They died of disease. The ratio was above two to one: more than twice as many Civil War soldiers died from disease as from enemy action. A modern source puts the figures for deaths from disease at 225,000 for the Union and 194,000 for the Confederacy.[27]

If we adjust the comparisons accordingly, the figures for deaths in the Civil War as a result of combat change dramatically: roughly 201,000, not 620,000. And to break that figure down into Union and Confederate dead proportionately would render the figures thus: 135,000 for the North and 66,000 for the South. In absolute numbers then, the North suffered deaths equal to about two and one half times the number of Americans killed in Vietnam, and the South experienced well below one and a half times the deaths of American soldiers in Vietnam. Neither figure begins to approach in magnitude the American casualties suffered in World War II.

Again, the point is not to belittle the losses incurred in the Civil War but to reveal that they were not magnitudes greater than the losses in any other conflict in which Americans fought. The point, put another way, is to show that the claims of "bloodiest" conflict can be qualified so as not to make the Civil War exist in some unfathomably violent category by itself.

That the Civil War was America's bloodiest war is probably still true, whatever distortions the figures have undergone in years of excited exploitation rather than close analysis of their meaning. But why apply only an American standard? In this book I have championed from the very first chapter an international approach to understanding the American Civil War. On the subject of numbers and losses, such an approach proves to be eye-opening. The French expedition to Mexico does not provide a useful comparison in this case, for total French forces in that under-strength operation never exceeded 35,553, the size of a modest army in one theater of the American Civil War.[28] But if we turn to the European war immediately preceding the American Civil War for comparison, the casualty figures are indeed instructive. Historians of the Crimean War of 1853–1856 put the death toll from that conflict at 640,000. In fact, the major European powers did not become fully engaged in combat in the Crimea until March 1854, and they signed the peace treaty ending the war on March 30, 1856. It would be fair to say that the Crimean War generated as many soldiers' deaths as the American Civil War did in about half the time, only two years, and the two wars were fought under the assumptions of roughly the same state of medical knowledge.[29]

In other words, it might be argued that the true significance of the Civil War casualty figures is quite the opposite of what has been asserted routinely about them in the past. In a strange way, they are a sign of how lucky America has been in its history. The country's bloodiest war pales in comparison to European and other wars fought elsewhere in the world.

And that is spectacularly true if we make the comparison with twentieth-century wars. The historian Niall Ferguson has at last alerted us that "the hundred years after 1900 were without question the bloodiest century in history, far more violent in relative as well as absolute terms than any previous era."[30] It is possible that one out of every twenty-two deaths in the century was caused by killing, he says. And the appalling figures, in the tens of millions, are more concentrated in particular places and times.[31] By comparison with the rest of the world at the same time or with the modern world, the Civil War cannot be singled out for bloodiness. In fact, Ferguson, in his

700 page book on increasing violence in warfare, never discusses the American Civil War.[32]

It is not the fault of the historians of the American Civil War that the meaning of the casualty figures remains uncertain. The systematic academic study of numbers and losses in war is in its infancy. The standard work on the general question remains J. David Singer and Melvin Small, *The Wages of War, 1816–1965: A Statistical Handbook,* published over thirty years ago. And that work excludes civil wars from its complicated comparative tables.[33] The general subject is ripe for serious reconsideration.

Approaching the more modest task of rethinking the significance of the death rate in the Civil War should at least make historians recognize the urge to exaggeration rather than to analysis with which we have embraced the statistics of numbers and losses. At this point, the assertion that it was the "bloodiest" war in American history no longer serves the end of valorizing valor for the sake of reuniting the nation or to prove America's worthy place among "militant nations" in the world. Originally, an emphasis on destructiveness, which was a part of the idea that the Civil War was a "total war," led to the broad consideration of economic, technological, and psychological aspects of the war, but that is no longer the case. Destructiveness, shorn of the greater overarching concept of "total war," now leads nowhere. Civil War historians writing in the academy have not really needed to do battle against sentimentalism since Schlesinger exposed it as a problem in writing on the war before the 1950s. Repeated assertion of the destructive nature of the Civil War may, in fact, serve only to remind readers of the provincial nature of American history-writing, since the world perspective from the Crimea to the end of the twentieth century would call into question the magnitude of the losses. The regular assertion of the death rate in the Civil War serves no end whatever. We are left with an empty cult of violence in writing abut the Civil War.

⤙⟶⟴ ⟴⟵⤙

If historians search the Civil War for something other than violence to describe, they will find it. As a concluding example, take the case of Missouri, once again, in 1865. Under the assumptions of modern interpretation, this would mean seeing the Civil War at the worst place and time. Missouri embodied the rule-less guerrilla conflict, and by 1865 attitudes had surely grown as hardened as possible in that war. By that late date President Lincoln had been wearied with reports of ceaseless internecine conflict in Missouri. Did the experiences in Missouri harden Lincoln's attitudes? Did the experiences in Missouri lead Lincoln to embrace some new and merciless approach to war in that state?

The president pressed the lessons of the civil war in Missouri on the newly elected governor of the state, Thomas C. Fletcher, in a long letter written on February 20, 1865:

> It seems there is now no organized force of the enemy in Missouri and yet that destruction of property and life is rampant every where. Is not the cure for this within easy reach of the people themselves? It cannot but be that every man, not naturally a robber or cut-throat, would gladly put an end to this state of things. A large majority in every locality must feel alike upon this subject; and if so they only need to reach an understanding one with another. Each leaving all others alone solves the problem. And surely each would do this but for his apprehension that others will not leave him alone. Can not this mischievous distrust be removed? Let neighborhood meetings be every where called and held, of all entertaining a sincere purpose for mutual security in the future, whatever they may heretofore have thought, said or done about the war or about anything else. Let all such meet and waiving all else pledge each to cease harassing others and to make common cause against whomever persists in making, aiding or encouraging fur-

ther disturbance. The practical means they will best know how to adopt and apply. At such meetings old friendships will cross the memory; and honor and Christian Charity will come in to help.

Please consider whether it may not be well to suggest this to the now afflicted people of Missouri.[34]

Historians have found it difficult in modern times—in the face of the ferocious language most commonly used to describe warfare in the Civil War—to take Lincoln's letter seriously. Michael Fellman commented after describing the contents of the letter, "The war was nearly over and Lincoln was tired." He was bereft of policy solutions, Fellman implies; all he could do was to urge "good men to come to their senses."[35]

On the contrary, President Lincoln was about to embark on his second term in office. He was obviously developing a consistent policy for the future. What he told Governor Fletcher about Christian charity and honor was of a piece with what he would say two weeks later about "malice toward none and charity for all" in his Second Inaugural Address. Lincoln was by no means throwing up his hands in despair at the continuing "destruction of property and life" in a state that ought to be at peace. He was putting together a policy to bring about peace despite the recalcitrant force in the government in Missouri.

In short, Lincoln expected Governor Fletcher to call those local meetings. Fletcher did not, so Lincoln sent him a prodding letter a week later: "Have you received my letter of the 20th? I think some such thing as therein suggested, is needed. If you put it before the people, I will direct the Military to cooperate. Please answer."[36] Fletcher was in no mood to take the advice. He said that he thought it impractical. He telegraphed an answer immediately after receiving the second message, saying he would "try the policy" but that he had "utter want of confidence in its success" and that he would be pre-

paring at the same time "for the only other policy" in the case of failure. He asked Lincoln not to say anything to the military authorities
until he heard from him again. Fletcher issued a vague proclamation
inviting Missourians to submit to the civil law on March 7, but his
sincere views, expressed in a long letter to Lincoln, left little room for
any means of governing but martial law. "It would but madden the
true men of this State," he said, "to talk to them of reliance on the
'honor' and 'christian charity' of these fiends in human shape."[37]

Lincoln proved to be as determined in his pursuit of honor and
charity as he is said to have been in his pursuit of military victory. He
decided to change Missouri from the outside if the foot-dragging
politicians inside would not do it themselves. He wasted no more
words on Fletcher. Instead, he directed the military authorities to
change policy in the state. He had already appointed General John
Pope as a new department commander, and Pope's mission now was
to see to it that the job got done.

⋯⟫ ⟪⋯

The experience of Missouri in the Civil War included much that was
hard, merciless, terrible, and destructive, and there were those like
Thomas C. Fletcher bent on instrumenting cruel practices to the bitter end. And so it was in some other places and times during the war.
But there were powerful countervailing forces, in the White House,
in the army, and in the culture generally, which tend to be ignored in
the modern cult of violence in writing on the Civil War. The image
of the conflict we are now being offered is distorted at best. Historians have been grappling realistically with the blood shed in the
great conflict for more than half a century now, at least. Doing battle
with sentimentalism constitutes beating a dead horse.

It is not clear what purpose the cult of violence in writing about
the Civil War now serves. It cannot possibly be true that we are now
at risk of underestimating the destructiveness of that war. Instead,

we consistently underestimate many other important features of the conflict because of the fixation on violence.

But I make no plea for the return of sentimentalism to the study of the Civil War—far from it. Honor and Christian charity had their place, all right, but it was a place reserved in that era mostly for white and "civilized" belligerents. International law had its place too, but racial assumptions underlay it as well. "In modern regular wars of the Europeans and their descendants in other parts of the globe," wrote Francis Lieber in his laws of war, "protection of the inoffensive citizen of the hostile country is the rule, privation and disturbance of private relations are the exceptions." He added, "Protection was, and still is with uncivilized people, the exception."[38] The central restraining force on the destructive abilities of Civil War soldiers was their visceral perceptions of racial identity. Surely our age can see nothing of sentimentality in that.

# Notes

## Introduction

1. Credit for recognizing the delicious appropriateness of this retribution on the South Carolina secessionists goes to the *New York Herald,* August 28, 1863. The standard work on the siege of Charleston, Stephen R. Wise's *Gate of Hell: Campaign for Charleston Harbor, 1863* (Columbia, S.C.: University of South Carolina Press, 1994), 148, 170, does not find much drama in the use of these incendiary shells.

2. Robert V. Bruce, *Lincoln and the Tools of War,* orig. pub. 1956 (Urbana: University of Illinois Press, 1989), 179–182. Short was from Buffalo, New York. Wise says that Gillmore had two kinds of shells with Greek Fire in them, one kind designed by Short, the other by Robert Parrott.

3. David Herbert Donald, Jean H. Baker, and Michael F. Holt, *The Civil War and Reconstruction* (New York: W. W. Norton, 2001), 736.

4. These are terms used to define "brutal" in *Webster's Ninth New Collegiate Dictionary* (Springfield, Mass.: Merriam-Webster, 1985), 183.

5. See Roger L. Ransom and Richard Sutch, *One Kind of Freedom: The Economic Consequences of Emancipation,* 2nd ed. (Cambridge: Cambridge University Press, 2001), esp. chap. 3, "The Myth of the Prostrate South," where they argue that the physical destruction wrought in the region by the war has been exaggerated in historical accounts and was quickly repaired. What set the Southern economy back after the war was the withdrawal of slave labor. The point of the second edition of this landmark

study of the Southern post–Civil War economy, first published in 1977, was to show how well their assertions had stood the test of time. Apparently no one challenged their claim that the "Prostrate South" was a "Myth" (see p. xix). Their sample counties did not include the Shenandoah Valley of Virginia, but they did study Georgia and South Carolina, areas crossed by William T. Sherman (see pp. 280, 317).

## 1. The Mexican-American War

1. Obviously this chapter owes a great debt to the new literature on the Mexican-American War, in particular to the fresh and bracing insights of Paul Foos, *A Short, Offhand, Killing Affair: Soldiers and Social Conflict in the Mexican-American War* (Chapel Hill: University of North Carolina Press, 2002), and to James M. McCaffrey, *Army of Manifest Destiny: The American Soldier in the Mexican War, 1846–1848* (New York: New York University Press, 1992), and Richard Bruce Winders, *Mr. Polk's Army: The American Military Experience in the Mexican War* (College Station: Texas A&M University Press, 1997). See also Alfred Hoyt Bill, *Rehearsal for Conflict: The War with Mexico, 1846–1848* (New York: Knopf, 1947).

2. See, for example, Foos, *A Short, Offhand, Killing Affair,* 113: "The propaganda surrounding the war effort was nakedly opportunistic and expressly promised plunder as the right of the volunteer." Foos locates the aggressive appeal at the level of the common soldier. At a level of government and official ideologies, see Thomas R. Hietala, *Manifest Destiny: Anxious Aggrandizement in Late Jacksonian America* (Ithaca: Cornell University Press, 1985).

3. Charles Winslow Elliott, *Winfield Scott: The Soldier and the Man* (New York: Macmillan, 1937), 448.

4. Joseph E. Chance traced the origin of the quotation from undated newspaper clippings kept by Curtis. See Chance, ed., *Mexico under Fire: Being the Diary of Samuel Ryan Curtis, 3rd Ohio Regiment, during the American Military Occupation of Northern Mexico, 1846–1847* (Fort Worth: Texas Christian University Press, 1994), xiv–xv. I first encountered the alleged Taylor quotation in Foos, *A Short, Offhand, Killing Affair,* 123. Foos makes the most critical case against the behavior of American soldiers in Mexico. Taylor's biographer, Holman Hamilton, apparently did not know about the issue.

5. *Memoirs of Lieut. General Scott . . . Written by Himself,* 2 vols., orig. pub. 1864 (Freeport, N.Y.: Books for Libraries Press, 1970), 2:393, 541; see also Foos, *A Short, Offhand, Killing Affair.*

6. Samuel E. Chamberlain, *My Confession* (New York: Harper & Brothers, 1956), 30. I first encountered the description of the officers' elections in Foos, *A Short, Offhand, Killing Affair,* 50.

7. Chance, ed., *Mexico under Fire,* 25.

8. Ibid., xvii, xii.

9. Ibid., 24.

10. George B. McClellan to his mother, November 14, 1846, quoted in William Starr Myers, ed., *The Mexican War Diary of George B. McClellan* (Princeton: Princeton University Press, 1917), 18n.

11. Ibid., 11–12, 69.

12. Letter of July 9, 1846, quoted in ibid., 18n.

13. Quoted in Holman Hamilton, *Zachary Taylor: Soldier of the Republic* (Indianapolis: Bobbs-Merrill, 1941), 201.

14. Ibid.

15. Hamilton, *Zachary Taylor,* 201; Chance, ed., *Mexico under Fire,* 92, 104, 140.

16. Allan Peskin, ed., *Volunteers: The Mexican War Journals of Private Richard Coulter and Sergeant Thomas Barclay, Company E, Second Pennsylvania Infantry* (Kent: Kent State University Press, 1991), 110.

17. Ibid., 180–182.

18. D. E. Livingston-Little, ed., *The Mexican War Diary of Thomas D. Tennery* (Norman: University of Oklahoma Press, 1970), 37–38, 76.

19. Mark L. Gardner and Marc Simmons, eds., *The Mexican War Correspondence of Richard Smith Elliott* (Norman: University of Oklahoma Press, 1997), 61, 190, 260n.

20. Myers, ed., *Mexican War Diary of George B. McClellan,* 91.

21. Foos, *A Short, Offhand, Killing Affair,* 92.

22. Peskin, ed., *Volunteers,* 97–98.

23. *American Poetry: The Nineteenth Century: Volume One: Freneau to Whitman* (New York: Library of America, 1993), 759–760.

24. H. K. Brands, *Lone Star Nation: The Epic Story of the Battle for Texas Independence* (New York: Random House, 2004), 393–407.

25. Peskin, ed., *Volunteers,* 113–114.

26. Neither do two of the newer books, those by Paul Foos and Richard

Winders. James McCaffrey gives the Mier influence serious treatment but overlooks the problems of constructed national identity in the memory of the episode: see *Army of Manifest Destiny,* 33–34.

27. Joseph E. Chance, ed., *The Mexican War Journal of Captain Franklin Smith* (Jackson: University Press of Mississippi, 1991), 115.

28. Nathaniel Cheairs Hughes, Jr., and Timothy D. Johnson, eds., *A Fighter from Way Back: The Mexican War Diary of Lt. Daniel Harvey Hill, 4th Artillery, USA* (Kent: Kent State University Press, 2002), 10.

29. Quoted in John S. D. Eisenhower, *So Far from God: The U.S. War with Mexico, 1846–1848* (New York: Random House, 1989), 87.

30. Chance, ed., *The Mexican War Journal of Captain Franklin Smith,* 236–237n.

31. Ibid., 200, 251n.

32. Eisenhower, *So Far from God,* 145–151.

33. Norman F. Tutorow characterizes Chamberlain's memoir as a "valuable work" in his standard bibliography. See Tutorow, ed., *The Mexican-American War: An Annotated Bibliography* (Westport, Conn.: Greenwood Press, 1981), 270. *My Confession,* which contains watercolor illustrations by Chamberlain as well as text, includes a description and an illustration of the scalping of Mexican citizens by Arkansas volunteers (p. 88). The scalping is not corroborated by any other source.

34. James M. McPherson, *For Cause and Comrades: Why Men Fought in the Civil War* (New York: Oxford University Press, 1997), 10.

35. Eric Foner vividly reconstructed the Republican critique of the Southern economy in *Free Soil, Free Labor, Free Men: The Ideology of the Republican Party before the Civil War* (New York: Oxford University Press, 1970).

36. The image of Mexico as an El Dorado will be explored in Chapter 3.

37. McCaffrey, *Army of Manifest Destiny,* 210. He compares the two wars in terms of race on pp. 137–138.

38. See Winders, *Mr. Polk's Army,* 62: "Ballentine and others mused that resentment over severe punishment might have motivated many a soldier's desertion."

39. McPherson, *For Cause and Comrades,* 47.

40. McCaffrey, *Army of Manifest Destiny,* 111–112, lists this as the third of four reasons but it should surely rank first.

41. John D. Billings, *Hardtack and Coffee: The Unwritten Story of Army Life,* orig. pub. 1887 (Lincoln: University of Nebraska Press, 1993), 161; see also p. 157.

42. *New York Evening Post,* September 20 and July 25, 1861.

43. Bell I. Wiley, *The Life of Billy Yank: The Common Soldier of the Union,* orig. pub. 1952 (New York: Charter Books, 1962), 203–204, 209–210.

44. Billings, *Hardtack and Coffee,* 146. An illustration depicting two men riding the horse appears on p. 150.

45. Harry S. Stout, *Upon the Altar of the Nation: A Moral History of the Civil War* (New York: Viking, 2006), esp. xvii.

46. Richard Shelly Hartigan, *Lieber's Code and the Law of War* (Chicago: Precedent, 1983), 1–2.

47. Oddly, Harry S. Stout is contemptuous of Lieber's code in *Upon the Altar of the Nation,* 192–193, 325.

48. See Gregory J. W. Urwin, ed., *Black Flag over Dixie: Racial Atrocities and Reprisals in the Civil War* (Carbondale: Southern Illinois University Press, 2004).

49. Mark Grimsley, "'A Very Long Shadow': Race, Atrocity, and the American Civil War," in Gregory J. W. Urwin, ed., *Black Flag over Dixie,* 233.

50. Gardner and Simmons, eds., *The Mexican War Correspondence of Richard Smith Elliott,* 117.

51. [Luther Giddings], *Sketches of the Campaign in Northern Mexico* (New York: George P. Putnam & Co., 1853), 228.

52. James Milgrim, "Civil War: Libby Prison Correspondence of Tattnall Paulding," *American Philatelist* 89 (December 1975), 1120.

53. Tattnall Paulding to Becca, November 14, 1863, in ibid., 1126.

54. T. Michael Parrish and Robert M. Willingham, Jr., *Confederate Imprints: A Bibliography of Southern Publications from Secession to Surrender* (Austin, Tex.: Jenkins Publishing, n.d.), 568 and facing page (item 6728).

## 2. Price's Raid

1. Michael Fellman, *Inside War: The Guerrilla Conflict in Missouri during the American Civil War* (New York: Oxford University Press, 1989); Daniel Sutherland, "Sideshow No Longer: A Historiographical Review of the Guerrilla War," *Civil War History* 46 (March 2000), 5–23.

2. *Punch,* October 24, 1863, 168–169. The cartoon is reproduced in Gary Bunker, *From Railsplitter to Icon: Lincoln's Image in Illustrated Periodicals, 1860–1865* (Kent: Kent State University Press, 2001), 224.

3. The Palmyra Massacre is not mentioned in E. B. Long, *The Civil War Day by Day: An Almanac, 1861–1865,* orig. pub. 1971 (New York: Da Capo, n.d.). Michael Fellman gives the incident brief mention in *Inside War,* 113–114. A chapter on the massacre appears in Lonnie R. Speer, *War of Vengeance: Acts of Retaliation against Civil War POWs* (Mechanicsburg, Pa.: Stackpole Books, 2002), 29–41, but it lacks reference to McNeil's correspondence in the Abraham Lincoln Papers, Library of Congress.

4. Lynda Lasswell Crist, ed., *The Papers of Jefferson Davis, Volume 8: 1861* (Baton Rouge: Louisiana State University Press, 1995), 482, 496, 524–525.

5. E. Kirby Smith to S. Cooper, June 3, 1863, *War of the Rebellion: A Compilation of the Official Records of the Union and Confederate Armies,* 128 vols. (Washington, D.C.: U.S. Government Printing Office, 1880–1901), I, 22, pt. 2, p. 852; this work is hereafter cited as *O.R.*

6. Lynda Lasswell Crist, ed., *The Papers of Jefferson Davis, Volume 10: October 1863–August 1864* (Baton Rouge: Louisiana State University Press, 1999), 104; Ezra J. Warner, *Generals in Blue: Lives of the Union Commanders,* orig. pub. 1959 (Baton Rouge: Louisiana State University Press, 1986), 511.

7. John McNeil to Samuel R. Curtis, December 12, 1862, Abraham Lincoln Papers, Library of Congress, microfilm reel 45.

8. R. E. Anderson to John B. Henderson, December 24, 1862, Abraham Lincoln Papers, Library of Congress, microfilm reel 46.

9. The Missouri petitions are at January 1, 1863, Abraham Lincoln Papers, Library of Congress, microfilm reels 46 and 47; New York State Citizens, December 12, 1862, Abraham Lincoln Papers, Library of Congress, microfilm reel 45.

10. John McNeil to Samuel R. Curtis, December 24, 1862, Abraham Lincoln Papers, Library of Congress, microfilm reel 46.

11. *O.R.,* I, 22, pt. 1, p. 292.

12. Ibid., 267; for reference to McNeil as a "murderer" see also p. 1065.

13. Ibid., 241.

14. Warner, *Generals in Blue,* 306. This biographical sketch makes no mention of the Palmyra Massacre.

15. See, for example, Lincoln's endorsement of the Missouri petitions in Roy P. Basler, ed., *Collected Works of Abraham Lincoln,* 9 vols. (New

Brunswick, N.J.: Rutgers University Press, 1953–1955), 6:531. Lincoln corresponded with Curtis at the same time about the arrest of a Confederate-sympathizing Protestant minister in St. Louis named McPheeters but did not bring up the McNeil case.

16. See McNeil's orders on assuming command of the District of Southwest Missouri, July 15, 1863, *O.R.*, I, 22, pt. 2, p. 378.

17. John McNeil to William Steele, December 9, 1863, *O.R.*, I, 22, pt. 2, p. 738.

18. *O.R.*, I, 41, pt. 1, p. 722. Figures given by the Confederate commanders vary. James McPherson puts Price's initial numbers at 12,000 in *Battle Cry of Freedom: The Civil War Era* (New York: Oxford University Press, 1988), 787. He does not mention the number who were unarmed. The best discussion of the problem of estimating troop strength in Price's army appears in Robert L. Kerby, *Kirby Smith's Confederacy: The Trans-Mississippi South, 1861–1865* (New York: Columbia University Press, 1972), 333–352. For the high figure of 4,000 unarmed men on the raid (supplemented by another 2,000 unarmed recruits later), see Christopher Phillips, "Price's Missouri Raid," entry in Richard N. Current, ed., *Encyclopedia of the Confederacy,* 4 vols. (New York: Simon & Schuster, 1993), 3:1252–1255.

19. Robert Shalhope calls the men the "dregs" of the military department, in *Sterling Price: Portrait of a Southerner* (Columbia: University of Missouri Press, 1971), 264.

20. Testimony of Major James R. Shaler, assistant adjutant-general, at the court of inquiry on Price's raid, May 2, 1865, *O.R.*, I, 41, pt. 1, p. 722.

21. Shalhope, *Sterling Price,* 263–264.

22. *O.R.*, I, 41, pt. 1, p. 722.

23. This was, of course, a matter of controversy, but see the inquiry at ibid., 722–723.

24. John N. Edwards, *Shelby and His Men, or the War in the West* (Cincinnati: Miami Printing and Publishing, 1867), published Reynolds's letter on the raid. This quotation appears on pp. 470–471.

25. Ibid., 471. See *The Columbia Encyclopedia in One Volume,* 2nd ed. (New York: Columbia University Press, 1950), 1033.

26. Price was forced to rely on Quantrill and Anderson to destroy a key railroad bridge. See *O.R.*, I, 41, pt. 1, p. 718.

27. The whole force was supposed to be mounted, as on a raid. Apparently horses could not be found for a thousand of the men at the start.

28. See Michael C. C. Adams, *Fighting for Defeat: Union Military Failure in the East, 1861–1865,* orig. pub. as *Our Masters the Rebels: A Speculation on Union Military Failure in the East, 1861–1865* in 1978 (Lincoln: University of Nebraska Press, 1992), 76–78.

29. Thomas Ewing to H. H. Williams, October 16, 1864, *O.R.,* I, 41, pt. 4, p. 9.

30. H. Hannahs to D. Q. Gale, October 16, 1864, ibid., 9.

31. See S. C. Charlot's special field order, Headquarters Army of the Border, October 20, 1864, ibid., 144.

32. William L. Shea and Earl J. Hess, *Pea Ridge: Civil War Campaign in the West* (Chapel Hill: University of North Carolina Press, 1992), 102, 323. The authors say the Indians' participation has lent the battle an "exotic" quality, but there was more significance than that in the perhaps false memory of the mounted Indian charge at the battle.

33. John W. Noble, note attached to Cyrus Bussey to Samuel R. Curtis, March 14, 1862, in *O.R.,* I, 8, p. 236.

34. T. I. McKenny to Earl Van Dorn, March 9, 1862, in *O.R.,* I, 8, p. 194.

35. Dabney H. Maury to Samuel R. Curtis, March 14, 1862, in *O.R.,* I, 8, p. 195.

36. Shea and Hess, *Pea Ridge,* 320.

37. D. H. Maury to Albert Pike, March 21, 1862, in *O.R.,* I, 8, pp. 795–796. Alvin Josephy surmises that Van Dorn was hinting "that he believed the enemy's exaggerations." See Josephy, *The Civil War in the American West,* 349.

38. Samuel R. Curtis to Benjamin F. Wade, May 21, 1862, in *O.R.,* I, 8, p. 206.

39. Samuel R. Curtis to D. H. Maury, March 21, 1862, in *O.R.,* II, 3, p. 399.

40. *O.R.,* I, 41, pt. 1, p. 722. The great political fear—of a large secret organized opposition within the state—never came true, however. See, for example, Chester Harding to H. Z. Curtis, March 25, 1863, *O.R.,* I, 22, pt. 2, p. 179.

41. *O.R.,* I, 41, pt. 1, pp. 714, 716. Albert Castel is skeptical that the Union general took civilian hostages into the fort and surmises that the civilian dead were Union refugees taken in for safety from the Confederate invaders; see *General Sterling Price and the Civil War in the West* (New York: Oxford University Press, 1989), 219.

42. *O.R.,* I, 41, pt. 1, pp. 682, 685–686.

43. Sterling Price has two able modern biographers, Robert Shalhope and Albert Castel, referred to in previous notes, but both historians were in-

terested more in strategic assessments of his military campaigns and with the history of the South than with characterizing the nature of the Civil War, which requires a rather different study of both Northern and Southern sides in the campaign. Michael Fellman, by contrast, was interested in the nature of warfare and probed the differences between the values of "honor" that drove Confederates like Price and the motivations of the guerrillas in Missouri. See *Inside War: The Guerrilla Conflict in Missouri during the American Civil War* (New York: Oxford University Press, 1989), 287n, 108–111. Fellman concluded that "an expedition meant to redeem Missouri and prove the nobility of the southern cause had instead devolved into a chaotic, large-scale enactment of the war on civilians which the guerrillas had developed."

44. *O.R.*, I, 41, pt. 1, p. 417.

45. *O.R.*, I, 41, pt. 1, p. 339.

46. Sterling Price said he was greeted by "a scene of devastation." Ibid., p. 627.

47. *O.R.*, I, 41, pt. 1, pp. 308–309. James McPherson gives the number of soldiers taken from the train and killed by Anderson at Centralia as 24, not 22; the date was actually September 27. McPherson, *Battle Cry of Freedom*, 787.

48. *O.R.*, I, 41, pt. 1, p. 317.

49. General Orders No. 100, section II, rule 45, stated that "all captures and booty belong . . . primarily to the government of the captor." Richard Shelly Hartigan, *Lieber's Code and the Law of War* (Chicago: Precedent, 1983), 54.

50. James Rainsford to W. H. Stark, October 31, 1864, *O.R.*, I, 41, pt. 4, p. 354. The orders were actually signed by Price's assistant adjutant-general, a Missourian, whose handwriting could be identified by locals.

51. One of them is illustrated in Fellman, *Inside War*, 187.

52. William S. Rosecrans to Sterling Price, October 22, 1864, *O.R.*, I, 41, pt. 4, p. 101.

53. James M. McPherson, "From Limited to Total War: Missouri and the Nation, 1862–1865," *Gateway Heritage* 12 (1992), 4–19, reprinted as "From Limited to Total War, 1861–1865," in McPherson, *Drawn with the Sword: Reflections on the American Civil War* (New York: Oxford University Press, 1996), 66–86 (quotations from p. 72).

54. *Chicago Tribune*, July 19, 1864.

55. These career sketches are based on the essential reference work by Warner, *Generals in Blue.*

56. Ibid., 127–128.

57. See, for example, G. M. Dodge to E. B. Brown, January 27, 1865, *O.R.,* I, 48, pt. 1, p. 659, and Dodge to C. T. Christensen, December 11, 1864, *O.R.,* I, 41, pt. 4, p. 829 (see also pp. 905–906 and 928–929).

58. Grenville M. Dodge, *The Battle of Atlanta and Other Campaigns, Addresses, etc.* (Council Bluffs, Iowa: Monarch Printing, 1911), 178.

59. I have left out Joseph T. Copeland, who commanded a prisoner of war camp at Alton, Illinois, and did not face combat duties.

60. Mark E. Neely, Jr., *The Fate of Liberty: Abraham Lincoln and Civil Liberties* (New York: Oxford University Press, 1991), 46–49. Rosecrans modified a later Ewing plan to "renovate" southeast Missouri by removing "the worst rebel families." See Thomas Ewing, Jr., to H. M. Hiller, October 27, 1864, *O.R.,* I, 41, pt. 4, pp. 275–276, and to Amos W. Maupin, November 8, 1864, ibid., p. 491.

61. *O.R.,* I, 41, pt. 1, pp. 59, 415; ibid., I, 48, pt. 1, p. 484. Fisk once protested that "no order for the destruction of the property or the killing of an unarmed citizen ever emanated from my headquarters."

62. General Orders No. 3, *O.R.,* I, 48, pt. 1, pp. 622–623.

63. John B. Sanborn to Sarah M. Scott, February 1, 1865, *O.R.,* I, 48, pt. 1, pp. 716–717.

64. John F. Phillips to J. F. Bennett, November 14, 1864, *O.R.,* I, 41, pt. 4, p. 562, and Phillips endorsement on D. Dale to Phillips, February 15, 1865, in *O.R.,* I, 48, pt. 1, p. 861.

65. Ibid., pp. 286–287.

66. Mark Grimsley, *The Hard Hand of War: Union Military Policy toward Southern Civilians, 1861–1865* (New York: Cambridge University Press, 1995).

67. *O.R.,* I, 41, pt. 1, pp. 339–340.

68. *O.R.,* I, 41, pt. 4, p. 257.

## 3. Emperor Maximilian's Black Decree

1. William Blair, "Editor's Note," *Civil War History* 49 (June 2003), 109–110.

2. Thomas Schoonover, discussing the efforts to sway U.S. opinion on the conflict in Mexico, states that "Maximilian's well-funded counter-

publicity proved unavailing, which suggests that sentiment was indeed overwhelmingly opposed to a foreign monarchy in Mexico." There remains no direct examination of American public opinion as expressed in the press and in private letters. See Schoonover, "Napoleon is Coming! Maximilian Is Coming?" in Robert E. May, ed., *The Union, the Confederacy, and the Atlantic Rim* (West Lafayette, Ind.: Purdue University Press, 1995), 120.

3. Amzi Wood to Phebe Wood, May 4, 1865, Amzi Wood Papers, Division of Rare and Manuscript Collections, Carl A. Kroch Library, Cornell University.

4. W. Harris Chynoweth, *Maximilian, Late Emperor of Mexico; with . . . a Particular Description of the Causes which Led to His Execution . . .* (London: privately published, 1872), 51n.

5. Jasper Ridley, *Maximilian and Juárez* (New York: Ticknor & Fields, 1992), 228.

6. Bertita Harding, *Phantom Crown: The Story of Maximilian and Carlota of Mexico* (New York: Halcyon House, 1914), 214–215.

7. Ridley, *Maximilian and Juárez* , 229–230.

8. Dexter Perkins, *A History of the Monroe Doctrine* (Boston: Little, Brown, 1955), 129–130. Alfred Jackson Hanna and Kathryn Abbey Hanna, *Napoleon III and Mexico* (Chapel Hill: University of North Carolina Press, 1971), celebrated the triumph of William H. Seward's foreign policy.

9. On this belief's continuing potency in mid-century politics see Michael F. Holt, *The Political Crisis of the 1850s* (New York: W. W. Norton, 1978), and J. Mills Thornton III, *Politics and Power in a Slave Society: Alabama, 1800–1860* (Baton Rouge: Louisiana State University Press, 1978). On its continuing legacy in the North during the Civil War, see Michael T. Smith, "The Enemy Within: Corruption and Political Culture in the Civil War North," Ph.D. diss., Pennsylvania State University, 2005. On its demise in American politics see Andrew L. Slap, "The Doom of Reconstruction: The Liberal Republicans in the Civil War Era," Ph.D. diss., Pennsylvania State University, 2003. Its relationships to foreign policy have never been well established, but the fit is definitely not tight. On the competing idea of Manifest Destiny, see Amy S. Greenberg, *Manifest Manhood and the Antebellum American Empire* (New York: Cambridge University Press, 2005), 18–87. Greenberg is persuasive in emphasizing "the persistence of Manifest Destiny" (p. 54).

10. Mark Wasserman, *Everyday Life and Politics in Nineteenth Century Mexico: Men, Women, and War* (Albuquerque, N.M.: 2000), 113.

11. Ibid., 129.

12. Amzi Wood to Phebe Ann Wood, May 7, 1865, Amzi Wood Papers, Cornell University.

13. Amzi Wood to Phebe Wood, July 10–11, 1865, Amzi Wood Papers. On the battles for Matamoros see Jerry Thompson and Lawrence T. Jones III, *Civil War and Revolution on the Rio Grande Frontier: A Narrative and Photographic History* (Austin: Texas State Historical Association, 2004), 100–123.

14. Amzi Wood to Sarah [Wood?], July 19, 1865, Amzi Wood Papers.

15. Amzi Wood to ?, ca. July 17, 1865, Amzi Wood Papers.

16. Amzi Wood to Phebe Ann Wood, May 7, 1865, Amzi Wood Papers.

17. Roy P. Basler, ed., *The Collected Works of Abraham Lincoln,* 9 vols. (New Brunswick, N.J.: Rutgers University Press, 1953–1955) 2:129–131.

18. Ibid., 3:358.

19. Francis P. Blair, memorandum, January 12, 1865, Abraham Lincoln Papers, Library of Congress, microfilm reel 90.

20. Francis P. Blair, Sr., "Suggestions," January 12, 1865, Abraham Lincoln Papers, Library of Congress, microfilm reel 90.

21. Alfred Jackson Hanna and Kathryn Abbey Hanna, *Napoleon III and Mexico: American Triumph over Monarchy* (Chapel Hill: University of North Carolina Press, 1971), 212.

22. For indications of his Whig affiliations see Joseph A. Fry, *Henry S. Sanford: Diplomacy and Business in Nineteenth-Century America* (Reno: University of Nevada Press, 1982), 10.

23. Henry Shelton Sanford to William Henry Seward, May 10, 1867, Papers of William Henry Seward, Rush Rhees Library, Department of Rare Books, Manuscripts, and Archives, University of Rochester, microfilm reel 100.

24. Ibid.

25. On the resilience of Manifest Destiny in public opinion in the United States past the time of the Mexican-American War see Amy S. Greenberg, *Manifest Manhood and the Antebellum American Empire,* 18–40 and 54–87.

26. Henry Shelton Sanford to William Henry Seward, May 10, 1867, Papers of William Henry Seward, microfilm reel 100.

27. William Need to William Henry Seward, October 8, 1865, Papers of William Henry Seward, microfilm reel 91.

28. Wilson's book was entitled *Mexico and Its Religion: With Incidents of Travel in that Country during Parts of the Years 1851–52–53–54* (1855). Paul Foos characterizes Wilson's book as "harsh commentary" on the republic. See Foos, *A Short, Offhand, Killing Affair: Soldiers and Social Conflict in the Mexican-American War* (Chapel Hill: University of North Carolina Press, 1997), 177.

29. Robert Anderson Wilson to William Henry Seward, September 24, 1864, Papers of William Henry Seward, microfilm reel 85. *The American Annual Cyclopaedia and Register of Important Events of the Year 1861* (New York: D. Appleton, 1864) put it at 7,665,420 in 1861 (p. 462).

30. Wasserman, *Everyday Life and Politics in Nineteenth Century Mexico*, 22.

31. Quoted in Robert M. Johannsen, *To the Halls of the Montezumas: The Mexican War in the American Imagination* (New York: Oxford University Press, 1985), 36. Johannsen notes that Marcy and Winfield Scott both treated guerrillas as prisoners of war nonetheless.

32. See Charles Gibson, ed., *The Black Legend: Anti-Spanish Attitudes in the Old World and the New* (New York: Alfred A. Knopf, 1971), and Philip Wayne Powell, *Tree of Hate: Propaganda and Prejudices Affecting United States Relations with the Hispanic World* (New York: Basic Books, 1971).

33. George J. Potts to William Henry Seward, November 21, 1865, Papers of William Henry Seward, microfilm edition, reel 92.

34. *Message from the President of the United States, of March 20, 1866: Relating to the Condition of Affairs in Mexico, in Answer to a Resolution of the House of December 11, 1865* (Washington, D.C.: Government Printing Office, 1866), 39 Cong., 1 sess., House Executive Document 73, pt. 1, Serial No. 1261, p. 203. The letter found its way into the published diplomatic correspondence of the United States via the agency of Matías Romero, the minister from the Juárez government to the United States.

35. George E. Church, *Mexico. Its Revolutions: Are They Evidences of Retrogression or of Progress?* (New York: Baker & Godwin, 1866), 83; Vine Wright Kingsley, *French Intervention in America; or, A Review of "La France, le Méxique, et les Etats-Conféderés"* (New York: C. B. Richardson, 1863).

36. [F. J. Parker], *The Mexican Empire: Its Actual Situation Briefly Explained*

*and Its Relations to the United States Considered* (New York: Sackett & Mackay, 1866), 13.

37. Henry M. Flint, *Mexico under Maximilian* (Philadelphia: National Publishing Company, 1867); Frederic Hall, *Life of Maximilian I, Late Emperor of Mexico, with a Sketch of the Empress Carlota* (New York: James Miller, 1868).

38. See his letter about Apaches in the *New York World,* July 8, 1867.

39. Sylvester Mowry to William Henry Seward, March 16, 1866, with undated newspaper clipping, Papers of William Henry Seward, microfilm reel 93.

40. Thomas D. Schoonover, ed., *Mexican Lobby: Matías Romero in Washington, 1861–1867* (Lexington: University Press of Kentucky, 1986), esp. xi. Robert Ryal Miller, "Matías Romero: Mexican Minister to the United States during the Juárez-Maximilian Era," *Hispanic American Historical Review* 45 (May 1965), 232, notes his "role . . . as a propaganda agent" in general but not this work in particular.

41. Alfred Jackson Hanna and Kathryn Abbey Hanna somehow overlooked the source in their otherwise comprehensive critical bibliography in *Napoleon III and Mexico: American Triumph over Monarchy* (Chapel Hill: University of North Carolina Press, 1971).

42. *Message,* 39 Cong., 1 sess., House Executive Document 73, pt. 1, Serial No. 1261, pp. 68, 89.

43. Ibid., 92.

44. Ibid., 115–116.

45. Ibid., 149–150; the event goes without mention in the extremely pro-French book by Jack Autrey Dabbs, *The French Army in Mexico, 1861–1867: A Study in Military Government* (The Hague: Mouton, 1963).

46. House Executive Document 73, pt. 1, Serial No. 1261, p. 169.

47. Ibid., 200.

48. Jose María Arteaga to Achille Bazaine, April 24, 1865, ibid., 229. For similar documents see p. 300.

49. William Henry Seward to John Bigelow, November 2, 1865, ibid., 479.

50. Ibid., 335, 482.

51. Ibid., 400, 401.

52. Ibid., 495–497.

53. William H. Seward to Matías Romero, March 14, 1866, ibid., 510.

54. Dabbs, *The French Army in Mexico, 1861–1867,* 236–237.

55. *New York Herald,* April 17, 1867.

56. *New York Herald,* June 1, 1867.

57. Quoted in the *New York Herald,* June 4, 1867.

58. Papers quoted in the *New York Herald,* June 4, 1867.

59. *New York Evening Post,* July 1, 1867; *Wilkes's Spirit of the Times,* July 6, 1867.

60. *New York Tribune,* July 4, 1867; *Chicago Tribune,* July 2, 7, 1867; *Washington National Intelligencer,* July 3 and 11, 1867; *New York Times,* July 2, 1867. "Sanguinary" was the Chicago newspaper's word. The *Times* had criticized the October 3 decree sharply in 1865.

61. *Richmond Dispatch,* July 2, 1867; *New Orleans Bee,* July 3, 1867. "Cold blooded murder" was the language employed by the *Bee,* which also excused the October 3 decree in its issue of July 7.

62. *Cong. Globe,* 40 Cong., 1 sess., 507–509, 598 (Senate debate). Opposition to the execution of Maximilian was Johnson administration foreign policy, and Radicals were predisposed to hate his works and those of his secretary of state and apologist, Seward. But the partisan divisions on the question in Congress and the press have never been explored systematically, and the reasons behind them are not easy to understand under the present state of the literature on the subject. But see William Blair, "The Problem of Mexico in Punishing Confederate Traitors," workshop paper, Civil War Era Center, Pennsylvania State University, November 11, 2005.

63. *Cong. Globe,* 40 Cong., 1 sess., 509 (July 8, 1867).

64. Ibid., 601 (July 12, 1867).

65. Ibid., 602 (July 12, 1867).

66. *New Orleans Bee,* July 10, 1867.

67. Henry Shelton Sanford, to William Henry Seward, June 25, 1867, Papers of William Henry Seward, microfilm reel 101.

68. Jack Autrey Dabbs, a sympathetic source, says of Dupin's unit: "Actually it was a troop of free lances who fought fire with more fire and achieved the worst reputation of any part of the French Army." See Dabbs, *The French Army in Mexico,* 85. The American historian of the French Foreign Legion termed Dupin "an upper-class thug." See Douglas Porch, *The French Foreign Legion: A Complete History of the Legendary Fighting*

*Force* (New York: HarperCollins, 1991), 145. For a close-up view of Dupin's reputation for butchery see also Thompson and Jones III, *Civil War and Revolution on the Rio Grande Frontier*, 101, 104–105.

69. Henry Shelton Sanford to William Henry Seward, June 25, 1867, Papers of William Henry Seward, microfilm reel 101.

70. Henry Shelton Sanford to William Henry Seward, July 5, 1867, Papers of William Henry Seward, microfilm reel 101.

71. Henry Shelton Sanford to William Henry Seward, July 20, 1867, Papers of William Henry Seward, microfilm edition, reel 101.

72. James M. McPherson has an estimate of 50,000 Southern civilian deaths in the war, including deaths of African Americans and deaths from war-related malnutrition and disease. If African Americans are included in the estimate, then the population of the Confederacy was half again as great as that of Mexico. There is no hint of the documentary basis for McPherson's figure. Records of civilian deaths encountered in Southern newspapers do not suggest a high figure, and neither does their occasional mention in the official records of the war. See *Battle Cry of Freedom: The Civil War Era* (New York: Oxford University Press, 1988), 619 and note. The French army in Mexico was very small, perhaps half the size of the Army of Northern Virginia in 1864. When compared, civilian deaths in the two wars were by no means proportionate to the size of armies in the field inflicting death.

73. For a rare instance, attributed to Confederates in the bitter civil war in East Tennessee, see William G. Brownlow, *Sketches of the Rise, Progress, and Decline of Secession: With a Narrative of Personal Adventures among the Rebels* (Philadelphia: George W. Childs, 1862), 302. For a mass hanging of Unionists in Texas by Confederates see Richard B. McCaslin, *Tainted Breeze: The Great Hanging at Gainesville, Texas* (Baton Rouge: Louisiana State University Press, 1994). Neither event, of course, was initiated by U.S. forces.

## 4. The Shenandoah Valley

1. Joseph T. Glatthaar, *The March to the Sea and Beyond: Sherman's Troops in the Savannah and Carolinas Campaigns* (Baton Rouge: Louisiana State University Press, 1985), 72, 140.

2. John L. Heatwole, *The Burning: Sheridan in the Shenandoah Valley* (Charlottesville, Va.: Rockbridge Publishing, 1998).

3. Michael Fellman, Lesley J. Gordon, and Daniel E. Sutherland, *This Terrible War: The Civil War and Its Aftermath* (New York: Longman, 2003), 271.

4. William G. Thomas, "Nothing Ought to Astonish Us: Confederate Civilians in the 1864 Shenandoah Valley Campaign," in Gary W. Gallagher, ed., *The Shenandoah Valley Campaign of 1864* (Chapel Hill: University of North Carolina Press, 2006), 239–240.

5. Thomas, "Nothing Ought to Astonish Us," 241.

6. Quoted in Michael G. Mahon, *The Shenandoah Valley, 1861–1865: The Destruction of the Granary of the Confederacy* (Mechanicsburg, Pa.: Stackpole Books, 1999), 115.

7. J. H. Kidd, *Personal Recollections of a Cavalryman with Custer's Michigan Cavalry Brigade in the Civil War,* orig. pub. 1908 (Alexandria, Va.: Time-Life Books, 1983), 398–399.

8. Mahon, *The Shenandoah Valley, 1861–1865,* esp. 117–126, 133–135. William G. Thomas dismisses Mahon's work as showing "little evidence to support his argument." Thomas, "Nothing Ought to Astonish Us," 255n.

9. Kidd, *Personal Recollections of a Cavalryman,* 397–398.

10. *War of the Rebellion: A Compilation of the Official Records of the Union and Confederate Armies,* 128 vols. (Washington, D.C.: U.S. Government Printing Office, 1880–1901), I, 43, pt. 1, p. 30; hereafter cited as *O.R.*

11. Philip H. Sheridan to Ulysses S. Grant, September 29, 1864, in *O.R.,* I, 43, pt. 1, p. 30. Sheridan learned later that he was misusing the expressions "lower" and "upper" in relation to the Shenandoah Valley. "Upper" means southern and "lower" means northern in referring to directions in the valley. Sheridan to Grant, October 7, 1864, in ibid., 31.

12. Mahon makes the assertion of drought. If one examines the diary of Jedidiah Hotchkiss, however, there seems to have been plenty of rain in the autumn of 1864: *O.R.,* I, 43, pt. 1, pp. 567–588.

13. James M. McPherson, *Battle Cry of Freedom: The Civil War Era* (New York: Oxford University Press, 1988), 778.

14. Quoted in Philip Henry Sheridan, *Personal Memoirs of P. H. Sheridan, General, United States Army,* 2 vols. (New York: Charles L. Webster, 1888), 1:486.

15. Ulysses S. Grant to Henry W. Halleck, July 14, 1864, *O.R.*, I, 40, pt. 3, p. 223.

16. Philip H. Sheridan to John A. Rawlins, February 3, 1866, *O.R.*, I, 43, pt. 1, p. 50.

17. Ulysses S. Grant to Philip H. Sheridan, August 5, 1864, in ibid., 57.

18. Jubal A. Early to Robert E. Lee, October 9, 1864, in ibid., 558.

19. Philip H. Sheridan to Ulysses S. Grant, October 7, 1864, in ibid., 30. Sheridan used the term "untenable" in giving orders to General Torbert, too. See Philip H. Sheridan to A. T. A. Torbert, August 16, 1864, in ibid., 43.

20. *O.R.*, I, 42, pt. 1, p. 1024. See also "burning in every direction" (p. 1029). Hotchkiss also kept a journal during the war. William G. Thomas noted the paucity of references to destruction in the valley in Hotchikiss's journal in "Nothing Ought to Astonish Us," 39–40. The journal entry is dated August 17 and thus preceded much of the destruction wrought by Sheridan's cavalry in the valley. Hotchkiss remained in the area for the whole campaign, and it is not clear why he offered no further comment on the Yankees' work. The journal entry has long been available in *O.R.*, I, 43, pt. 1, p. 569. Thomas refers to the modern separate edition: Archie P. McDonald, ed., *Make Me a Map of the Valley: The Civil War Journal of Stonewall Jackson's Topographer* (Dallas: Southern Methodist University Press, 1973), 222.

21. Sheridan, *Memoirs*, 2:17.

22. On the importance of corn to Southern freed people's diets, see Roger L. Ransom and Richard Sutch, *One Kind of Freedom: The Economic Consequences of Emancipation,* 2nd ed. (Cambridge: Cambridge University Press, 2001), 11–12. The diet of white yeomen would not likely have been greatly different under the straitened circumstances of war. Corn was so central to the Southern diet that the economic historians Ransom and Sutch measured food production in "corn-equivalent bushels" (p. 153).

23. Wesley Merritt to William Russell, Jr., October 5, 1864, *O.R.*, I, 43, pt. 1, p. 443.

24. *O.R.*, I, 42, pt. 1, p. 37.

25. William H. Powell to William Russell, Jr., October 27, 1864, *O.R.*, I, 43, pt. 1, p. 510.

26. Eric J. Wittenberg, *One of Custer's Wolverines: The Civil War Letters of*

*Brevet Brigadier General James H. Kidd, 6th Michigan Cavalry* (Kent: Kent State University Press, 2000), 120–121.

27. Wesley Merritt, "Sheridan in the Shenandoah Valley," in Robert Underwood Johnson and Clarence Clough Buel, eds., *Battles and Leaders of the Civil War . . .* , 4 vols., orig. pub. 1887–1888 (New York: Thomas Yoseloff, 1956), 4:513.

28. *O.R.,* I, 42, pt. 1, p. 54.

29. Ibid., 40–41.

30. It had dawned on him by October 7 what the moral effect was. "The people here are getting sick of the war," he told Grant; "heretofore they have had no reason to complain, because they have been living in great abundance." Sheridan to Grant, October 7, 1864, *O.R.,* I, 43, pt. 1, p. 30.

31. Jubal A. Early to Robert E. Lee, October 21, 1864, *O.R.,* I, 43, pt. 1, p. 563. In terms of want of supplies and equipment the most striking complaint on the Confederate side came from the cavalry commanders who needed sabers and pistols (p. 613).

32. James McPherson writes: "The guerrilla fighting in Missouri produced a form of terrorism that exceeded anything else in the war . . . Jayhawkers initiated a scorched-earth policy against rebel sympathizers three years before Sheridan practiced it in the Shenandoah Valley." *Battle Cry of Freedom,* 784.

33. Sheridan, *Memoirs,* 1:353–356, 368–369. On fear of the Confederate cavalry, see Michael C. C. Adams, *Fighting for Defeat: Union Military Failure in the East, 1861–1865,* orig. published as *Our Masters the Rebels: A Speculation on Union Failure in the East, 1861–1865* in 1978 (Lincoln: University of Nebraska Press, 1992), 76–78 and 161–162.

34. John Bigelow, Jr., *The Campaign of Chancellorsville: A Strategic and Tactical Study* (New Haven: Yale University Press, 1910), 74. Apparently the quotation is apocryphal, but its currency during the Civil War, whatever its origins, still reveals the reputation of the cavalry.

35. Sheridan, *Memoirs,* 1:347.

36. A. T. A. Torbert to F. A. Forsyth, November 1864, *O.R.,* I, 43, pt. 1, p. 426.

37. Wesley Merritt to William Russell, Jr., October 12, 1864, *O.R.,* I, 43, pt. 1, pp. 445–446.

38. Wesley Merritt to William Russell, Jr., October 12, 1864, *O.R.,* I. 43, pt. 1, p. 444. See also p. 447 ("sabering everyone who made resistance").

39. George A. Custer to A. E. Dana, September 28, 1864, *O.R.*, I, 43, pt. 1, p. 458.

40. Thomas C. Devin to A. E. Dana, October 13, 1864, *O.R.*, I, 43, pt. 1, p. 482.

41. Thomas C. Devin to A. E. Dana, October 23, 1864, *O.R.*, I, 43, pt. 1, p. 478.

42. Kidd, *Personal Recollections of a Cavalryman*, 380–382.

43. James H. Wilson to J. W. Forsyth, February 18, 1865, *O.R.*, I, 43, pt. 1, p. 518. Custer was promoted to command of the Third Division during the campaign.

44. W. H. Powell to William Russell, Jr., November 17, 1864, *O.R.*, I, 43, pt. 1, p. 512.

45. Philip H. Sheridan to Henry W. Halleck, August 17, 1864, *O.R.*, I, 43, pt. 1, p. 19. See also the same correspondents on August 28, 1864, p. 22. Sheridan used a slightly different tone in describing the cavalry charges years later in his *Memoirs*, 2:58. There he described the Battle of Tom's Brook, where Torbert inflicted defeat on General Thomas Rosser and the Confederate cavalry, this way: "The open country permitting a saber fight, both sides seemed bent on using that arm."

46. McPherson, *Battle Cry of Freedom*, 777. For a different view of the Union cavalry under Sheridan, see Paddy Griffith, *Battle Tactics of the Civil War* (New Haven: Yale University Press, 1989), 184–188. He focuses on the 1865 campaign for Appomattox; his standard of judgment is utility and nothing is said of psychological factors derived from the history of the army.

47. Wesley Merritt to William Russell, Jr., October 5, 1864, *O.R.*, I, 43, pt. 1, p. 440. August 17 was the day that Jedidiah Hotchkiss noted in his journal seeing destruction of farms, hay, and crops in the valley.

48. Philip H. Sheridan to A. T. A. Torbert, August 16, 1864, *O.R.*, I, 43, pt. 1, p. 43.

49. Edwin M. Stanton to Philip H. Sheridan, October 12, 1864, *O.R.*, I, 43, pt. 1, p. 62.

50. Ulysses S. Grant to Philip H. Sheridan, September 22, 1864, *O.R.*, I, 43, pt. 1, p. 57.

51. For this description of the tactics I am indebted to Allan L. Tischler, "Sabers Glistening on the Ride to Victory," *America's Civil War*, November 2005, esp. p. 25.

52. Merritt, "Sheridan in the Shenandoah Valley," 507.

53. William Tecumseh Sherman, *Memoirs of General W. T. Sherman*, orig.

pub. 1875 (New York: Library of America, 1990), 810. The general was careful to offer a more serious explanation of foraging on the campaign elsewhere in his memoirs (at pp. 658–659).

54. In a retrospective illustrated history of the campaign (which he witnessed) put together near the end of the century, the artist James E. Taylor did offer a humorous image of chasing pigs. See Taylor, *The James E. Taylor Sketchbook* (Dayton: Morningside House, 1989), 272.

55. William Thompson to Eliza [?], August 22, 1864, Baldridge-Thompson Collection, Pennsylvania State University Archives and Rare Books.

56. For more evidence of reluctance on the part of soldiers to put property to the torch see H. A. DuPont, *The Campaign of 1864 in the Valley of Virginia and the Expedition to Lynchburg* (New York: National Americana Society, 1925), 51. The action preceded Sheridan's campaign and occurred further west in Virginia.

57. John P. Suter to his wife, October 2, 1864, John P. Suter Papers, Harrisburg Civil War Round Table Collection, Box 5, Army Heritage Center, Carlisle, Pennsylvania.

58. John P. Suter to his wife, November 10, 1864, ibid.

59. John W. Elwood, *Elwood's Stories of the Old Ringgold Cavalry, 1847–1865* (Coal Center, Pa.: priv. pub., 1914), 246. Elwood justified the work as retribution for Early's campaign in Maryland and concluded as well that only the destruction of Early's army made the valley "untenable" for a Confederate army (pp. 246–247).

60. Ann Hartwell Britton and Thomas J. Reed, eds., *To My Beloved Wife and Boy at Home: The Letters and Diaries of Orderly Sergeant John F. L. Hartwell* (Madison, N.J.: Fairleigh Dickinson University Press, 1997), 293 (cavalry's destruction), 272, 276, 281, 282, 286 (things eaten).

61. Beverly Hayes Kallgren and James L. Crouthamel, eds., *"Dear Friend Anna": The Civil War Letters of a Common Soldier from Maine* (Orono: University of Maine Press, 1992) (made no comment); Julie Holcomb, ed., *Southern Sons, Northern Soldiers: The Civil War Letters of the Remley Brothers, 22nd Iowa Infantry* (DeKalb: Northern Illinois University Press, 2004), 153; Richard L. Kiper, ed., *Dear Catharine, Dear Taylor: The Civil War Letters of a Union Soldier and His Wife* (Lawrence: University Press of Kansas, 2002), 279, 282; John S. Collier and Bonnie B. Collier, eds., *Yours for the Union: The Civil War Letters of John W. Chase, First Massachusetts Light Artillery* (New York: Fordham University Press, 2004),

366; E. R. Hagemann, ed., *Fighting Rebels and Redskins: Experiences in Army Life of Colonel George B. Sanford, 1861–1892* (Norman: University of Oklahoma Press, 1969), 300; Edward W. Emerson, *The Life and Letters of Charles Russell Lowell* (Boston: Houghton, Mifflin, 1907), 324, 353. (All made only slight mentions.)

62. J. M. Campbell, General Order, July 17, 1863, John P. Suter Papers. See also General Order No. 3, November 27, 1863.
63. W. H. Powell to William Russell, Jr., October 27, 1864, *O.R.*, I, 43, pt. 1, pp. 508, 509, 510–511.
64. Sheridan, *Memoirs*, 2:52.
65. Philip Henry Sheridan to Wesley Merritt, September 28, 1864, *O.R.*, I, 43, pt. 2, p. 202.
66. Philip Henry Sheridan to Ulysses S. Grant, October 9, 1864, *O.R.*, I, 43, pt. 1, p. 31.
67. Philip Henry Sheridan to Ulysses S. Grant, October 11, 1864, *O.R.*, I, 43, pt. 1, p. 32.
68. Philip Henry Sheridan to John A. Rawlins, February 3, 1866, *O.R.*, I, 43, pt. 1, pp. 55–56.
69. Sheridan, *Memoirs*, 1:465.
70. Ibid., 1:486–487n.
71. Ibid., 1:487n.
72. Ibid., 1:486–488.

### 5. The Sand Creek Massacre

1. Michael Fellman, "At the Nihilist Edge: Reflections on Guerrilla Warfare during the American Civil War," in Stig Förster and Jörg Nagler, eds., *On the Road to Total War: The American Civil War and the German Wars of Unification, 1861–1871* (Washington, D.C.: Cambridge University Press, 1997), 522, 532.
2. Mark Grimsley, "'Rebels' and 'Redskins': U.S. Military Conduct toward White Southerners and Native Americans in Comparative Perspective," in Mark Grimsley and Clifford J. Rogers, eds., *Civilians in the Path of War* (Lincoln: University of Nebraska Press, 2002), 137–139.
3. Grimsley, "'Rebels' and 'Redskins,'" 151, 152.
4. Mark Grimsley, *The Hard Hand of War: Union Policy toward Southern Civilians, 1861–1865* (New York: Cambridge University Press, 1995), 225.

5. *Cong. Globe,* 40 Cong., 1 sess., 601 (July 8, 1867).

6. Nat Brandt, *The Man Who Tried to Burn New York* (Syracuse, N.Y.: Syracuse University Press, 1986); Edwin G. Burrows and Mike Wallace, *Gotham* (New York: Oxford University Press, 1999), 902–903. See also the entry "Greek Fire" in the eleventh edition of *The Encyclopaedia Britannica* (New York: Encyclopaedia Britannica, 1910), 12:492–493. For more on the attempt to set fires in New York and on Greek Fire see Mark E. Neely, Jr., "Terror in the Civil War: A Reconsideration in the Light of 9/11," in Ellen Fitzpatrick, ed., *Terror and Liberal Democracy: Lessons from the Past* (forthcoming).

7. *Chicago Times,* October 8, 1863.

8. Robert V. Bruce, *Lincoln and the Tools of War,* orig. pub. 1956 (Urbana: University of Illinois Press, 1989), 181. Bruce does not say what the chemical composition of the compound in Levi Short's shells was.

9. Ibid., 181–182.

10. "Greek Fire or Pyrophori," *Scientific American* 9 (December 19, 1863), 391.

11. See especially able comparisons of the Civil War and Indian wars in Fellman, "On the Nihilist Edge," 519–540, and Grimsley, "'Rebels' and 'Redskins,'" 137–162.

12. For application to the Sand Creek Massacre itself, see David Svaldi, *Sand Creek and the Rhetoric of Extermination: A Case Study in Indian-White Relations* (Lanham, Md.: University Press of America, 1989).

13. Philip Henry Sheridan, *Personal Memoirs of P. H. Sheridan, General, United States Army,* 2 vols. (New York: Charles L. Webster, 1888), 1:44.

14. William T. Sherman to John Sherman, January 25, 1863, in Rachel Sherman Thorndike, ed., *The Sherman Letters: Correspondence between General and Senator Sherman from 1837 to 1891* (New York: C. Scribner's Sons, 1894), 185.

15. *War of the Rebellion: A Compilation of the Official Records of the Union and Confederate Armies,* 128 vols. (Washington, D.C.: U.S. Government Printing Office, 1880–1901), I, 41, pt. 1, pp. 830–831; hereafter cited as *O.R.*

16. See the maps "Operations on the Northern Plains 1865" and "The Southern Plains and the Southwest, 1862–1865," in Robert M. Utley, *Frontiersmen in Blue: The United States Army and the Indian, 1848–1865* (New York: Macmillan, 1967), 305, 321.

17. *O.R.,* I, 41, pt. 1, p. 831.

18. Eugene F. Ware, *The Indian War of 1864,* orig. pub. 1911 (New York: St. Martin's Press, 1960), 355–356.

19. Charles Royster, *The Destructive War: William Tecumseh Sherman, Stonewall Jackson, and the Americans* (New York: Alfred A. Knopf, 1991), 291.

20. *O.R.,* I, 41, pt. 1, p. 172.

21. Shepard Krech III, *The Ecological Indian: Myth and History* (New York: W. W. Norton, 1999), 101–122.

22. *O.R.,* I, 48, pt. 1, p. 96.

23. *Charleston Courier,* August 15, 1863.

24. *Charleston Courier,* August 25, 1863.

25. For two examples of such thinking see Utley, *Frontiersmen in Blue,* 345–346, and Lance Janda, "Shutting the Gates of Mercy: The American Origins of Total War," *Journal of Military History* 59 (January 1995), 7–26. For a different view see Mark E. Neely, Jr., "'Civilized Belligerents': Abraham Lincoln and the Idea of 'Total War,'" in John Y. Simon and Michael E. Stevens, eds., *New Perspectives on the Civil War: Myths and Realities of the National Conflict* (Madison, Wis.: Madison House, 1998), 16–18.

26. John M. Blum et al., *The National Experience: A History of the United States,* 5th ed. (New York: Harcourt, Brace, Jovanovich, 1981), 76.

27. Michael T. Smith, "Battles or Massacres?" in Richard W. Slatta, ed., *The Mythical West: An Encyclopedia of Legend, Lore, and Popular Culture* (Santa Barbara, Calif.: ABC-CLIO, 2001).

28. Scott J. Anthony to J. E. Tappan, December 15, 1864, in *O.R.,* I, 41, pt. 1, p. 954.

29. Edward W. Wynkoop to J. E. Tappan, January 15, 1865, in ibid., 960.

30. *Cong. Globe,* 38 Cong., 2 sess., pt. 1, pp. 251–252 (January 13, 1865).

31. Utley, *Frontiersmen in Blue,* 116–117.

32. *Cong. Globe,* 38 Cong., 2 sess., pt. 1, pp. 251–252. Utley says only that 160 women and children were "captured" at Bear River; *Frontiersmen in Blue,* 223–224.

33. The terminology rankled most Western soldiers. Eugene Ware, for example, sneered: "Among the humanitarians of Boston it was called the 'Chivington Massacre,' but there was never anything more deserved than that massacre." See *The Indian War of 1864,* 309.

34. The description of Cheyenne warfare is based on George Bird Grinnell,

*The Cheyenne Indians: Their History and Ways of Life,* 2 vols. (New Haven: Yale University Press, 1923; Lincoln: University of Nebraska Press, 1972), 2:1–48, and David Svaldi, *Sand Creek and the Rhetoric of Extermination,* 317n.

35. Stan Hoig, *The Sand Creek Massacre* (Norman: University of Oklahoma Press, 1961), 95–107. The exchange actually involved Cheyennes held as hostages and not the prisoners to whom Black Kettle originally referred.

36. Robert L. Monkres, "Indian-White Contact before 1870: Cultural Factors in Conflict," *Journal of the West* 10 (July 1971), 457; Grinnell, *The Cheyenne Indians,* 4–7.

37. Samuel R. Curtis to Henry W. Halleck, January 12, 1865, in *O.R.,* I, 48, pt. 1, pp. 502–503.

38. Samuel R. Curtis to Abraham Lincoln, February 28, 1864, Abraham Lincoln Papers, Library of Congress, microfilm reel 69.

39. Randall M. Miller and William Pencak, eds., *Pennsylvania: A History of the Commonwealth* (University Park: Pennsylvania State University Press, 2002), 132.

40. Bruce Tap, *Over Lincoln's Shoulder: The Committee on the Conduct of the War* (Lawrence: University Press of Kansas, 1998), 193–208.

41. *Report of the Joint Committee on the Conduct of the War at the Second Session Thirty-eighth Congress* (Washington, D.C.: Government Printing Office, 1865), 121.

42. Ibid., i.

43. Michael A. Sievers says even the fact of the flag-raising is in doubt. He dismisses it as a "trivial" question, but the flag is far too symbolic in war to be dismissed from consideration. See Sievers, "Sands of Sand Creek Historiography," *Colorado Magazine,* 49 (Spring 1972), 140.

44. *Report of the Joint Committee on the Conduct of the War,* ii, iv.

45. Condition of the Indian Tribes. Report of the Joint Special Committee appointed under Joint Resolution of March 3, 1865, 39 Cong., 2 sess., Senate Executive Document 156 (1867), serial no. 1279.

46. Report of the Secretary of War . . . , 39 Cong., 2 sess., Senate Executive Document 26 (1867), serial no. 1277.

47. Helen Hunt Jackson, *A Century of Dishonor: A Sketch of the United States Government's Dealings with Some of the Indian Tribes,* orig. pub. 1881 (Williamstown, Mass.: Corner House Publishers, 1979). Conestoga re-

ferred to the action of the "Paxton boys," colonial militia, against Butler's Rangers (Tories) and Indians in New York near the end of the Revolution.

48. George W. Manypenny, *Our Indian Wards,* orig. pub. 1880 (New York: Da Capo, 1972), 158–159.

49. Condition of the Indian Tribes. Report of the Joint Special Committee appointed under Joint resolution of March 3, 1865, 39 Cong., 2 sess., Senate Executive Document No. 156, serial no. 1279, p. 5.

50. Ibid.

51. Brown diary, entry for May 1, 1861. Harrisburg Civil War Round Table Collection, Box 6, Army Heritage Center, Carlisle, Pennsylvania.

52. *O.R.,* I, 22, pt. 1, p. 83.

## 6. Avenging Andersonville

1. Andrew Delbanco, ed., *The Portable Abraham Lincoln* (New York: Penguin Books, 1992), 230.

2. Edmund Wilson, *Patriotic Gore: Studies in the Literature of the American Civil War* (New York: Oxford University Press, 1966), 117.

3. *Cong. Globe,* 38 Cong., 2 sess., pt. 1, p. 73.

4. As late as 1930 the historian William Best Hesseltine thought a balanced account necessary to defuse the passions still prevailing over the issue of Andersonville. See his *Civil War Prisons: A Study in War Psychology* (Columbus: Ohio State University Press, 1930), esp. vii.

5. Roy P. Basler, ed., *Collected Works of Abraham Lincoln,* 9 vols. (New Brunswick, N.J.: Rutgers University Press, 1953–1955) 7:302–303.

6. *New York Evening Post,* January 12, 1865.

7. Richard Shelly Hartigan, *Lieber's Code and the Law of War* (Chicago: Precedent, 1983), 50, 57.

8. *Cong. Globe,* 38 Cong., 2 sess., pt. 1, p. 268 (January 16, 1865).

9. Ibid., 292, 307 (January 17, 1865).

10. *Cong. Globe,* 38 Cong., 2 sess., pt. 1, pp. 363–364 (January 23, 1865).

11. Historians have not altogether ignored the debate. See Bruce Tap, *Over Lincoln's Shoulder: The Committee on the Conduct of the War* (Lawrence: University Press of Kansas, 1998), 207–208 and William C. Harris, *Lincoln's Last Months* (Cambridge: Harvard University Press, 2003), 102–103. The retaliation debate has often been obscured by the struggle in the

other house to pass the resolution for the Thirteenth Amendment to the Constitution. In press coverage at the time it was obscured somewhat by reports of the many rumors of peace initiatives.

12. *Cong. Globe,* 38 Cong., 2 sess., pt. 1, p. 364 (January 23, 1865).

13. Ibid., 387 (January 24, 1865).

14. Ibid., 387–388 (January 24, 1865).

15. Ibid., 365 (January 23, 1865)

16. Ibid., 364 (January 23, 1865).

17. Ibid., 428 (January 26, 1865).

18. Ibid., 434, 452 (January 26, 27, 1865).

19. Ibid., 384 (January 24, 1865).

20. Ibid., 386 (January 24, 1865).

21. Ibid., 459 (January 27, 1865).

22. David H. Donald, *Charles Sumner and the Rights of Man* (New York: Alfred A. Knopf, 1960), does not mention it.

23. David Donald, *Charles Sumner and the Coming of the Civil War* (New York: Alfred A. Knopf, 1960), 352–363.

24. *Report of the Joint Committee on the Conduct of the War at the Second Session Thirty-eighth Congress,* 8 vols. (Washington, D.C.: Government Printing Office, 1865), 3:449; "Rebel Barbarities, and the Barbarism of Slavery. Resolution . . . April 1, 1862," in *Charles Sumner: His Complete Works,* 20 vols. (Boston: Lee and Shepard, 1900), 8:301–302.

25. "The Issues of the War. Dedication of a New Edition of the Speech on the Barbarism of Slavery, July 4, 1863," in *Charles Sumner,* 9:322–324.

26. *Cong. Globe,* 38 Cong., 2 sess., pt. 1, p. 381 (January 24, 1865). Sumner intended the renewed emphasis on the barbarism of slavery during the war to place foreign powers in the position of supporting the cause of civilization in the United States. Despite his virulent rhetoric, he never intended his depiction of the enemy as failing to exist on the same plane of civilization to lead to unrestrained treatment in warfare.

27. Ibid., 382 (January 24, 1865).

28. For confirmation of that point from a church historian, see Harry S. Stout, *Upon the Altar of the Nation: A Moral History of the Civil War* (New York: Viking, 2006).

29. Mark Grimsley, *The Hard Hand of War: Union Military Policy toward Southern Civilians, 1861–1865* (New York: Columbia University Press, 1995), 190–204, and "'Rebels' and 'Redskins': U.S. Military Conduct to-

ward White Southerners and Native Americans in Comparative Perspective," in Grimsley and Clifford J. Rogers, eds., *Civilians in the Path of War* (Lincoln: University of Nebraska Press, 2002), esp. pp. 147–148.

30. E. M. Furness to Charles Sumner, January 24, 1865; Israel Washburn to Sumner, January 25, 1865; James Butler to Sumner, February 25, 1865; Orville N. Wilder to Sumner, February 27, 1865; Mary Schoolcraft to Sumner, March 2, 1865; Robert Anderson to Sumner, March 4, 1865—all in the Papers of Charles Sumner, Houghton Library, Harvard University, microfilm edition, reel 32.

31. F. W. Newman to Charles Sumner, March 20, 1865; James E. Harvey to Sumner, February 17, 1865; James H. Campbell to Sumner, March 19, 1865, Papers of Charles Sumner, microfilm reel 33 (Harvey letter, reel 32).

32. John L. Maxwell to Charles Sumner, January 27, 1865, ibid., reel 32.

33. James Butler to Charles Sumner, February 27, 1865, ibid., reel 32.

34. Orville N. Wilder to Charles Sumner, February 27, 1865, ibid., reel 32.

35. J. S. Donaldson to Charles Sumner, January 26, 1865, ibid., reel 32.

36. Charles Francis Adams, Jr., to Charles Sumner, February 7, 1865, with clipping, ibid., reel 32. Adams, an officer in an African American cavalry regiment was home recuperating from an illness. See Worthington Chauncey Ford, ed., *A Cycle of Adams Letters, 1861–1865,* 2 vols. (Boston: Houghton, Mifflin, 1920), 2:194–195, 250–251.

37. Mrs. A. Moor to Abraham Lincoln, January 13, 1865, Abraham Lincoln Papers, Library of Congress, microfilm reel 90.

38. Mrs. C. Greene Brayton to Abraham Lincoln, February 1, 1865, Abraham Lincoln Papers, microfilm reel 91.

39. *Harper's Weekly,* June 18, 1864.

40. Tap, *Over Lincoln's Shoulder,* 201–208.

41. See, for example, William Frank Zornow, *Lincoln and the Party Divided* (Norman: University of Oklahoma Press, 1954), and David E. Long, *The Jewel of Liberty: Abraham Lincoln's Re-Election and the End of Slavery* (Mechanicsburg, Pa.; Stackpole Books, 1994).

42. Harris, *Lincoln's Last Months,* 102–103, and Tap, *Over Lincoln's Shoulder,* 201–208. The groundwork had been laid even earlier, in 1862, when the Joint Committee on the Conduct of the War reported rebel atrocities in the first Bull Run campaign. See "Rebel Barbarities," *Report of the Joint Committee on the Conduct of the War,* 3:449–491.

43. Charles F. Mitchell to William H. Seward, September 3, 1864, Papers of William Henry Seward, microfilm edition, reel 85.

44. Michael F. Holt, *The Political Crisis of the 1850s* (New York: W. W. Norton, 1978), 5.

45. Mark E. Neely, Jr., *The Union Divided: Party Conflict in the Civil War North* (Cambridge: Harvard University Press, 2002), esp. p. 116.

46. *New York Evening Post,* January 12 and February 1, 1865. It had recently said that if Confederate peace commissioners were hung with their heads upside down until death, the fate would be too good for them because they shared responsibility as leaders for the torture of Union prisoners of war.

47. *New York World,* February 7, 1865.

48. James Kelley to William H. Seward, April 3, 1865, Papers of William Henry Seward, microfilm edition, reel 88.

49. *New York Herald,* January 8, 1865.

50. Ernest A. McKay, *The Civil War and New York City* (Syracuse, N.Y.: Syracuse University Press, 1990), 287–290; Edwin G. Burrows and Mike Wallace, *Gotham: A History of New York City to 1898* (New York: Oxford University Press, 1999), 902–903. The fullest treatment can be found in Nat Brandt, *The Man Who Tried to Burn New York* (Syracuse, N.Y.: Syracuse University Press, 1986).

51. Donald, *Charles Sumner and the Rights of Man.*

52. "Relations with Great Britain: The St. Albans Raid," in *Charles Sumner,* 7:41–745.

53. On various reductions of rations—one of them apparently ordered in retaliation on April 20, 1864, for reports of Confederate abuses of Union prisoners—see Lonnie R. Speer, *War of Vengeance: Acts of Retaliation against Civil War POWs* (Mechanicsburg, Pa.: Stackpole Books, 2002), 124–127. The reductions do not appear to be related to the congressional resolution.

54. Basler, ed., *Collected Works of Abraham Lincoln,* 6:408.

55. Ibid., 7:493. Grant's reply to Lincoln, cited in this source, though defiant, proved that he too had a firm sense of the proper limits of such destruction. See the footnote to the entry in *Collected Works of Abraham Lincoln.*

56. Abraham Lincoln to Joseph J. Reynolds, January 20, 1865, in ibid., 8:229.

57. *Cong. Globe,* 38 Cong., 2 sess., pt. 1, p. 408. The incidents were raised in debate by Gratz Brown, a Missouri Radical.

58. Basler, ed., *Collected Works of Abraham Lincoln,* 4:506.

59. *Cong. Globe,* 38 Cong., 2 sess., pt. 1, p. 496 (January 30, 1865).

60. Abraham Lincoln to Orville Hickman Browning, September 22, 1862, in Basler, ed., *Collected Works of Abraham Lincoln,* 4:532.

61. *Cong. Globe,* 38 Cong., 2 sess., pt. 1, p. 388 (January 24, 1865).

62. Basler, ed., *Collected Works of Abraham Lincoln,* 6:357.

63. Essayists in Gregory J. W. Urwin, ed., *Black Flag over Dixie: Racial Atrocities and Reprisals in the Civil War* (Carbondale: Southern Illinois University Press, 2004) appear to agree that Lincoln did not enforce the order rigorously but that it was well known to the Confederates and might well have deterred even worse incidents of atrocity than those that occurred.

## Conclusion

1. Charles Royster, *The Destructive War: William Tecumseh Sherman, Stonewall Jackson, and the Americans* (New York: Alfred A. Knopf, 1991), 79–80.

2. I focus on professional historians in the academy in order to show that these trends do not represent commercial sensationalism.

3. David Donald, ed., *Why the North Won the Civil War* (Baton Rouge: Louisiana State University Press, 1960), 35.

4. Ibid., 31.

5. Arthur M. Schlesinger, Jr., "The Causes of the Civil War: A Note on Historical Sentimentalism," *Partisan Review* (October 1949), 969–981.

6. Donald, ed., *Why the North Won the Civil War,* 30, 38.

7. Royster, *The Destructive War,* 39.

8. John B. Walters, *Merchant of Terror: General Sherman and Total War* (Indianapolis: Bobbs-Merrill, 1973).

9. Mark E. Neely, Jr., "'Civilized Belligerents': Abraham Lincoln and the Idea of 'Total War,'" in John Y. Simon and Michael E. Stevens, eds., *New Perspectives on the Civil War: Myths and Realities of the National Conflict* (Madison, Wisc.: Madison House, 1998), 10. See also my first essay on the subject, "Was the Civil War a Total War?" *Civil War History* 27 (March 1991), 5–28.

10. James M. McPherson, *Battle Cry of Freedom: The Civil War Era* (New York: Oxford University Press, 1988), 338.

11. John Keegan, *The Face of Battle* (New York: Viking, 1976).

12. Gerald F. Linderman, *Embattled Courage: The Experience of Combat in the American Civil War* (New York: Free Press, 1987), 180.

13. Phillip S. Paludan, *Victims: A True Story of the Civil War* (Knoxville: University of Tennessee Press, 1981), xv.

14. Ayers is quoted on the jacket of the book. Fellman, *Inside War: The Guerrilla Conflict in Missouri during the American Civil War* (New York: Oxford University Press, 1989).

15. Daniel Sutherland, "Sideshow No Longer: A Historiographical Review of the Guerrilla War," *Civil War History* 46 (March 2000), 16, 19, 23.

16. James M. McPherson, "From Limited to Total War: Missouri and the Nation, 1862–1865," *Gateway Heritage* 12 (1992), 4–19, reprinted as "From Limited to Total War, 1861–1865," in McPherson, *Drawn with the Sword: Reflections on the American Civil War* (New York: Oxford University Press, 1996), 66–86 (quotations here from p. 72).

17. Frank Freidel, *Francis Lieber: Nineteenth-Century Liberal* (Baton Rouge: Louisiana State University Press, 1947), chap. 14.

18. Richard Shelly Hartigan, *Lieber's Code and the Laws of War* (Chicago: Precedent, 1983), 58.

19. William F. Fox, *Regimental Losses in the American Civil War, 1861–1865: A Treatise on the Extent and Nature of the Mortuary Losses in the Union Regiments, with Full and Exhaustive Statistics Compiled from the Official Records on File in the State Military Bureaus and at Washington* (Albany, N.Y.: Albany Publishing, 1889), 1.

20. Thomas L. Livermore, *Numbers and Losses in the Civil War in America, 1861–1865*, 2nd ed. (Boston: Houghton, Mifflin, 1901), iv.

21. Ibid., 77.

22. Drew Gilpin Faust, "'Numbers on Top of Numbers': Counting the Civil War Dead," *Journal of Military History* 70 (October 2006), 997, 1000–1001.

23. Ibid., 997.

24. James M. McPherson and William J. Cooper, Jr., eds., *Writing the Civil War: The Quest to Understand* (Columbia: University of South Carolina Press, 1998), 2.

25. Phillip S. Paludan, *"A People's Contest": The Union and Civil War, 1861–*

*1865* (New York: Harper & Row, 1988), 316–317. Paludan uses as the Civil War total the figure 623,000.

26. Faust, "'Numbers on Top of Numbers,'" 997.

27. Michael Fellman, Lesley J. Gordon, and Daniel E. Sutherland, *This Terrible War: The Civil War and Its Aftermath* (New York: Longman, 2002), 188.

28. Gustave Niox, *Expedition du Mexique, 1861–1867: recit politique & militaire* (Paris: Librairie Militaire de J. Dumaine, 1874), 750.

29. Winfried Baumgart, *The Crimean War, 1853–1856* (London: Oxford University Press, 1999), 9, 208, 216.

30. Niall Ferguson, *The War of the World: History's Age of Hatred* (London: Allen Lane [Penguin]: 2006), 647.

31. Ibid., 649.

32. "Civil War" is not an index entry of its own or listed under "United States," and I did not see the Civil War figure in the analysis. The book, of course, is about the twentieth century.

33. J. David Singer and Melvin Small, *The Wages of War, 1816–1965: A Statistical Handbook* (New York: John Wiley & Sons, 1972).

34. Abraham Lincoln to Thomas C. Fletcher, February 20, 1865, in Roy P. Basler, ed., *Collected Works of Abraham Lincoln,* 9 vols. (New Brunswick, N.J.: Rutgers University Press, 1953–1955), 8:308.

35. Fellman, *Inside War,* 85. I dismissed it too. See Mark E. Neely, Jr., *The Fate of Liberty: Abraham Lincoln and Civil Liberties* (New York: Oxford University Press, 1991), 49.

36. Abraham Lincoln to Thomas C. Fletcher, February 27, 1865, in Basler, ed., *Collected Works of Abraham Lincoln,* 8:319.

37. Ibid., 8:319–320n.

38. Hartigan, *Lieber's Code and the Law of War,* 50.

⋆⇒◯⇐⋆

# Selected Bibliography

## Primary Sources

Manuscripts

Abraham Lincoln Papers, Library of Congress. Microfilm edition.

Amzi Wood Papers, Division of Rare and Manuscript Collections, Carl A. Kroch Library, Cornell University.

Baldridge-Thompson Collection, Archives and Rare Books, Paterno Library, Pennsylvania State University.

Brown Diary, Harrisburg Civil War Round Table Collection, Box 6, Army Heritage Center, Carlisle, Pennsylvania.

John P. Suter Papers, Harrisburg Civil War Round Table Collection, Box 5, Army Heritage Center, Carlisle, Pennsylvania.

Papers of Charles Sumner, ed. Beverly Wilson Palmer, Houghton Library, Harvard University. Microfilm edition, 1988.

Papers of William Henry Seward, Rush Rhees Library, Department of Rare Books, Manuscripts, and Archives, University of Rochester. Microfilm edition.

Newspapers (Especially 1864–1867)

*Charleston Courier*
*Chicago Tribune*
*London Times*

## Selected Bibliography

*New York Evening Post*
*New York Herald*
*New York Times*
*New York Tribune*
*New York World*
*Richmond Dispatch*
*Washington National Intelligencer*
*Wilkes's Spirit of the Times* (New York)

### OFFICIAL DOCUMENTS

*Condition of the Indian Tribes. Report of the Joint Special Committee appointed under Joint Resolution of March 3, 1865.* 39 Cong., 2 sess., Senate Executive Document No. 156, serial no. 1279.

*Congressional Globe*

*Message from the President of the United States, of March 20, 1866: Relating to the Condition of Affairs in Mexico, in Answer to a Resolution of the House of December 11, 1865.* Washington, D.C.: Government Printing Office, 1866. 39 Cong., 1 sess., House Executive Document 73, serial no. 1261.

*Report of the Joint Committee on the Conduct of the War at the Second Session Thirty-eighth Congress.* Washington, D.C.: Government Printing Office, 1865.

*Report of the Secretary of War.* 39 Cong., 2 sess., Senate Executive Document No. 26 (1867), serial no. 1277.

*War of the Rebellion: A Compilation of the Official Records of the Union and Confederate Armies.* 128 vols. Washington, D.C.: U.S. Government Printing Office, 1880–1901.

## Secondary Sources

### WARFARE AND THE CIVIL WAR

Adams, Michael C. C. *Fighting for Defeat: Union Military Failure in the East, 1861–1865.* (Originally titled *Our Masters the Rebels: A Speculation on Union Military Failure in the East, 1861–1865.*) Originally published in 1978. Lincoln: University of Nebraska Press, 1992.

Billings, John D. *Hardtack and Coffee: The Unwritten Story of Army Life.* Originally published in 1887. Lincoln: University of Nebraska Press, 1993.

Brady, Lisa M. "The Wilderness of War: Nature and Strategy in the American Civil War." *Environmental History* 10 (July 2005), 421–447.

Bruce, Robert V. *Lincoln and the Tools of War.* Originally published in 1956. Urbana: University of Illinois Press, 1989.

Dawes, James. *The Language of War: Literature and Culture in the U.S. from the Civil War through World War II.* Cambridge: Harvard University Press, 2002.

Dawson, Joseph G., III. "The First of Modern Wars?" In *The American Civil War: Explorations and Reconsiderations,* ed. Susan-Mary Grant and Brian Holden Reid, pp. 121–141. London: Longman, 2000.

Donald, David H., ed. *Why the North Won the Civil War.* Baton Rouge: Louisiana State University Press, 1960.

Dyer, Frederick H. *A Compendium of the War of the Rebellion . . .* 1908. New York: Thomas Yoseloff, 1959.

Faust, Drew Gilpin. "'Numbers on Top of Numbers': Counting the Civil War Dead." *Journal of Military History* 70 (October 2006), 995–1010.

Fellman, Michael. "At the Nihilist Edge: Reflections on Guerrilla Warfare during the American Civil War." In *On the Road to Total War: The American Civil War and the German Wars of Unification, 1861–1871,* ed. Stig Förster and Jörg Nagler, pp. 519–540. Cambridge: Cambridge University Press, 1997.

Fellman, Michael, Lesley J. Gordon, and Daniel E. Sutherland. *This Terrible War: The Civil War and Its Aftermath.* New York: Longman, 2003.

Ferguson, Niall. *The War of the World: History's Age of Hatred.* London: Penguin, 2006.

Fox, William F. *Regimental Losses in the American Civil War, 1861–1865: A Treatise on the Extent and Nature of the Mortuary Losses in the Union Regiments. . .* Albany, N.Y.: Albany Publishing, 1889.

Glatthaar, Joseph T. *The March to the Sea and Beyond: Sherman's Troops in the Savannah and Carolinas Campaigns.* Baton Rouge: Louisiana State University Press, 1985.

Griffith, Paddy. *Battle Tactics of the Civil War.* New Haven, Conn.: Yale University Press, 1987.

Grimsley, Mark. *The Hard Hand of War: Union Military Policy toward Southern Civilians, 1861–1865.* Cambridge: Cambridge University Press, 1995.

————"'A Very Long Shadow': Race, Atrocity, and the American Civil War." In *Black Flag over Dixie: Racial Atrocities and Reprisals in the Civil War,* ed. Gregory J. W. Urwin, pp. 231–244. Carbondale: Southern Illinois University Press, 2004.

Hartigan, Richard Shelly. *Lieber's Code and the Law of War.* Chicago: Precedent, 1983.

Janda, Lance. "Shutting the Gates of Mercy: The American Origins of Total War, 1860–1880." *Journal of Military History* 59 (January 1995), 7–26.

Keegan, John. *The Face of Battle.* New York: Viking, 1976.

Linderman, Gerald. *Embattled Courage: The Experience of Combat in the American Civil War.* New York: Free Press, 1987.

Livermore, Thomas L. *Numbers and Losses in the Civil War in America, 1861–1865.* Boston: Houghton, Mifflin, 1900.

Mackey, Robert C. *The Uncivil War: Irregular Warfare in the Upper South, 1861–1865.* Norman: University of Oklahoma Press, 2004.

Mahon, Michael. *The Shenandoah Valley, 1861–1865: The Destruction of the Granary of the Confederacy.* Mechanicsburg, Pa.: Stackpole Books, 1999.

McPherson, James M. *Battle Cry of Freedom: The Civil War Era.* New York: Oxford University Press, 1988.

————*For Cause and Comrades: Why Men Fought in the Civil War.* New York: Oxford University Press, 1997.

Milgrim, James. "Civil War: Libby Prison Correspondence of Tattnall Paulding." *American Philatelist* 89 (December 1975), 1113–1135.

Neely, Mark E., Jr. "'Civilized Belligerents': Abraham Lincoln and the Idea of 'Total War.'" In *New Perspectives on the Civil War: Myths and Realities of the National Conflict,* ed. John Y. Simon and Michael E. Stevens, pp. 3–23. Madison, Wis.: Madison House, 1998.

————"Was the Civil War a Total War?" *Civil War History* 37 (March 1991), 5–28.

Paludan, Phillip Shaw. *"A People's Contest": The Union and Civil War, 1861–1865.* New York: Harper & Row, 1988.

————*Victims: A True Story of the Civil War.* Knoxville: University of Tennessee Press, 1981.

Parrish, T. Michael, and Robert M. Willingham, Jr. *Confederate Imprints: A Bibliography of Southern Publications from Secession to Surrender.* Austin: Jenkins Publishing, n.d.

Phisterer, Frederick. *Statistical Record of the Armies of the United States.* New York: Charles Scribner's Sons, 1883.

Royster, Charles. *The Destructive War: William Tecumseh Sherman, Stonewall Jackson, and the Americans.* New York: Alfred A. Knopf, 1991.

Schlesinger, Arthur M., Jr. "The Causes of the Civil War: A Note on Historical Sentimentalism." *Partisan Review,* October 1949, 969–981.

Sebald, W. G. *On the Natural History of Destruction.* New York: Random House, 2003.

Sherman, William T. *Memoirs of General William T. Sherman.* 2 vols. 2nd ed. published in 1885. New York: Library of America, 1990.

Speer, Lonnie R. *War of Vengeance: Acts of Retaliation against Civil War POWs.* Mechanicsburg, Pa.: Stackpole Books, 2002.

Stout, Harry S. *Upon the Altar of the Nation: A Moral History of the Civil War.* New York: Viking, 2006.

Sutherland, Daniel E. "Abraham Lincoln, John Pope, and the Origins of Total Warfare." *Journal of Military History* 56 (October 1992), 567–586.

———"Sideshow No Longer: A Historiographical Review of the Guerrilla War." *Civil War History* 46 (March 2000), 5–23.

Tap, Bruce. *Over Lincoln's Shoulder: The Committee on the Conduct of the War.* Lawrence: University Press of Kansas, 1998.

Thorndike, Rachel Sherman, ed. *The Sherman Letters: Correspondence between General and Senator Sherman from 1837 to 1891.* New York: C. Scribner's Sons, 1894.

Urwin, Gregory J. W., ed. *Black Flag over Dixie: Racial Atrocities and Reprisals in the Civil War.* Carbondale: Southern Illinois University Press, 2004.

Walters, John B. *Merchant of Terror: General Sherman and Total War.* Indianapolis: Bobbs-Merrill, 1973.

Warner, Ezra. *Generals in Blue: Lives of the Union Commanders.* Baton Rouge: Louisiana State University Press, 1964.

———*Generals in Gray: Lives of the Confederate Commanders.* Baton Rouge: Louisiana State University Press, 1959.

Wiley, Bell I. *The Life of Billy Yank: The Common Soldier of the Union.* Originally published in 1952. New York: Charter Books, 1962.

## Selected Bibliography

Wilson, Edmund. *Patriotic Gore: Studies in the Literature of the American Civil War.* New York: Oxford University Press, 1966.

Wise, Stephen R. *Gate of Hell: Campaign for Charleston Harbor.* Columbia: University of South Carolina Press, 1994.

### THE MEXICAN-AMERICAN WAR

Brands, H. W. *Lone Star Nation: The Epic Story of the Battle for Texas Independence.* New York: Random House, 2004.

Chamberlain, Samuel. *My Confession.* New York: Harper & Brothers, 1956.

Chance, Joseph E., ed. *The Mexican War Journal of Captain Franklin Smith.* Jackson: University Press of Mississippi, 1991.

Chance, Joseph E., ed. *Mexico under Fire: Being the Diary of Samuel Ryan Curtis, 3rd Ohio Regiment, during the American Military Occupation of Northern Mexico, 1846–1847.* Fort Worth: Texas Christian University Press, 1994.

Eisenhower, John S. D. *So Far from God: The U.S. War with Mexico, 1846–1848.* New York: Random House, 1989.

Elliot, Charles Winslow. *Winfield Scott: The Soldier and the Man.* New York: Macmillan, 1937.

Foos, Paul. *A Short, Offhand, Killing Affair: Soldiers and Social Conflict in the Mexican-American War.* Chapel Hill: University of North Carolina Press, 2002.

Gardner, Mark L., and Marc Simmons, eds. *The Mexican War Correspondence of Richard Smith Elliott.* Norman: University of Oklahoma Press, 1997.

Garrett, Jenkins. *The Mexican-American War of 1846–1848: A Bibliography of the Holdings of the Libraries of the University of Texas at Arlington.* College Station: Texas A & M University Press, 1995.

Giddings, Luther. *Sketches of the Campaign in Northern Mexico.* New York: George P. Putnam & Co., 1853.

Hamilton, Holman. *Zachary Taylor: Soldier of the Republic.* Indianapolis: Bobbs-Merrill, 1941.

Hietala, Thomas R. *Manifest Destiny: Anxious Aggrandizement in Late Jacksonian America.* Ithaca: Cornell University Press, 1985.

Hughes, Nathaniel Cheairs, Jr., and Timothy D. Johnson, eds. *A Fighter from Way Back: The Mexican War Diary of Lt. Daniel Harvey Hill, 4th Artillery, USA.* Kent: Kent State University Press, 2002.

*Selected Bibliography*

Johannsen, Robert M. *To the Halls of the Montezumas: The Mexican War in the American Imagination.* New York: Oxford University Press, 1985.

Livingston-Little, D. E., ed. *The Mexican War Diary of Thomas D. Tennery.* Norman: University of Oklahoma Press, 1970.

McCaffrey, James M. *Army of Manifest Destiny: The American Soldier in the Mexican War, 1846–1848.* New York: New York University Press, 1992.

Myers, William Starr, ed. *The Mexican War Diary of George B. McClellan.* Princeton: Princeton University Press, 1917.

Peskin, Allan, ed. *Volunteers: The Mexican War Journals of Private Richard Coulter and Sergeant Thomas Barclay, Company E, Second Pennsylvania Infantry.* Kent: Kent State University Press, 1991.

Scott, Winfield. *Memoirs of Lieut. General Scott . . . written by Himself.* 2 vols. Originally published in 1864. New York: Books for Libraries Press, 1970.

Tuturow, Norman F., ed. *The Mexican-American War: An Annotated Bibliography.* Westport, Conn.: Greenwood Press, 1981.

Winders, Richard Bruce. *Mr. Polk's Army: The American Military Experience in the Mexican War.* College Station: Texas A & M University Press, 1997.

Missouri

Castel, Albert. *General Sterling Price and the Civil War in the West.* Baton Rouge: Louisiana State University Press, 1968.

Crist, Lynda Lasswell, ed. *The Papers of Jefferson Davis, Volume 8: 1861.* Baton Rouge: Louisiana State University Press, 1995.

Edwards, John N. *Shelby and His Men: or, the War in the West.* Cincinnati: Miami Printing and Publishing, 1867.

Fellman, Michael. *Inside War: The Guerrilla Conflict in Missouri during the American Civil War.* New York: Oxford University Press, 1989.

Josephy, Alvin M., Jr. *The Civil War in the American West.* New York: Alfred A. Knopf, 1991.

Kerby, Robert L. *Kirby Smith's Confederacy: The Trans-Mississippi South, 1861–1865.* New York: Columbia University Press, 1972.

McPherson, James M. "From Limited to Total War, 1861–1865." (Originally titled "From Limited to Total War: Missouri and the Nation, 1862–1865".) In McPherson, *Drawn with a Sword: Reflections on the American Civil War,* pp. 66–86. New York: Oxford University Press, 1996.

Oates, Stephen B. *Confederate Cavalry West of the River.* Austin: University of Texas Press, 1961.

Parrish, William E. *Missouri under Radical Rule, 1865–1870.* Columbia: University of Missouri Press, 1965.

Shalhope, Robert E. *Sterling Price: Portrait of a Southerner.* Columbia: University of Missouri Press, 1971.

Shea, William L., and Earl J. Hess. *Pea Ridge: Civil War Campaign in the West.* Chapel Hill: University of North Carolina Press, 1992.

MEXICO UNDER MAXIMILIAN

*American Annual Cyclopaedia and Register of Important Events of the Year 1861.* New York: D. Appleton, 1864.

*American Annual Cyclopaedia and Register of Important Events of the Year 1864.* New York: D. Appleton, 1865.

Bancroft, Hubert Howe. *History of Mexico. Vol. VI, 1861–1867.* In *The Works of Hubert Howe Bancroft.* Originally published in 1888. New York: McGraw-Hill, n.d.

Blair, William. "Editor's Note [on internationalizing study of the Civil War]." *Civil War History* 49 (June 2003), 109–110.

Church, George E. *Mexico. Its Revolutions: Are They Evidences of Retrogression or of Progress?* New York: Baker & Godwin, 1866.

Chynoweth, W. Harris. *The Fall of Maximilian, the Emperor of Mexico; with . . . a Particular Description of the Causes which Led to His Execution.* London: privately printed, 1872.

Clarke, Henry C. "A Day's Fighting in Querétaro." *Harper's New Monthly Magazine* 37 (December 1867), 31–36.

Dabbs, Jack Autrey. *The French Army in Mexico, 1861–1867: A Study in Military Government.* The Hague: Mouton, 1963.

Flint, Henry M. *Mexico under Maximilian.* Philadelphia: National Publishing Company, 1867.

Frazier, Robert W. "Maximilian's Propaganda Activities in the United States." *Hispanic American Historical Review* 24 (February 1944), 4–29.

Fry, Joseph A. *Henry S. Sanford: Diplomacy and Business in Nineteenth-Century America.* Reno: University of Nevada Press, 1982.

Gibson, Charles, ed. *The Black Legend: Anti-Spanish Attitudes in the Old World and the New.* New York: Alfred A. Knopf, 1971.

Greenberg, Amy S. *Manifest Manhood and the Antebellum American Empire.* New York: Cambridge University Press, 2005.

Hall, Frederic. *Life of Maximilian I, Late Emperor of Mexico, with a Sketch of the Empress Carlota.* New York: James Miller, 1868.

Hanna, Alfred Jackson, and Kathryn Abbey Hanna. *Napoleon III and Mexico: American Triumph over Monarchy.* Chapel Hill: University of North Carolina Press, 1971.

Harding, Bertita. *Phantom Crown: The Story of Maximilian and Carlota of Mexico.* New York: Halcyon House, 1934.

Johannsen, Robert W. *To the Halls of the Montezumas: The Mexican War in American Imagination.* New York: Oxford University Press, 1985.

Kingsley, Vine Wright. *French Intervention in America: or, A Review of "La France, le Méxique, et les Etats-Confédérés."* New York: C. B. Richardson, 1863.

Miller, Robert Ryal. "Matías Romero: Mexican Minister to the United States during the Juárez-Maximilian Era." *Hispanic American Historical Review* 45 (May 1965), 228–245.

Parker, F. J. ["An American"]. *The Mexican Empire, Its Actual Situation Briefly Explained and Its Relations to the United States Considered.* New York: Sackett & Mackay, 1866.

Porch, Douglas. *The French Foreign Legion: A Complete History of the Legendary Fighting Force.* New York: HarperCollins, 1991.

———*Wars of Empire.* 2000. American ed. Washington, D.C.: Smithsonian Books, 2006.

Powell, Philip Wayne. *Tree of Hate: Propaganda and Prejudices Affecting United States Relations with the Hispanic World.* New York: Basic Books, 1971.

Ridley, Jasper. *Maximilian and Juárez.* New York: Ticknor & Fields, 1992.

Salm-Salm, Felix. *My Diary in Mexico in 1867: Including the Last Days of the Emperor Maximilian. . .* 2 vols. London: R. Bentley, 1868.

Scheina, Robert L. *Santa Anna: A Curse upon Mexico.* Washington, D.C.: Brassey's, 2002.

Schoonover, Thomas D. "Napoleon Is Coming! Maximilian Is Coming?" In *The Union, the Confederacy, and the Atlantic Rim,* ed. Robert E. May, pp. 101–130. West Lafayette, Ind.: Purdue University Press, 1995.

Schoonover, Thomas D., ed. *Mexican Lobby: Matías Romero in Washington, 1861–1867.* Lexington: University Press of Kentucky, 1986.

Thompson, Jerry, and Lawrence T. Jones III. *Civil War and Revolution on the Rio Grande Frontier: A Narrative and Photographic History.* Austin: Texas State Historical Association, 2004.

Wasserman, Mark. *Everyday Life and Politics in Nineteenth Century Mexico: Men, Women, and War.* Albuquerque: University of New Mexico Press, 2002.

Wilson-Bareau, Juliet. *Manet: The Execution of Maximilian: Painting, Politics and Censorship.* London: National Gallery Publications in association with Princeton University Press, 1992.

### THE SHENANDOAH VALLEY CAMPAIGN

Brandt, Nat. *The Man Who Tried to Burn New York.* Syracuse, N.Y.: Syracuse University Press, 1986.

Britton, Ann Hartwell, and Thomas J. Reed, eds. *To My Beloved Wife and Boy at Home: The Letters and Diaries of Orderly Sergeant John F. L. Hartwell.* Madison, N.J.: Fairleigh Dickinson University Press, 1997.

Burrows, Edwin G., and Mike Wallace. *Gotham.* New York: Oxford University Press, 1999.

Collier, John S., and Bonnie B. Collier, eds. *Yours for the Union: The Civil War Letters of John W. Chase, First Massachusetts Light Artillery.* New York: Fordham University Press, 2004.

Dodge, Grenville M. *The Battle of Atlanta and Other Campaigns, Addresses, Etc.* Council Bluffs, Iowa: Monarch Printing, 1911.

Elwood, John W. *Elwood's Stories of the Old Ringgold Cavalry, 1847–1865.* Coal Center, Pa.: privately published, 1914.

Emerson, Edward W. *The Life and Letters of Charles Russell Lowell.* Boston: Houghton, Mifflin, 1907.

Hagemann, E. R., ed. *Fighting Rebels and Redskins: Experiences in Army Life of Colonel George B. Sanford, 1861–1892.* Norman: University of Oklahoma Press, 1969.

Heatwole, John L. *The Burning: Sheridan in the Shenandoah Valley.* Charlottesville, Va.: Rockbridge Publishing, 1998.

Holcomb, Julie, ed. *Southern Sons, Northern Soldiers: The Civil War Letters of the Remley Brothers, 22nd Iowa Infantry.* DeKalb: University of Northern Illinois Press, 2004.

Kallgren, Beverly Hayes, and James L. Crouthamel, eds. *"Dear Friend*

*Anna": The Civil War Letters of a Common Soldier from Maine.* Orono: University of Maine Press, 1992.

Kidd, J. H. *Personal Recollections of a Cavalryman with Custer's Michigan Cavalry Brigade in the Civil War.* Originally published in 1908. New York: Time-Life Books, 1983.

Kiper, Richard L., ed. *Dear Catharine, Dear Taylor: The Civil War Letters of a Union Soldier and His Wife.* Lawrence: University Press of Kansas, 2002.

Mahon, Michael G. *The Shenandoah Valley, 1861–1865: The Destruction of the Granary of the Confederacy.* Mechanicsburg, Pa.: Stackpole Books, 1999.

McDonald, Archie P., ed. *Make Me a Map of the Valley: The Civil War Journal of Stonewall Jackson's Topographer.* Dallas: Southern Methodist University Press, 1973.

Merritt, Wesley. "Sheridan in the Shenandoah Valley." In *Battles and Leaders of the Civil War,* ed. Robert Underwood Johnson and Clarence Clough Buel, 4:500–521. Originally published in 1887–1888. New York: Thomas Yoseloff, 1956.

Sheridan, Philip Henry. *Personal Memoirs of P. H. Sheridan, General, United States Army.* 2 vols. New York: Charles L. Webster, 1888.

Thomas, William G. "Nothing Ought to Astonish Us: Confederate Civilians in the 1864 Shenandoah Valley Campaign." In *The Shenandoah Valley Campaign of 1864,* ed. Gary W. Gallagher, pp. 222–256. Chapel Hill: University of North Carolina Press, 2006.

Tishler, Allan L. "Sabers Glistening on the Ride to Victory." *America's Civil War,* November 2005, 22–28.

Wittenberg, Eric J. *One of Custer's Wolverines: The Civil War Letters of Brevet Brigadier General James H. Kidd, 6th Michigan Cavalry.* Kent: Kent State University Press, 2000.

INDIANS

Cheek, Lawrence. *The Navajo Long Walk.* Tucson: Rio Nuevo Publishers, 2004.

"Destructive Fire Shells." *Scientific American* 6 (January 11, 1862): 25.

"Experiments with 'Greek Fire.'" *Scientific American* 8 (June 27, 1863), 195.

"Greek Fire—Incendiary Shells." *Scientific American* 9 (September 9, 1863), 81.

## Selected Bibliography

"Greek Fire or Pyrophori." *Scientific American* 9 (December 19, 1863), 391.

"Greek Fire—Shell and Shot." *Scientific American* 9 (October 24, 1863), 265.

Greene, Jerome A., and Douglas D. Scott. *Finding Sand Creek: History, Archaeology, and the 1864 Massacre Site.* Norman: University of Oklahoma Press, 2004.

Grimsley, Mark. "'Rebels' and 'Redskins': U.S. Military Conduct toward White Southerners and Native Americans." In *Civilians in the Path of War,* ed. Mark Grimsley and Clifford J. Rogers, pp. 137–162. Lincoln: University of Nebraska Press, 2002.

Grinnell, George Bird. *The Cheyenne Indians: Their History and Ways of Life.* 2 vols. Originally published in 1923. Lincoln: University of Nebraska Press, 1972.

Hoffert, Sylvia D. "Gender and Vigilantism on the Minnesota Frontier: Jane Grey Swisshelm and the U.S.-Dakota Conflict of 1862." *Western Historical Quarterly* 29 (Autumn 1998), 343–362.

Hoig, Stan. *The Sand Creek Massacre.* Norman: University of Oklahoma Press, 1961.

Jackson, Helen Hunt. *A Century of Dishonor: A Sketch of the United States Government's Dealings with Some of the Indian Tribes.* Originally published in 1881. Williamstown, Mass.: Corner House Publishers, 1979.

Josephy, Alvin M., Jr. *The Civil War in the American West.* New York: Alfred A. Knopf, 1991.

Krech, Shepard, III. *The Ecological Indian: Myth and History.* New York: W. W. Norton, 1999.

Manypenny, George W. *Our Indian Wards.* Originally published in 1880. New York: Da Capo Press, 1972.

Monkres, Robert L. "Indian-White Contact before 1870: Cultural Factors in Conflict." *Journal of the West* 10 (July 1971), 439–473.

Sievers, Michael A. "Sands of Sand Creek Historiography." *Colorado Magazine* 49 (Spring 1972), 116–142.

Smith, Michael T. "Battles or Massacres?" In *The Mythical West: An Encyclopedia of Legend, Lore, and Popular Culture,* ed. Richard W. Slatta. Santa Barbara: ABC-CLIO, 2001.

Svaldi, David. *Sand Creek and the Rhetoric of Extermination: A Case Study in Indian-White Relations.* Lanham, N.Y.: University Press of America, 1989.

Utley, Robert M. *Frontiersmen in Blue: The United States Army and the Indian, 1848–1865.* New York: Macmillan, 1967.

Ware, Eugene F. *The Indian War of 1864,* ed. Clyde C. Walton. Originally published in 1911. New York: St. Martin's Press, 1960.

West, Elliott. *The Contested Plains: Indians, Goldseekers, and the Rush to Colorado.* Lawrence: University Press of Kansas, 1998.

RETALIATION

Basler, Roy P., ed. *The Collected Works of Abraham Lincoln.* 9 vols. New Brunswick, N.J.: Rutgers University Press, 1953–1955.

*Charles Sumner: His Complete Works.* 20 vols. Boston: Lee and Shepard, 1900.

Donald, David Herbert. *Charles Sumner and the Coming of the Civil War.* New York: Alfred A. Knopf, 1965.

———*Charles Sumner and the Rights of Man.* New York: Alfred A. Knopf, 1970.

Freidel, Frank. *Francis Lieber: Nineteenth Century Liberal.* Baton Rouge: Louisiana State University Press, 1947.

Harris, William C. *Lincoln's Last Months.* Cambridge: Harvard University Press, 2004.

Hartigan, Richard Shelly. *Lieber's Code and the Laws of War.* Chicago: Precedent, 1983.

Hesseltine, William Best. *Civil War Prisons: A Study in War Psychology.* Columbus: Ohio State University Press, 1930.

Neely, Mark E., Jr. *Retaliation: The Problem of Atrocity in the American Civil War.* Gettysburg, Pa.: Gettysburg College, 2002.

———*The Union Divided: Party Conflict in the Civil War North.* Cambridge: Harvard University Press, 2002.

# Acknowledgments

I want to thank people who have helped me with this book. Among my colleagues at Penn State, Professor Amy Greenberg read the chapter on Maximilian. Professor Adam Rome read the chapter on Plains Indian warfare. Both had their reservations about what they saw, but they held nothing back in offering constructive suggestions for revision. Professor Gabor Boritt of Gettysburg College gave me permission to use much of the material that formed the Forty-first Fortenbaugh Memorial Lecture, which I gave in Gettysburg on November 19, 2002. It was published as a pamphlet under the title *Retaliation: The Problem of Atrocity in the American Civil War* (Gettysburg: Gettysburg College, 2002). I am especially thankful for the opportunity he gave me to try my first ideas on the subject out in a public forum. Dr. Richard Summers of the U.S. Army Historical Center at Carlisle, Pennsylvania, guided me to sources for the Shenandoah Valley campaign and taught me how to use them efficiently. Another Penn State colleague, Professor William Blair, who heads the Richards Civil War Era Center, of which I am a part, is always helpful in discussions about the period. Sylvia Neely reads every word I write and criticizes a lot of them.

# Illustration Sources

Information about and interpretation of the illustrations are based on the following books: Michael C. C. Adams, *Fighting for Defeat: Union Military Failure in the East, 1861–1865* (Lincoln: University of Nebraska Press, 1992); Amy Greenberg, *Manifest Manhood and the Antebellum American Empire* (New York: Cambridge University Press, 2005); George Wilkins Kendall, *The War between the United States and Mexico Illustrated* (New York: D. Appleton, 1851); W. Michael Mathes, *Mexico on Stone: Lithography in Mexico, 1826–1900* (San Francisco: The Book Club of San Francisco, 1984); Mark E. Neely, Jr., and Harold Holzer, *The Union Image: Popular Prints of the Civil War North* (Chapel Hill: University of North Carolina Press, 2000); Martha A. Sandweiss, Rick Stewart, and Ben W. Huseman, *Eyewitness to War: Prints and Daguerreotypes of the Mexican War, 1846–1848* (Fort Worth: Amon Carter Museum and Washington, D.C.: Smithsonian Institution Press, 1989); William L. Shea and Earl J. Hess, *Pea Ridge: Civil War Campaign in the West* (Chapel Hill: University of North Carolina Press, 1992); and Ronnie C. Tyler, *The Mexican War: A Lithographic Record* (Austin: Texas State Historical Association: 1973).

The sources for the illustrations themselves are:

1. *Mexico* (New York: J. H. Colton, 1855).
2. Lithograph (New York: D. Appleton & Co., 1851). This lithograph formed part of a portfolio executed in France by Adolphe-Jean-Baptiste Bayot

after Carl Nebel and published with accompanying text by the journalist George Wilkins Kendall of New Orleans as *The War between the United States and Mexico Illustrated.* Division of Rare and Manuscript Collections, Carl A. Kroch Library, Cornell University.

3. John D. Billings, *Hardtack and Coffee: The Unwritten Story of Army Life* (Boston: George M. Smith, 1887), p. 150.

4. Cartoon from *Punch,* London, October 24, 1863.

5. Chromolithograph (Chicago: Kurz & Allison, 1889). Reproduced from the Collections of the Library of Congress, LC-USZ62-5454.

6. Chromolithograph (Chicago: Kurz & Allison, 1889). Reproduced from the Collections of the Library of Congress, LC-USZ62-19554.

7. Lithograph (Mexico City: Decaen, 1863–1864).This is part of a portfolio of lithographs entitled *México y sus Alrededores* that was published in Mexico during the French occupation.

8. Lithograph (Mexico City: Decaen, 1863–1864).

9. Lithograph (Mexico City: Decaen, 1863–1864).

10. Chromolithograph (Chicago: Kurz & Allison, 1890).

11. Chromolithograph (Chicago: Kurz & Allison, 1892).

12. Carte-de-visite photograph. Reproduced from the Collections of the Library of Congress, LC-B8184-5526.

# Index

# Index